"We used to eat people"

"We used to eat people"
Revelations of a Fiji Islands Traditional Village

R. M. W. Dixon

McFarland & Company, Inc., Publishers
Jefferson, North Carolina

Unless otherwise noted all illustrations
are from the author's collection.

LIBRARY OF CONGRESS CATALOGUING-IN-PUBLICATION DATA

Names: Dixon, Robert M. W., 1939– author.
Title: "We used to eat people" : revelations of a Fiji Islands
traditional village / R. M. W. Dixon.
Description: Jefferson, North Carolina : McFarland & Company, Inc.,
Publishers, 2018 | Includes bibliographical references and index.
Identifiers: LCCN 2017048643 | ISBN 9781476671819
(softcover : acid free paper) ∞
Subjects: LCSH: Ethnology—Fiji. | Fijian language. | Cannibalism—Fiji. |
Dixon, Robert M. W., 1939—-Anecdotes.
Classification: LCC GN671.F5 D59 2018 | DDC 305.80099611—dc23
LC record available at https://lccn.loc.gov/2017048643

BRITISH LIBRARY CATALOGUING DATA ARE AVAILABLE

**ISBN (print) 978-1-4766-7181-9
ISBN (ebook) 978-1-4766-3070-0**

© 2018 R.M.W. Dixon. All rights reserved

*No part of this book may be reproduced or transmitted in any form
or by any means, electronic or mechanical, including photocopying
or recording, or by any information storage and retrieval system,
without permission in writing from the publisher.*

Front cover: Tui Nasau, literally "King of Nasau," or village chief;
background pattern by Joachim Angeltun (iStock)

Printed in the United States of America

*McFarland & Company, Inc., Publishers
Box 611, Jefferson, North Carolina 28640
www.mcfarlandpub.com*

Table of Contents

Maps vi

Author's Note 1

1. Getting There — 3
2. "This is paradise" — 22
3. Our Village — 42
4. "No cyclone today!" — 66
5. "Do you want to live or do you want to die?" — 91
6. Becoming a Part of the Village — 110
7. A Divine Visitor — 127
8. A New House and a New Baby — 158
9. "Oh dear! Roopate is getting ready to go!" — 183

Epilogue 205

References by Chapter 207

Index 209

Maps

vi

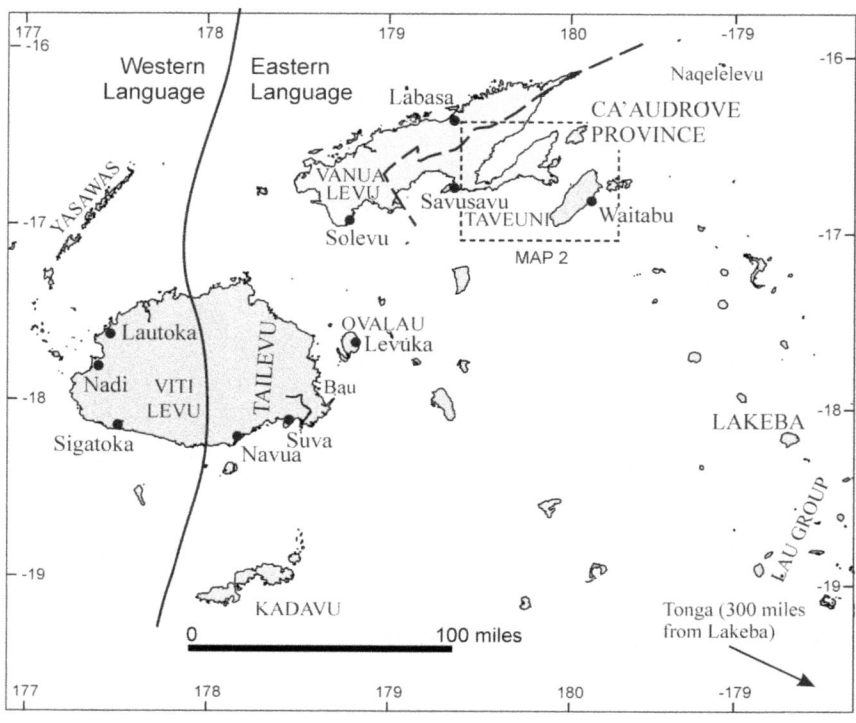

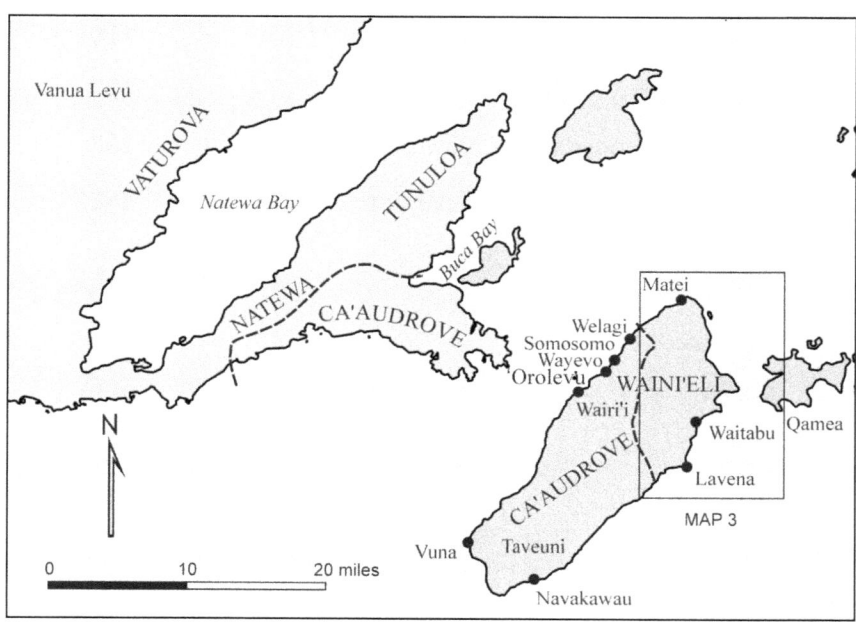

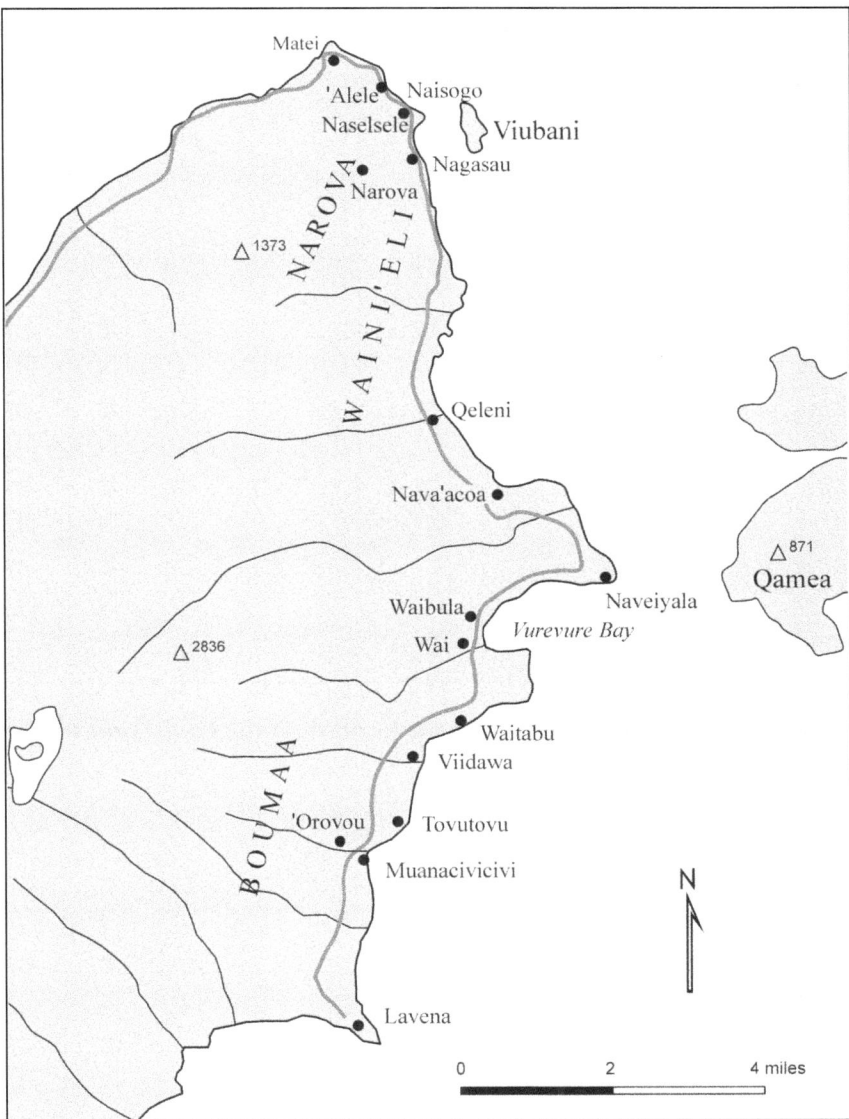

Map 3. Northeast part of Taveuni, showing places mentioned in the legend of the Prince of Boumaa and the Princess of Waini'eli ("Do you want to live or do you want to die?").

Opposite, top: Map 1. Fiji Islands. There are about a hundred inhabited islands. *Bottom:* Map 2. Southeast Vanua Levu and Taveuni.

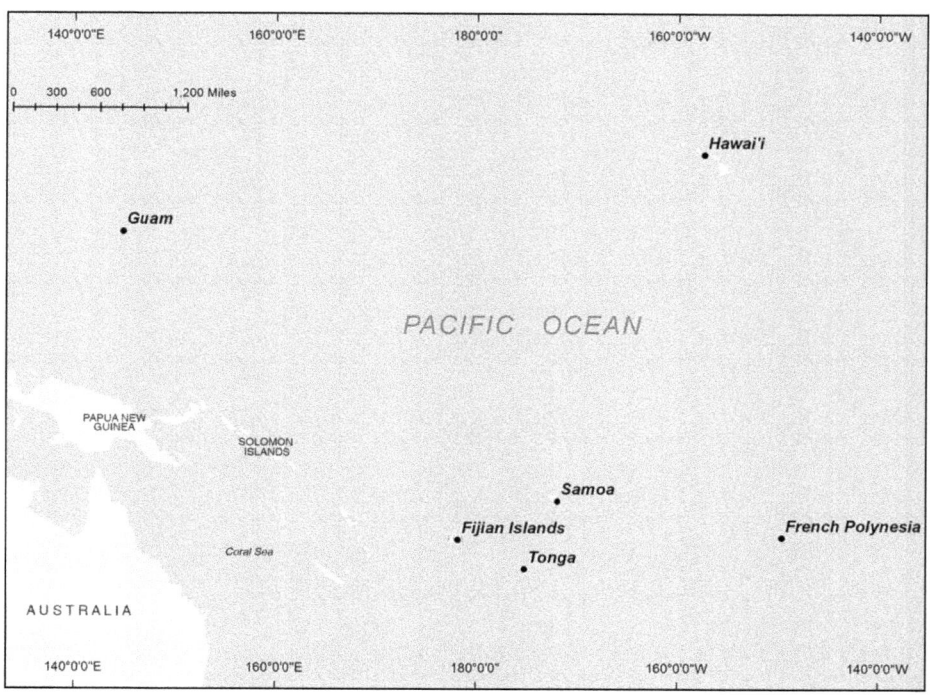

Map 4. The West Pacific, showing the location of the Fiji Islands (courtesy Bai Junwei).

Author's Note

This account of my six-month sojourn in a monolingual Fijian village in 1985 was written, in pencil, in three notebooks, between October 30 and December 18, 1988. It was keyboarded by Angela Lansdown between January and June 2016, and then revised by the author. Apart from the pseudonyms Charlotte Ferreiro (Koleta), Qito, and Father Hendricks, everyone is referred to by their real name. My name Robert became Roopate in Fijian.

1

Getting There

The wind was just beginning to howl like a witch.

Tap. Tap. Tap.

Our roof was only a few pieces of corrugated iron, tied on with twine. But at least it was tied on a bit more securely than for the previous cyclones in that summer of 1985.

Koleta and I were doing linguistic fieldwork in Waitabu, on the "garden isle" of Taveuni. We lived in a small hut belonging to Sepo (or Josefa), Koleta's adopted father, who was younger brother of the village chief.

The walls were made of *gasau*, thick reeds from the local forest, fastened together with wire. The doors were the sides of old packing cases. And the roof was held down by large sticks, lying across the corrugated iron, tied at each end to a parallel stick coming out of the house frame.

Tap. Tap. Tap.

"There's someone at the door," Koleta suggested.

"Surely not. Isn't it just the wind shifting things around?"

Peteroo, Sepo's eldest son, was home on leave from the Fijian Battalion of the UN Peace-Keeping force in Lebanon. Pete and his ten-year-old brother Elia had climbed up the hill on the east side of the village to chop down three large bamboo canes, each as thick as your arm. They'd thrown them over the cliff toward the village and Sepo had tied the bamboo across our roof, one at each end and one in the middle. After he'd finished I put a few further twists of twine around each extremity.

Tap. Tap. Tap.

The sound came louder, jagging into the rising roar of wind.

"It is someone there."

"Yes," I agreed, "they must be at the front door."

We'd lashed a sheet of corrugated iron over each of the side entrances. Since it was necessary to get into the house, the front door had been left unprotected on the outside. From the inside, though, it was tied in place with more of the thickest twine we could buy on the island.

"Whoever would want to knock on a door at this time?" Koleta asked. As if in agreement, the wind honed in on us, lifting one sheet of roofing iron six inches above its neighbor, providing a clear view of stars and moon. "Don't open it!"

"No. I certainly won't."

A Fijian house has no furniture. We lay on woven mats, on the ground, looking up at the roof. Another burst of wind, once more selectively lifting pieces of iron, making a noise like a washboard played by a giant thimbled hand.

Tap. Tap. Tap. The knocking became more peremptory. And there was a voice. We strained to hear the Fijian (hardly anyone in the village spoke English). "Tui Nasau here."

"Oh goodness." We both spoke at once. "It won't do to ignore him."

Tui Nasau (literally "King of Nasau") was the village chief. In the old cannibal days, a chief could order someone killed and roasted just because he felt like a morsel of human flesh. The missionaries had stopped all that, but the King of Nasau still had total power (much more than the Queen of England could have in Britain). He had the power to help or frustrate our fieldwork. Or he could just order us out of his village.

"Please excuse—." I began to undo the string that tied the packing case side into place (there was nothing in the nature of hinges). "Please excuse my slowness, Big Uncle."

Sepo was Koleta's father and thus my father-in-law or classificatory uncle (according to how one is supposed to marry, in the Fijian way of things). Tui Nasau was thus my uncle's older brother. *Moomoo Levu* or "Big Uncle." I know he liked to be addressed in this way.

"Have you any—ugh!" Tui Nasau's rasping cough blended into the next bluster of wind. He cleared his throat. "Any tobacco?"

He knew that earlier in the day we'd said that we had none left.

"There is one for emergencies. Better give it to him." Koleta pointed: "In the bag on the wall, under the clothes pegs."

I eased one side of the door an inch ajar and slipped a packet of cigarettes into the waiting royal hand. "Last one, Big Uncle."

"Very good. I offer great thanks, Roopate and Koleta. Now I must go and barricade myself in my own house." In Fiji the protocol of politeness must never be shortened, not even in the presence of a "murdering wind" (which is a literal translation of the Fijian for cyclone), so he added: "I am most grateful to you for this fine tobacco."

He went off the dozen yards to his own front door as the rain began, gushing onto our roof like a burst city main.

"It's a bit like the Queen of England knocking on the door and asking to borrow a cup of sugar, don't you think?" My words were swallowed up by another giant rasp of wind on our washboard roof.

We'd already sealed our precious linguistic notebooks into plastic bags. It didn't matter if clothes or books blew away, but the fruits of two months of language study must be preserved if the roof should blow off (as did seem to be rather in the cards).

There was nothing left to do but simply endure the fifth cyclone of the season.

* * *

It really began with the Queen of England. Or her coronation, to be precise. There was just one other queen present. The English press made a great fuss of Salote of Tonga, whose girth was surpassed only by the brightness of her smile.

She was actually a real monarch, who ruled her kingdom. Oh sure, there were prime minister and cabinet, but they were appointed by the queen, and their job was to put into practice her policies.

The image of Queen Salote stayed with me as I finished school, in Nottingham, and went on to study mathematics at Oxford. The court of Tonga, I imagined, might be like one of those medieval courts in Europe. I'd read that some of the German princes had employed a court mathematician. It became a joke at Oxford that my ambition was to be court mathematician to the Queen of Tonga.

Then I switched to linguistics and came to Australia to study Aboriginal languages. I'd spent twenty years on this, recording stories, writing grammars, and compiling vocabularies of languages from the rain forest of northeast Queensland.

In the early 1980s, things started to go a little bit wrong. Work didn't seem as satisfying as it usually was. Then, after years of indecision, I jumped out of a marriage that had gone stale. This was totally traumatic. I'd taken the step but I felt slugged, drained, beaten.

Charlotte Ferreiro, who later adopted the Fijian name of Koleta (let us call her thus), and with whom I was having a romantic relationship, suggested that I go with her to Fiji.

Tonga had always been there, in the back of my mind. Once I'd switched to linguistics there was a definite plan, one day, to go and write a grammar of Tongan. Tonga, Fiji—what's the difference? Aren't they both idyllic lands in the south seas? It seemed like an invitation to visit paradise. I certainly needed a spell away from Canberra, which held the ghost of my old life. I'd been at the Australian National University for fourteen years without any time off (all my recent work in Aboriginal languages had been done during the vacations) and they now granted me a semester free of teaching to undertake fieldwork—from December 1984 to July 1985.

Charlotte had studied Japanese and linguistics before working with an Aboriginal language which was fast being replaced by English, and seeing how the last generation of semi-speakers used an attenuated form of the traditional language. She had now decided to undertake fieldwork for a Ph.D. The plan was to do a sociolinguistic study of a place where a number of different varieties of language were used, investigating how they were employed and in what circumstances. She wanted to get experience of working outside Australia, and Fiji seemed the answer—there's the standard language, the local dialect, the variety of Hindi used by Indians, and various pidgins used for communication between Fijians and Indians.

At that stage, the main thing I thought about was getting away. I also had it in mind to write a novel. And—of course—study the language. There'd been a number of grammars written of Fijian but I could see that many topics hadn't been covered and there were a great number of things that could profitably be studied in the field.

There were all sorts of preparations necessary before beginning fieldwork. The most important was to try and learn as much as we could of the language. Milner's *Fijian Grammar* is a well-written introduction, introducing vocabulary and grammatical topics in a measured way, with examples that illustrate Fijian culture. During 1984, Charlotte and I worked through Milner at the rate of a chapter each week, assiduously doing all the translation exercises and then checking we'd got them right by the key at the back of the book. Any that weren't right we'd go back and do again the next week, until we had fully mastered that particular point of language.

The Fijian alphabet is quite straightforward. One just has to remember that g is used for the "ng" sound which only comes at the end of words in English, that c is a sound like the beginning of English *that*, and that d, b and q are pronounced "nd," "mb" and "ng-g" respectively. The alphabet uses the principle of "one letter for one sound"; a Fijian pronounces each of "nd," "mb" and "ng-g" as a single sound, and writes them this way. An international traveler arrives at the airport that is written Nadi, but pronounced "Nandi." It's all pretty easy once you get used to it.

Most of the words given in Milner are easy to remember: *vale* "house," *waqa* "boat," *koro* "village." But I remember expostulating when on page 18 he had introduced *cauravou* "young man." "That's got five vowels," I grumbled. "It's too long a word to give in Lesson 5, surely!"

What you can't get from a book is the correct pronunciation of a language, and that's the most important thing of all. We just called at the Fijian High Commission, in an ordinary house in the Canberra suburb of Red Hill, where the Third Secretary, Akuila Waradi, accepted a blank cassette and promised to record the sentences at the end of chapters 8 and 9 of Milner, as well as the four short texts at the end of the book. Mr. Waradi turned out to be a real find—he even had us over to dinner and provided all sorts of hints about how to get on in Fiji.

During May 1984 Charlotte made a short experimental trip to Fiji. She met Paul Geraghty, an Irishman who worked for the Monolingual Dictionary Project in Suva and—following his introduction—she visited two villages in search of a likely field site. Neither seemed quite suitable, but it was useful in letting her see what could be done and what the problems might be.

For fieldwork proper, we'd each need a research visa which Mr. Waradi warned would take a fair while to get. The original plan was for Charlotte to go in late October and I'd follow in December once I'd finished marking end-of-year examinations. So she applied in late May. And waited. And waited. Early October came and she called Mr. Waradi. "Yes," he acknowledged. "I think we do have a problem." It wasn't that anyone expected the visa application to be refused; that apparently never happened. It was just that the bureaucratic machinery which Britain had bequeathed to Fiji ground around very slowly.

Eventually Charlotte got the go-ahead in early November—but by then we'd decided to leave together in December. They said that since the time was so short she could pay the visa fee on arrival.

I'd applied in July and also just got the go-ahead in November. Only I was told to send the fee in advance, and then the visa would be mailed to me. There seemed time enough for that to happen—I sent off the fee about the 8th of November and told them I was hoping to arrive on the 8th December.

Only, of course, the visa didn't come. I was allowed to enter the country on a short-stay visitor visa and confidently waited in Suva for the research visa to be forwarded from Canberra (I assumed it would have got there just after I left). Nothing arrived. So, just before Christmas I went to the immigration office in Suva. After an hour or so they found the file. My visa had been posted to me in Canberra on the 15th of December, a week after I'd actually arrived in Suva. What with cyclones and such, it didn't actually catch up with me until February. And then, I was officially given permission to do "A sociolinguistic study of the language in a Fijian village." This was Charlotte's topic; mine had been a quite different one, "The semantic basis of Fijian syntax." The funny thing was that we'd applied for research visas quite separately, a couple of months apart. There should have been nothing to connect us. It became apparent that what the Fijian bureaucracy lacked in speed and efficiency it more than made up for in terms of perspicuity.

Before leaving Canberra, Charlotte had a fair idea of where she wanted a field site. It should be a village where the local dialect was mutually intelligible with standard Fijian, but had its own distinctive and easily recognisable characteristics. How about the island of Taveuni, which was supposed to be one of the most beautiful parts of Fiji, with soft, sandy beaches…? Sounded okay to me.

* * *

Besides Milner and a number of other Fijian grammars, we'd also read all sorts of anthropological and historical books about Fiji. I'd picked up Lorimer Fison's *Tales from Old Fiji* in a second-hand bookshop. The tales themselves were ordinary enough. But Fison's introduction mentioned a few Fijian customs that seemed a little extreme. When a new house was being built for a chief "it used be no uncommon occurrence for a living man to be placed standing in each post-hole, and then buried alive by the side of the post, the hole being filled up and the earth rammed down over him." It seems that the chief "would be dishonored if no human life were taken when the posts were set up."

Many Australian Aborigines used to be cannibals. They would eat parts of a dead enemy, or some member of their own tribe who was judged to have committed a capital offense. Aborigines would never kill someone just because they felt hungry. But Fijian chiefs did. A commoner may have done no wrong whatsoever, and be marked down for the roasting pit just to satisfy a chief's whim (or his ego!).

Fison also tells of how when a man died his wives might be strangled and placed in the ground with him. There is even an illustration of widow-strangling, with the lady placing her head in a noose the ends of which were held by two seated men. (To strangle someone while sitting down! But we later found that in Fiji almost everything is done sitting down.) "It was a disgrace," Fison stated, for "a woman to show the slightest unwillingness to be strangled when her lord and master died."

The Fijians also practised euthanasia. "Aged parents would walk to the grave which had already been dug by their own children, or offer themselves to a cord which was held in the hands of their eldest son, with no more apparent resistance or emotion on either side than is manifested by a pauper family in England when the old folks have to be removed to the work house." We later learned the reason for this custom. The Fijians believed in a heaven very similar to the Christian idea, except that you arrived at heaven in the physical state in which you left earth. So it was sensible to make the transition while you still had a bit of life left in you.

All of these practices were now firmly in the past, since Fiji had been thoroughly missionized during the second half of the nineteenth century. Every village was firmly Wesleyan or Catholic (they'd even fought a few wars over the difference between these Christian sects!). Charlotte, on her visit in May, had had to attend church service. One Sunday when she was staying in a Wesleyan village there had been four services, each lasting several hours, together taking up the entire day.

Now I'm an atheist and proud of it. I respect other people's beliefs and in return I expect them to respect my belief that there is no god. Charlotte said that I'd have to go to church, in order to get accepted. "No no," I replied, "when I tell them I don't feel any need for a god they'll accept that. They won't make me go to church just for the surface show of it." Anyway, we agreed to wait and see.

One other custom had been mentioned by Mr. Waradi—that of *kerekere*. Apparently if someone takes a fancy to anything belonging to someone else all they have to say is "I *kerekere* that," and the person has to give it to him. *Kerekere* can be translated "humbly ask for" or "beg for." But the cultural demand—not conveyed by these translations—is that the societal norm doesn't permit you to refuse a *kerekere*. The only valuable thing I had was an Omega watch and it seemed safest to leave that behind in Canberra. After all, who needs to know the time in a tropical paradise?

All these warnings and stories were drowned out by a feeling of adventure and excitement as we actually arrived in Nadi, on the west side of the main island of Viti Levu. Not that this is a typical Fijian town. There are lots of duty free shops, catering to foreign visitors. And there are many more Indians than Fijians.

The status of Fijian Indians is an interesting topic. After the native chiefs ceded the sovereignty of Fiji to Britain in 1874, Queen Victoria sent out Sir Arthur Gordon as the first governor. During the previous decade some of the chiefs had sold tracts of land (about 17 percent of the whole area of Fiji) to Europeans, who established sugar and copra plantations.

Gordon forbade further sales: all the land which still remained to Fijians was to belong to them in perpetuity. He also thought that if Fijians went to work as laborers on plantations their own social systems would break down, and so they were encouraged to stay in their home village to work their own land.

This led the plantation owners to inquire where they were supposed to get labor. Well, there was a large pool of potential workers in the Raj, some of whom had already been siphoned off to such places as the British West Indies and Mauritius. Between 1879 and 1916 perhaps sixty thousand Indians were brought to Fiji under indenture. Some returned home at the end of their contract but most stayed on. And they propagated faster than the Fijians so that, by 1984, slightly more than half of the population was Indian. These immigrants who were brought in by Sir Arthur Gordon to protect the lifestyle of the native Fijians were now threatening this, by sheer weight of numbers.

On that first day in Nadi we didn't think too hard about racial relations. We took off our shoes and wandered round an ornate Hindu temple on the bank of the Nadi river. And then had a goat curry. It was slightly more expensive than the lamb curry—and a little tougher—but we'd never tried it before. Might as well start straight away on experiencing new things; there'd be plenty of it ahead.

On her visit in May, Charlotte had discovered that there are two sides to Fiji. One is put on for the benefit of overseas visitors, who stay in posh hotels—often run by Indians but with Fijian staff (for the indispensable local color)—with their own beaches, tennis courts, golf courses. There's really no need to leave the hotel grounds. Our phonetics technician in Canberra had won a vacation for himself and his wife in Fiji. Air fare and accommodation were covered but he had to pay for his own meals and, he grumbled, it was twenty dollars for a little bit of steak! The restaurant we patronized in Nadi belonged to the other side, the Fiji that local people live in, and the goat curry plus all sorts of side dishes had come to two dollars, fifty cents.

There were two ways of traveling along the south side of Viti Levu to Suva, the capital. One was with a luxury air-conditioned limousine that would be full of tourists. We preferred to catch the regular bus, which was much cheaper, a bit slower, not quite as comfortable but much more fun. It stopped for twenty minutes at the open market in Sigatoka and then in Navua where the passengers bought little savory snacks, for ten and twenty cents, from stalls run by Indians.

And so to Suva, a city of about a hundred thousand people. Warm and muggy, feeling as if it's always just about to rain. The Australian National University had a couple of apartments a mile or two outside town, close to the University of the South Pacific. They are comfortable places to stay, with a sea breeze wafting between the window bars (crime being a considerable problem in Suva). The apartments were under the control of a rather fearsome white lady who owned a local nursery garden, and there was a sweet old Fijian lady, Sei, as resident caretaker. Sei would do washing and ironing for visitors for which she invariably charged ten dollars. It didn't seem to matter whether one gave her two items or twenty to wash—always ten dollars. Sei's English was quite rudimentary and it may be that "ten" was the only English number she knew.

* * *

Fiji has about a hundred inhabited islands and a population of over half-a-million people, at that time nearly half of them ethnic Fijians. There are perhaps a hundred local dialects which can be grouped into two, closely related languages (a bit like German and Dutch). One is spoken around Nadi and the offshore islands and in the western half of Viti Levu, the other in the eastern half of the main island and in all the other islands to the south, northeast, and east.

Missionaries settled first on Tonga, which was rather less bloodthirsty and thus more hospitable. They gradually infiltrated, in 1835, into Lakemba, on the nearby Lau Group of islands of Fiji, and thence into Viti Levu. Within a few years they realized that it would be an impossible task to translate the Bible into every single local dialect. The most important chief at that time came from Bau—a small island off the east coast of Viti Levu—and Bauan had something of the status of a lingua franca. This was chosen as the medium through which evangelical work would be conducted. In addition to the Bible, all radio broadcasts, newspapers, government documents and school books were in Standard Fijian, which is based upon—but not today exactly the same as—the dialect of Bau.

Our plan was to spend the rest of December in Suva taking intensive language lessons in order to be able to converse—at least a bit—in the standard dialect before setting off on fieldwork. But where to find a teacher? We were recommended to a man who worked for the Catholic church but he'd gone off to Bau for some important business. Why not try the Peace Corps?, someone suggested.

They were between language courses but, by great good luck, one of their teachers happened to have called into the office that day. A handsome, moustachioed Fijian with a confident air, in his mid-thirties. "My name," he wrote it on a piece of paper "is Jone Caginiliwalala." "Aha," I pronounced it "Thang-i-nili-wala-la."

"Well," Jone looked relieved that he wouldn't have to start right from scratch. "You know to pronounce 'c' as *th* and 'g' as *ng*."

"We've read Milner's grammar," Charlotte explained, "so we know the language in theory. Now what we have to do is learn to speak it."

Jone explained that he charged three dollars an hour for a single pupil, two dollars each an hour if there were two or more in the class. We said we'd like to come to his house each weekday morning for three hours. "No, better make it four," Jone suggested, "if you want to talk Fijian in three weeks."

And so, at nine o'clock the next day, it was Lesson One—Greetings. Followed by Names, How to introduce yourself, Where (question and response), Simple Verbs, Subject pronoun and then, in Lesson Seven, "Golden phrases." These were things like "What might be the Fijian word for—." After this there was no excuse for not speaking Fijian all through each lesson. If we didn't know a word, then use a golden phrase and ask, in Fijian, what it was.

Jone was a natural teacher and he used the intensive drills that had been devised by professional linguists for the Peace Corps courses. When we got into colors, for instance, Jone would sit down opposite us with a collection of objects. Each one would be described and we'd repeat the color. Then he'd hold them up, in random order, and we'd have to supply the right adjective—as quickly as we could. After a half-hour of this the names of colors were as firmly embedded in our brain as if we'd known them all our lives. We'd have a cup of tea and a substantial mid-morning snack and then Jone would pin a sheet of butcher's paper on the wall and we'd each have to write a simple story relating to what we'd learned that day.

In the afternoon we tried to consolidate what had been learned in the morning. Conversation at normal speed was still way beyond our understanding, but I recorded the news off Radio Fiji and then played it back a phrase at a time, trying to transcribe and translate. There was one phrase, *ranadi levu*, which was a puzzle. I knew *levu* "big" and Capell's dictionary explained *ranadi* as "a woman of chiefly rank." Ah—suddenly it clicked into place. *Ranadi levu* must be referring to the Queen of England. The Fijians have always had a strong sense of hierarchy and the English monarch fitted in, quite naturally, at the top of the tree.

Then there was Suva to explore. It had an excellent museum, one reasonable department store, five or six cinemas that have the sound turned up incredibly loud, some excellent Chinese restaurants, and also lots of Indian eating places. It was possible to get a reasonable curry lunch for one dollar. There was also the Hare Krishna coffee shop which sold good vegetarian snacks and also—wonderful to relate—good quality American-style ice cream. (Only no rum and raisin—nothing that smacks of alcohol!)

What Suva lacked was a decent bookshop. There were several branches of Desai's, with a few schoolbooks and blood-and-thunder paperbacks. The selection was rather worse than that of the average newsagent in a Canberra suburb—and this was the best bookshop in the nation. The Fiji Museum had just reissued a number of nineteenth century classics, such as *Life in Feejee, Or, Five Years Among the Cannibals by a Lady*. It cost $5 at the museum, about $7 at Desai's and $12 at the souvenir shop at one of the tourist hotels.

The most important person in Suva, as far as we were concerned, was Paul Geraghty. He'd been educated at Rugby, the famous public school. This was not because he was rich or aristocratic; Paul's parents were Irish immigrants who'd lived in the town of Rugby, and a few scholarships were offered to local lads. Then, at the age of seventeen, Paul had spent a year teaching in a school in Fiji as the prize for winning an essay competition at Rugby.

He'd been hooked. After taking a degree in modern European languages at Cambridge, Paul returned to Fiji and had been there ever since, except for a period at the University of Hawai'i where he completed a masterly Ph.D. dissertation on "The history of the Fijian languages" which described all the dialectal features and how they evolved. Paul Geraghty worked at an unusual institution called the Monolingual Fijian Dictionary Centre. The actor Raymond Burr had given money to start the institution, and it had been going for a dozen years, with a staff of six or eight.

What was odd when we first visited the Centre was that little or no work was being done on the dictionary; the staff sat and chatted or read newspapers or did their own handicrafts. When you asked the director, Teevita Nawadra, when it would be finished he'd say, "next year," but everyone knew that that had as much relation to any real period of time as a harassed mother saying she'll do something "in a minute," really meaning in two or three hours time. Things perked up once Teevita Nawadra retired and Paul took over as director. The staff actually worked on dictionary entries, which must have been much more satisfying for them. When the dictionary was more-or-less finished, a committee was set up by the government to decide on how to organize the publication. Members of the committee received "sitting fees" which were a useful addition to income and not something to be terminated. (That's how life works in Fiji.)

Paul Geraghty would sit—wearing a skirt-like isulu and no shoes—in a ground floor room in an old prefabricated building, just next to the Government Offices (on the other side from the Parliamentary chamber, where coups take place). I've said there are a hundred or so local dialects of the two Fijian languages. Paul Geraghty speaks most of them, far more than anyone else. The phone would ring and he'd answer it in the dialect of his interlocutor. People would pass by the window all the time, relaying titbits of news and gossip. A street vendor came along at the same time each day and Paul passed out thirty or fifty cents for a savory snack. Fijians brought him plays and poems they had written for literary and linguistic appraisal. The immigration department sought his opinion on applications for research visas and such like.

Every Monday afternoon Paul went across the road to Radio Fiji to record a half-hour program called "Our language," which people listened to all over the islands at ten o'clock on Tuesday evening. He talked about regional linguistic features, illustrated by recordings he had made, or by interviews.

The following July, after I had returned to Canberra, Paul interviewed Charlotte on "Our language." She's a natural, extrovert language learner and chatted happily about her work and life in Fiji with a personal greeting for all senior people in our village (I'd have been far too scared to go on, even if I'd been there). A few weeks later Charlotte was at Nadi airport and a couple of Fijian ladies, hearing the lilt of her voice, said "We heard you talking with Paul on 'Our language,' gee you can talk Fijian well." There is a tremendous interest in language among Fijians, which was fanned by Paul Geraghty and his weekly radio broadcast.

Paul has one characteristic in common with Queen Elizabeth II—neither of them is very fond of dinner parties. But he broke the rule one evening to come with us to the Lantern Palace. We also invited along Father David Arms, who works for the Catholic Church in Suva and did a superb descriptive and historical study of the grammar of standard Fijian for a Ph.D. dissertation at the University of Michigan. We chatted about all sorts of linguistic points that had been bothering us. Paul and David seemed to have studied or thought about every aspect of Fijian and were full of information and advice.

* * *

Learning a language all week is hard work, so one weekend we decided on a trip to the town of Levuka, on the island of Ovalau. This had been the first capital of the British Administration in Fiji, from 1874 until 1882, until it was moved to Suva. There was a two- or three-hour bus journey to Natovi, on the coast of Viti Levu opposite Ovalau, to catch the boat across.

We were a bit naive at first about how things are done in Fiji. The bus drew in and we stood meekly in the line waiting to board. But what the Fijians in the queue did was to shove their bags, packages and children through the open windows, as a way of reserving seats. By the time we actually got on, there was nowhere left for us to sit together. Charlotte got a single seat toward the back, next to a young white girl while I sat a few seats ahead with some Fijians.

I'd brought along a book to read and it was a good one—Churchward's *A New Fijian Grammar*, published in 1941. The reason I hadn't read it before was that in *The Languages of Fiji*, which has a sort-of survey of all the literature in Fijian by Albert J. Schütz, he rubbishes Churchward, suggesting that it has little value. Paul Geraghty put me right on that, saying that he didn't agree with Schütz and that Churchward had all sorts of useful insights into the workings of Fijian.

Suddenly I heard Charlotte calling down the aisle (in the Australian Aboriginal language which we both have a working knowledge of) "What are you reading?" I passed Churchward down the aisle and she seemed to be showing it to the girl in the next seat before handing it back.

Charlotte explained what it had all been about when we moved from bus to boat. Apparently, a new Wesleyan church was to be opened in Suva, and it was being dedicated to Churchward, who had been missionary as well as linguist. The church had invited across two of Churchward's daughters, and they'd brought along their daughters. Charlotte had been sitting next to a granddaughter of the man whose grammar I was reading.

We sat inside the boat but after a while Charlotte went out onto the prow to watch Ovalau come into view. I didn't follow for a while, being rather absorbed in the grammar, marking interesting passages with a pencil.

The two Churchward daughters were sitting on a cross-bench. One of them pointed at me: "Look at that man. He's annotating the book he's reading with a pencil just like father used to."

"Yes," replied her sister, who was the mother of the girl Charlotte had been sitting next to on the bus. "And you won't believe this, but it's father's book he's reading!"

The Reverend Dr. Clerk Maxwell Churchward (his father had named him after the famous physicist) spent the 1920s as a missionary on Rotuma,

The daughters of the Reverend Dr. C. Maxwell Churchward outside the study in which he wrote *A New Fijian Grammar* 45 years earlier.

a small island about 200 miles north of Fiji. He published a collection of *Tales of a Lonely Island* and also a grammar and dictionary of Rotuman, which is a dauntingly difficult language. After independence, Rotuma became part of Fiji politically and lots of the people moved to Suva. The new Wesleyan church had been erected by the Rotuman community, which held Churchward's linguistic work and Bible translation in the highest regard.

During the 1930s, Churchward worked in Fiji as a pastor, and wrote *A New Fijian Grammar.* Then, after the war, he went to Tonga where he completed a grammar and a substantial dictionary of that language. He'd died in Sydney just a few years back and his widow was too old and frail to travel.

Levuka had a special meaning for the Churchward daughters because the family had lived there in the 'thirties, in a home high on the hillside, reached by what seemed an interminable flight of steps. Marjorie Churchward told us that she'd once run away from home, at the age of eight or so, and got to the bottom of the steps before feeling lonely and climbing very slowly back up again. When we reached the top, we saw that the old house had been pulled down, except for one wing; and that was the study in which Churchward had written his Fijian grammar. It was in poor repair but we could visualize a preoccupied scholar pouring over the latest linguistic books that had arrived from England, and working into the night on verb endings and possessive pronouns in Fijian. Marjorie confirmed that he'd left the bringing up of the children very much to his wife.

Levuka probably looked much as it did a hundred years prior, except that some of the firms who traded there had left, the population had shrunk (to about 1,500) and there were gaps where houses once stood. We stayed at the Royal Hotel, which was like something out of Somerset Maugham. Large, high ceilings, lots of ferns and other plants, and a somnambulant air, so that one scarcely dared talk in more than a whisper.

After exploring the town and climbing the steep hillside that comes to within a couple of hundred yards of the wharf, we made for the bar of the Royal Hotel. It took a while to attract attention. "A gin and tonic and a rum and coke," I requested. The barman looked at Charlotte. "Sorry, can't serve ladies in the public bar. That's the law in Fiji. Go 'round to the lounge, in the front of the hotel and I can serve through the side window there."

It took a while to find it and then we stood at the side window for quite a time. Eventually he came over and I repeated the order. "Sorry, we don't have any Coca Cola or any other cola." The barman held up a hand as I began to suggest a substitute. "And I think we are out of tonic water." We wondered about asking him why he couldn't have told us this back in the bar, but decided against. "What do you have?" Charlotte asked, in a positive spirit. "Lemonade," the barman replied, with mild assurance. "Yes, well we'll have a gin and lemonade and a rum and lemonade."

There were comfortable cane chairs on the front verandah and we could watch little bits of Levuka going by outside. It was no more than twenty minutes later that the barman appeared in the front door with an expression of triumph. "There," he couldn't have shown more pride at unearthing the Koh-I–Noor diamond, "I found one in the bottom of the fridge." Held aloft was the treasure—a small bottle of Coca Cola.

* * *

Our lessons with Jone progressed through how to say "this" and "that" and "when" and "where"; how to say "I want" or "I need" something; what to say at meal times (a very important part of Fijian culture) things like "It smells nice," "I've had enough," "I'm full up" and how to say grace. We practiced describing types of pain and sickness, providing directions, telling the time, giving our family trees (parents, brothers, sisters). And then we were taught how to make a presentation.

On going to a strange village, Jone explained, one must take a valued gift for presentation to the chief. This could be a yaqona plant (what is called kava in English, from its Tongan name), the roots of which are pulverized to make an intoxicating drink. But if we were planning to stay a fair while then the gift must be a tabua or whale's tooth, the most prized wealth in Fiji.

Our lessons with Jone were light-hearted affairs, with lots of jokes and laughter. But with this, we had to be very serious. The visitor must place the gift before him, say who he is and where he comes from, explain the purpose of the visit and then finish by saying *asosoratu* in a high rising voice. The local chief will respond, accept the gift (which means that he is welcoming you into the village) and he will finish by saying *e-e-e-e*. Only then does the yaqona and tabua actually change hands.

It seemed an awful ordeal, far above our present competence in Fijian. But Jone said not to worry, we wouldn't actually have to do it ourselves. Every village had an official presenter who would act on our behalf. We'd just have to sit cross-legged behind him, look very solemn, join in on the responses and clap our hands in rhythm at the end. (The actual beat of the hand-clapping varied in different parts of Fiji, Jone explained, and we'd just have to imitate what everyone else did.)

Then it was necessary to prepare for visiting a village. Yaqona could be bought locally but we'd also need one or two whale's teeth. How were these to be acquired? (First locate your whale?) It seemed that every Fijian had a stock of tabuas and they passed back and forth in ceremony all the time—when two people were betrothed both parties would present whale's teeth; if you'd done some misdeed it would be expiated by presenting a tabua to the wronged party; and so on.

That was all very well for Fijians, but how were we to break into the circle? It turned out that pawn shops—run by Indians, of course—often had a few tabuas for sale. We walked up and down Marks Street and eventually located a nice selection in one shop. The big ones were forty or fifty dollars and the smaller ones twenty or twenty-five dollars each. Now I love bargaining and there's lots of opportunity for it in Fiji. We picked out one large tabua and two small ones, which would have added up to ninety dollars. "Sixty dollars," I offered. "No, seventy five," the shopkeeper said. He remained quite fixed at that figure, not prepared to come down another cent. Then I tried a trick that nearly always works. I pulled out three twenty-dollar bills and laid them on the counter. "Sixty dollars, take it or leave it." The actual sight of the money was too much for him. He snatched up the notes, we picked up the whale's teeth, and the deal was completed.

Okay. We had tabuas, and needed village to present them to. Charlotte had decided on Taveuni, the third largest island (but much smaller than Viti Levu or Vanua Levu). Her plan was to live as a member of a Fijian family in order to study language use from the inside, as it were. I value privacy and so I intended to wait until she was settled somewhere, then rent a house nearby to live on my own, working with interested speakers for perhaps a few hours each day. That way Charlotte could come and see me at weekends, or whenever she wanted.

Teevita Nawadra, head of the dictionary project, was going to spend Christmas and New Year's at his wife's village of Vuna on the south end of Taveuni. He said he'd ask whether they'd be interested in having Charlotte come and stay. Teevita seemed a bit vague about dates. First of all, he thought he'd be coming back to Suva early in the New Year. Then, next time we spoke he said he might stay for a week or two longer. Charlotte was given a phone number in Vuna and told not to call him there before the evening of Thursday, January 3rd. (The specificity of this seemed oddly out of keeping with the vagueness of the rest of the conversation.)

Jone also came up with an introduction, to Veronika, who worked in the Suva branch of Barclay's Bank. Vero turned out to be extremely helpful. She said her father, Josefa Cookanacagi, who lived in the village of Waitabu on the northeast side of Taveuni, loved having foreigners come and stay. (Although it was generally for two or three days, not six months!) She promised to call him up—if the village telephone was working—and explain about us.

Jone Cagi-ni-liwa-lala (the first name is of course an adaptation from English John, and the second means "wind of empty blowing," which describes some sort of mariner's nightmare) was then teaching us how to actually use the language. One morning we had a mock shop on his dining table, with Charlotte and I taking turns to be shopkeeper and customer. It developed a surrealistic hilarity. I moved the telephone onto the table. "You're not going to sell that?" Jone asked. "Oh yes we are," I countered.

We made a few elementary mistakes, like the shopkeeper telling the customer to "Go away" instead of "Come in," but they got sorted out. And in bargaining, each of us became so enmeshed in our own role that we didn't always pay attention to what the other was saying. "What will you offer me for this teapot—not fifty dollars, not thirty, not even twenty-five..." "I'll offer forty." "But we've already gone below that!"

This was just a practice for the real thing. The language of cooking was to be dealt with in two days' time, but first it was necessary to buy the ingredients. Jone took us to the open-air market in Suva with strict instructions to speak nothing but Fijian. He prodded us into plucking up the courage to go up to an old lady squatting on the ground to ask, "What might the name of this vegetable be?" or, "What is the cost of this vegetable?" Sometimes we didn't want to buy but instead explained that we were just practicing as part of language lessons. The ladies smiled in approval.

Then it was the language of cooking, which can of course only properly be learned while you're actually doing it. There was much more to learn than words. How to crack open a coconut, for instance. Jone did it with one blow of the coconut on the angle of a stair, or of a knife on the coconut. This turned out to be much harder than it looked. It was easier to scrape the flesh out (verb: *kari-a*), knead the flesh with hands under water (*boso-ka*), fold what was left in a cloth (*lobi-ka*), twist it round to squeeze out the last drops of milk (*loba-ka*). Our heads were reeling with verbs by the time we came to sit down for a lunch of taro leaves, cassava, fish and shell-fish.

Jone's wife Wai (literally "water") joined us for the meal. She was a nursing sister—trained at the hospital in Broken Hill, Australia—who had a full-time position as medical supervisor for the Peace Corps. Jone had mentioned to us the previous week that he'd told his wife he didn't want a Christmas present that year. "That means that you wouldn't buy anything for her, either?" we asked. "Yes," he grinned, "that's the whole idea, but I don't think she's tumbled to it."

I think she would have. Wai was a most impressive lady; obviously an excellent organizer. We were able to carry on a stumbling conversation in Fijian over the meal, much to Wai's surprise. She told us that the Peace Corps put on an intensive language course for its new recruits in Fiji and that some people went on to speak the language fluently but most didn't. They just sat on the edge of their assigned village, not being able to communicate with the people except a handful who might know a little English.

It was then getting near the end of December and Jone was preparing us for going out into the Fijian world, as it were. There were a number of rules about how to behave in a village—things that might have seemed trivial to us but had to be followed if we were not to offend cultural sensibilities. Don't yell within the confines of the village. Don't smoke or eat while walking around. Don't ever sit in a doorway. "Why?," we asked. "Because each house has its guardian god, who lives above the doorway, and would be offended if anyone sat there. You shouldn't even stand or talk in a doorway—only either inside or outside a house." Another rule concerned foundations—an old house might have been pulled down but the foundations (a raised rectangle of earth) would remain, and would belong to someone; never walk over foundations.

And, perhaps most important of all, never have anything on your head or shoulders within the boundaries of a village. Take off your hat, don't have a rucksack on your back, or even a towel over your shoulder. It seemed that this prohibition went back to warlike times when a visiting warrior was not allowed to have a spear on his shoulder. Anyway, whatever the origin, it was a custom that should most strictly be followed.

He also told us that in presentations the donor would disparage his gift and the recipient would magnify its size and value. Anyone presenting a whale's tooth would say *E lailai* "it's small" but the accepting chief would insist *E levu* "it's large." (One time, a few months later, we were watching the presentation of the smallest whale's tooth we'd ever seen, and it was hard to remain poker-faced at the description *E levu*. The whole point of course is that this verbal exchange is completely stylized.)

Anyway, we tried to get into the swing of things right there in Jone's house. I gave him a final check in payment for the lessons, which was perhaps a little more than a strict calculation would have given (but he was a superb teacher, as well as a most helpful friend). "Oh," Jone looked at the check, "*E levu.*" I shook my head: "*E lailai.*"

Back in May, Charlotte had made friends with a Fijian girl who lived in the middle of Suva and she had been visiting her once or twice each week, partly to practice conversation. Now about this time Charlotte was trying to choose a Fijian name for herself. I was all right, since Roopate is the accepted equivalent of Robert (I do prefer to be called Bob, but that wouldn't be possible here)—my Fijian name is pronounced "Row-*bah*-te"; every word must end in a vowel. It seemed that Koleta (let us say) was an appropriate Fijian version of Charlotte. So from then on she was Koleta.

Koleta's friend invited us both for Christmas dinner, which was both enjoyable and a useful sample of what village life would be like. We all sat cross-legged along an extended eating mat, laid along the floor, men at one end of the room and women at the other. After grace, we ate with our fingers, using both hands. It seemed that people held a huge chunk of yam or taro in the left hand, while using the right one for fish, chicken or greens.

2

"This is paradise"

On Wednesday, January 2, 1985 we caught the tiny Fiji Air plane from Nausori, just north of Suva, to Matei, at the apex of Taveuni. The accommodation guide had listed just two places in Taveuni—the Castaway International Hotel which cost $54 single, $60 double per night, and Kaba's Guest House, which was $8 single and $15 double.

Mr. Kaba (that wasn't his real name but we always called him that) was an Indian who ran the only modern-style supermarket on the island, just outside the village of Somosomo. This town had been notorious in the nineteenth century as perhaps the most bloodthirsty place in the whole Fiji group. Within a few weeks of the first missionaries arriving in 1839, sixteen young women were ceremoniously strangled and buried close to the missionaries' door, this being in honor of the chief's son who had been shipwrecked and eaten on a hostile island nearby.

The guest house had three twin bedrooms, with a communal sitting room, dining room and kitchen. There was a shower and washtub, with cold water only, and electricity was switched on by the parsimonious Kaba from 5:30 until about 9:30 each night. (It was powered by his private generator, since Taveuni had no regular electricity supply.) Mostly the guest house was pretty full, with a strange and ever-changing variety of people. There was usually an Indian family, who monopolized the two-ring gas burner in the kitchen and seemed to eat large meals of curry five times each day. An eye specialist from Labasa was on his monthly visit to the local hospital. And there was a young Englishman who had resigned from his diplomatic service at the end of a tour of duty in Uganda. Kampala was so marvelous, he said, that anywhere else would be anticlimactic, so he was backpacking around the world before trying to see whether he could make a career as a singer-pianist, somewhat in the Noel Coward style.

2. "This is paradise"

We wandered down into the village and Koleta, who had such a sunny, open personality that she made friends wherever she went, was soon surrounded by a gaggle of children. They took us around the village, explaining this and that, all talking at once. We were given ripe mangoes at one house and invited inside for a cup of tea and halting conversation at another. Somosomo seemed a peaceful village, far different from its murderous history. But what is it they say?—you see an angel on the surface, there's a devil lurking beneath. Only a few months later an old Indian woman was walking along the main road early one morning when she was murdered by a group of youths from Somosomo who'd been drinking yaqona all night.

The island of Taveuni is about twenty-six miles long and seven wide. There is a high mountain range in the middle so you can only travel around the outside (and then only around three-quarters of the perimeter, since there are high cliffs on the southwestern edge). Somosomo is in the middle of the western side, about mid-distant from our two possible field locations—Vuna, on the southern tip, and Waitabu, around the top on the northeastern shore.

We'd arranged that first Koleta should decide on where she could best do her work. It was a case of finding a family who would adopt her. Since a traditional Fijian house consists of one large room, in which everyone lives in close contact, this would involve a degree of adjustment by both sides. I'd then try and find a house to live in somewhere nearby, or at least somewhere on the island. I was keen that Koleta should start checking out the two villages straight away, then we could embark on actual fieldwork without any more delay.

Vuna, where Teevita Nawadra was staying, seemed the most likely location. My suggestion was that Koleta should call him up that first evening at Kaba's and see if it would be all right for her to catch the bus down to Vuna the next day. She demurred—Teevita had said not to ring him until the following day, the evening of Thursday, January 3. He *had* said that on one occasion but he'd generally been vague about how long he was staying away from Suva. He had been at Vuna since Christmas and there had been ample time to ask his wife's family whether they would welcome Koleta. What could it matter if she called on Wednesday or Thursday? But Koleta was firm—Teevita had said not to call until Thursday evening, and she didn't want to cause offense by not doing as he requested.

Then there was the lead we'd had from Jone's friend Vero—to Josefa Cookanacagi at Waitabu. Koleta was able to get through on the phone and he said "Yes, do come tomorrow." Apparently Waitabu wasn't actually on the main road so Josefa would send one of his daughters to meet Koleta off the ten o'clock bus.

Matei airport is on the way to Waitabu and when the bus stopped there the following morning who should Koleta see, sitting waiting for the plane back to Suva? That's right, it was none other than Teevita Nawadra. He was forced to come over to the bus, smile meekly at Koleta and say hello. Nothing was said about her staying at Vuna, or those strict instructions. But at least Koleta now knew it was Waitabu or nothing.

Fijian society is very male-oriented and as it was Koleta who was to choose a field location we had deemed it best for her to make the first exploratory trip to Waitabu alone. I was happy to stay back at Kaba's, explore a little locally, and relax. Six months away from the hustle and bustle of university administration and teaching had seemed the perfect opportunity to read all sorts of books I'd always wanted to. First of all, Plato's *Republic*.

I walked a couple of miles down the dusty road to Waiyevo, where the island's post office and hospital are located. Past the Castaway International Hotel, which looked deserted. Then another mile to Wairi'i, with a grand Catholic church built of stone, a Catholic high school, and a large wooden cross high on the hill. Fijian children coming out of school asked where I was from and then, apparently to test my language competence, asked me to count in Fijian (maybe that's what they'd been doing in school that day). I was permitted to stop at about eighteen.

The following morning, I took Plato for a stroll to the north. It was about midday, just by the Morris Hedstrom all-purpose store that the bus pulled up and, seeing me there, Koleta jumped out.

"Hey, Waitabu is a great place, just perfect. Josefa has adopted me as a daughter and there is his daughter Qito, she's my sister, who is so lovely. She'll teach me everything I want to know. Gee it's funny to be talking English again, I've only spoken Fijian for the past twenty-four hours."

Things were working out better than we had hoped. It seemed that Josefa had a small house that was vacant next to his own family home. We could live in that and have all our meals with the family. It might be the perfect combination of privacy and interaction, for both of us. Anyway, it wasn't at all the done thing in Fijian eyes for a couple to live anywhere but together. I said I'd be prepared to give it a go.

Since we'd be at Waitabu for at least three months in the first place (a short trip back to Suva had been provisionally planned for about April), Koleta thought we should see something of the western side of the island first, and not move out to Waitabu until Monday.

"Oh, and..." she added, hesitantly, "And I said you were five years younger than you are."

"Why?"

Numbers in Fijian are rather long-winded. Forty-five is *vaa-sagavulo 'a lima. Vaa* is "four," *sagavulo* is equivalent to "–ty," followed by *'a* "and" and finally *lima* "five." Koleta had said she was 26 (in fact she looked younger). Then they wanted to know my age. When Koleta said *vaa-sagavulo* "forty" there was a gasp of astonishment, so she left it at that and didn't add the extra *'a lima* "and five." It didn't make all that much difference to me. (We later discovered, in fact, that when Fijian people give their age—or anyone else's—there tends to be a wide margin for error.)

The next day we decided to catch the bus down to Soqulu, an old copra plantation south of Wairi'i which had been developed into housing units for foreign tourists. On the way we passed a plaque that marked where the International Date Line—180° east or west of Greenwich—crosses the Taveuni coast. Every so often magazines print funny stories about people on the island whose houses straddle the date line, so that they can wake up on Monday then go into the next room to have breakfast on Sunday. In fact, the actual date line is diverted away from 180° at this point, so that all the Fiji islands lie in the same time zone, just to the west of 180°. (The *Fiji Times* has a banner proclaiming that it is "the first newspaper published in the world today.")

Soqulu had been developed at tremendous expense, with paved roads criss-crossing up a hillside. But only a few of the blocks had been sold, only some of those had houses built on them, and quite a few of the houses that were there bore "for sale" notices. A couple of months back I'd seen an advertisement by the Soqulu developers in the *Australian Financial Review* offering a free air trip to Taveuni for anyone thinking of buying a block—they were that desperate! But who from Australia would want to build a house at Soqulu—to visit perhaps two or three times a year—when the nearest good beach was a dozen miles away, so you'd have to keep a car there? Also, the local hospital was said to be rather rudimentary; they had a dentist who visited once a month but all he did was extract bad teeth, no such thing as fillings.

We wandered around shuttered houses, across the golf-course, had a drink in the almost deserted clubhouse and caught the bus back to Kaba's. An Indian schoolteacher from Labasa on the north coast of Vanua Levu, had just arrived with his family. That evening, as we sat around Kaba's sitting room, he expounded on the desirability of speaking with a really good accent, like a pukka Englishman. This seemed surprising since he himself had a broad Indian pronunciation that was sometimes hard to make out. "That's what I teach my pupils," he insisted.

"What do you teach them?" we asked.

"This is a banana." These four words were articulated with a perfect BBC accent. He said them again "This is a banana." It turned out that our schoolteacher friend could only pronounce the one short sentence in the English manner. "This is a banana." But he did it very well indeed. An extreme example of specialization.

At about ten o'clock we tried to excuse ourselves. "No," he commanded, "you must stay. We will talk all night. Where else in the world would there be the opportunity for two such minds as yours and mine to communicate? We must make the most of it." (Ignoring Koleta was part of the chauvinism which Indians adhered to just as much as Fijians. Earlier in the day he'd offered a plate of curry just to me.)

Then it was necessary to buy supplies for living in Waitabu. Brightly colored cotton sheets and pillow cases, two pillows in a huge cardboard box, a bucket, a screw-top bottle for drinking water, a kerosene lamp, toilet paper, some lengths of cloth as presents for Koleta's new family and a couple of boxes of groceries as our contribution to the larder.

* * *

By that time, we had a rather incredible array of luggage, but Koleta said it was best to take the bus around to Waitabu—as a Fijian would—rather than a taxi. The one thing we wanted to avoid was arriving in a manner typical of tourists.

The bus garage was right next to Kaba's; from there the buses traveled to the south through Vuna and on to Navakawau. And then to the north, through the airport at Matei, past Waitabu, and on to the end of the road at Lavena. One bus spent the night at Lavena, leaving there at about 6:15 a.m. to bring people from the villages into the administrative center of the island, turning around at Somasomo at 8:30. There were three trips each way (two on Sundays) with the bus finishing up back at Lavena at about 6:30 p.m. I was able to persuade the man at the garage to dig out a set of timetables, but they turned out to be only a rough guide. The bus could be running half-an-hour or an hour behind schedule, especially late in the day, and sometimes it could be up to half-an-hour early. Occasionally the bus driver left Lavena ten minutes or so before he was supposed to and then would miss potential passengers, getting earlier and earlier along the route. One compensation was that the bus would stop anywhere. So, when we hadn't much luggage, we used to get onto the bus route ahead of time and then just start walking in the direction we were going, hailing the bus whenever it happened to reach us. (Sometimes if the journey was only three or four miles and the bus was very late, we arrived at our destination ahead of it.)

Buses in Taveuni didn't have any windows, but there were blinds that could sometimes be let down to keep out the sun or rain. There were open luggage racks—with rails to keep things from falling out—on the outside level with the wheel. We loaded some of our boxes and cases into these and hauled others inside the bus with us.

The main road—which had an asphalt surface only for a few hundred yards through Somosomo—ran close to the coast. We went past places the taxi driver had pointed out when we'd arrived five days before. The Fijian village of Welagi. A road leading up to a small settlement of Indian farmers who grew yaqona for sale to Fijians in the Suva market. Prince Charles Beach which had good bathing.

The road wound in and out of the cliffs. Past Matei airport then into the Vanua of Waini'eli (a Vanua is a confederation of three or four villages, with the chief of the leading village having authority over all of them.) Naselesele—a village with a large grassy green and a crescent of houses on the far side. The scenery was breathtaking; open forest on one side, clear blue ocean on the other, as our Indian driver swung around the bends. Qeleni village, almost hidden in the forest off to the right. Another couple of miles to Nava'acoa on flat ground between road and sea.

After half-a-dozen miles of Fijian land which had been left as forest—except for garden plots that were cleared as needed—we came to another plantation, a block of land that one of the older chiefs had sold to a European before the first English governor banned all further sales, a hundred and ten years earlier. There were rows of coconut palms, and cattle grazing between. Then it was forest again. A tiny village, straddling the road, up on a steep hill.

An hour and fifteen minutes after leaving Somosomo the bus stopped, apparently at nowhere. There were a few Fijian children standing by the side of the road and a rough track off to the left.

"We're here," Koleta stood up, arms full of parcels. "This is the turn-off for Waitabu. That's my sister Qito and those children with her must be some more of my brothers and sisters."

The bus driver was happy to wait while we unloaded everything. (There's never any "rush" or "go" about things on Fiji.) Qito—pronounced Ng-gito—was a buxom seventeen year-old with a winning smile. She'd been to school in Suva and knew a little English; none of the children

The "main road" leading from the bus route down to Waitabu village.

understood anything but Fijian. Well, it was going to be Fijian, Fijian and more Fijian from now on.

The road to Waitabu was downhill with a high wooded bank rising from one side and falling away on the other. Our welcome party were willing carriers but none of them could manage very much. About halfway down I had to leave one suitcase on the edge of the road and struggle on with just a couple of things in each hand.

We came onto a flat stretch with a bamboo pipe projecting a stream of pure water from a seven-foot high ledge. (As we soon discovered this was called *Paipo Wa'olo Levu*, or the Main Road Pipe, one of the three places where villagers went to bathe.) Ahead was a traditional house with high thatched roof. To the right, twenty or thirty men were erecting a building out of concrete blocks.

"This is the edge of the village," Koleta warned, taking off her own hat. I grabbed mine. "And the backpack too," she advised.

There was a man sitting right on top of the far wall, slapping mortar into place. He waved and came over.

"This is Roopate," Koleta said in Fijian. I smiled, trying to get used to the name. "And Josefa, who is my father." (In fact, everyone called him Sepo, which is a kind-of short form of Josefa.)

The village, approached from the bottom of the "main road."

"We are building a new store," Sepo explained. "The old one is close to falling down. I am the storekeeper, along with many other responsibilities. Come along now to my house."

A Fijian house is not a place to be approached casually. There are three distinct areas. The back portion is the "private" part, for sleeping, and only family members may venture there. The part nearest the front door is the public area, where visitors may sit. Between the two is a rather difficult region. The head of the house may sit there when talking to visitors. He may even invite a guest to join him in the middle portion but it is considered good manners—a gesture of humility—to refuse and insist on sitting near the front door.

There are also two side doors but those are exclusively for use by members of the family. You may be invited, as a form of politeness, to enter or leave by a side door but to be equally polite you should decline, and use the main door.

I must admit that after struggling across the village with backpack and hat in hand as well as all the bags and parcels, I went in through the front door and just sat in the place Sepo pointed to, not thinking about it.

Fijians had no furniture. Even then, houses in many villages had a bit but Waitabu was very traditional. Sepo had a table and a couple of chairs pushed against one wall (it was one of only two tables, in a village of twenty houses) but he only used them occasionally, for doing accounts or writing letters.

We sat on the plank floor, facing the middle of the room. And we sat cross-legged, as Jone had instructed, foot under opposite knee, hands on ankles and back kept straight. I wondered where our own house was; it would be nice to unpack and relax. But that, apparently, came much later.

Before anything else there must be a presentation. Among our impedimenta Koleta had a bundle of yaqona roots, bought from an Indian trader next to Kaba's. Sepo put it firmly on one side. "I have the complete plant. More appropriate if you are going to stay for a while." It was six feet long from the ends of the hairs on the root to the top most leaf. "And you have a tabua, Koleta?" I scrambled in what I hoped was the right bag and produced, as we'd agreed, the largest whale's tooth. Sepo weighed it approvingly in one hand.

All sorts of people came in and out of the house. There was Sepo's wife, Aqela Bogi (wife and husband have quite different names in Fiji) who offered us a cup of tea and dry scones. It seemed that the presentation wouldn't take place for a while yet (nothing ever really does in Fiji). Koleta had mentioned that the chief was Sepo's elder brother, so surely it should be reasonably informal.

An oldish person wearing a green T-shirt that bore the legend PHANTOM CLUB CALIFORNIA came in and sat down. I was still a bit dazed by everything and couldn't quite decide whether the new arrival was male or female—flabby chest and a slightly high voice (high for a man or low for a woman). He/she addressed a few words to Sepo in Fijian and plainly didn't understand the bits of English that Koleta's new father was directing at us, translating what he had just said in Fijian.

"You have all your bags?"

Oh no, I remembered the one by the roadside. Sepo spoke a couple of words to a man in his early twenties—must be one of his sons—who slipped out of a side door. We'd been able to understand Jone, and the ladies in the Suva market, but I could pick up nothing at all of the conversation going on around us now. There were some dialect differences, such as using a glottal stop (like the sound in the middle of a cockney pronunciation of *butter* as *bu'er*) where standard Fijian would have a "k." The word for "good," also used for "thank you," is *vina'a* in Waitabu compared with *vinaka* in Suva. It should be possible to adjust to this substitution. But all the speech in that room seemed so fast, vowels and consonants merging together into what sounded like one long slur.

Sepo was explaining terms of address. Koleta would use *Tata* "father" for him and *Nana* "mother" for Bogi. I should call Sepo *Moomoo*, which could be roughly translated as both "uncle" and "father-in-law," and Bogi would be my *Nei*. I tried to memorize at least this.

Our missing suitcase was brought in and put just inside the front door. Tea cups were taken away. Why didn't they get the presentation business over? Was the chief out of the village, or what?

Sepo said something to Koleta and she passed on the information that there were two Mataqalis (or clans) in the village. The chief belonged to one but there must also be a senior member of the other Mataqali present at any ceremony.

I wondered if people would get changed for what appeared to be an important event. Sepo had been bare-chested at the building site but now donned a rather nice blue T-shirt that said SUVA ELECTRIC LAUNDRY on the back. He was to make the presentation on our behalf.

A man came in through the front entrance, someone with a bit of a limp and a tic on one side of his face. Obviously the man we'd been waiting for. But how to behave toward such an important person? I half rose from the cross-legged position and shook hands (both of which were the wrong thing to do, but no one seemed annoyed). He sat down next to PHANTOM CLUB CALIFORNIA. I'd now decided that that person must be a man, probably the senior member of the other Mataqali.

Sepo motioned us to sit behind him, near the door. And then proceeded to make the most solemn and serious speech, really as if addressing an important monarch. He chose his words deliberately; then some hesitation, then a stream of high-blown language. The cheering thing was that I could understand quite a lot of it. He explained who we were, about our coming from a university in *Ositerelia* (which is *Australia*, in proper phonetic form), about wanting to study the language of the Vanua of Boumaa (of which Waitabu is a constituent village), that we would respect the laws and customs of the village. There was even a gratuitous mention about our being solid Christians and bits of references all through to *'Alou*, which is "God." Sepo pushed forward the yaqona plant and then our best whale's tooth, at various stages of the lengthy introduction. At last he uttered the ritualized ending phrase *asosovatu* and we joined in the rhythmic clapping.

Both the man in the green Californian T-shirt and the man with a tic made speeches of acceptance. These were a bit shorter than Sepo's peroration but spoken much faster so that I couldn't pick up anything except references to the exceptional size of the tabua. More clapping in unison.

Suddenly it was all finished; everyone relaxed. We moved back to sitting in a circle.

"Try and chat a bit with the chief," Koleta whispered.

My Fijian went as far as commenting on the weather and saying what a nice village it was. But then it turned out that he knew some English and was able to explain about his recent stroke, which accounted for the limp and the tic. He was no longer able to go to the garden. I sympathized. The man in the green Phantom Club shirt plainly couldn't understand English. He just sat and grinned, rather like a Cheshire cat. I was a little bit uneasy about him being left out of the conversation but at least the chief seemed happy to be talking about his affliction.

Koleta was chatting with Sepo. Then he went over to say something to the two older men.

"I said talk to the chief," she hissed.

"Well, I have."

"No, that's not him. The one in the Phantom Club shirt is the chief, Sepo's brother."

Oh dear! The person I'd thought might be a woman was actually the chief. He'd been there all the time, while we were waiting for the ceremony to begin, while we'd been waiting for the representative of the other Mataqali—the man who'd had a stroke (who was called Pelasio). And for the last fifteen minutes I'd been talking with Pelasio in English, completely ignoring the chief.

I *ought* to have realized. He had come through the side door as would be appropriate for a member of the family, Sepo's brother. Looking back it should have been obvious. But at the time my mind, traumatized by transfer into a new culture, just didn't work in the way that it should.

A new conversation started up, about the battalion of the Royal Fiji Army that was serving on the UN Peace-Keeping Force in the Middle East. I resolved to keep a low profile, to smile at the chief and nod whenever he said anything (really not being able to understand whatever he was telling us). Someone took down, from a hook on the opposite wall, a photograph of Sepo's oldest son who was currently in Lebanon. They gave it to Koleta who then passed it on to me. The conversation turned to something else—it wasn't clear to me exactly what the topic was now. I was left holding the photo. so I very quietly tiptoed across the room and put it back on its hook.

Everyone stopped talking and there was a sharp intake of breath. Oh-oh, I'd done it again. Broken two taboos all in one movement. I'd moved across in front of the chief, and I'd risen to a position higher than him, standing while he was sitting.

"You can do it," Sepo explained, mercifully in English, "but you must say *tulou* which is like your "excuse me."" It did ring a bell. A great big loud clattering one. Jone had rehearsed us in that very word when he had been acting as chief, at our pretend ceremonies in Suva.

The chief smiled, as if to say he could see I was confused and now sorry, and that he was still making allowances. But he obviously wouldn't continue to do so for much longer. I'd wanted to be accepted as part of the village, and now seemed to be in imminent danger of being summarily ejected.

Everyone was getting up and moving outside. "A little yaqona party," Sepo explained.

The party was in the next-door house and our host was Elia Waqa, a man with a round face surrounded by what looked like a solid halo of very black frizzy hair, and a deep, mellow voice. He was the leader of the Waiso'i Mataqali, the one to which Pelasio belonged. The senior Mataqali—to which the chief and Sepo (and Koleta, as his daughter) belonged—was called Vuunivesi.

We sat around a large carved wooden bowl called a tanoa, full of yaqona (looking the color of dirty washing-up water). A cup made out of a half coconut shell was dipped in and handed around the participants, according to a strictly determined order, by Mataqali and by seniority. It was offered and accepted and drunk and returned in formulaic manner. We were each given just a quarter-cup full since as Sepo said, we wouldn't be used to yaqona and it was best to begin slowly.

Where did I fit into the Mataqalis of Waitabu? The normal rule was that one should marry someone of the opposite Mataqali. Since Koleta was Vuunivesi did that make me automatically Waiso'i, she asked. "Oh no, no," people looked down as they explained, you could only belong to a Mataqali by blood ties.

It seemed I was a nobody, some stranger that Koleta—now accepted as a member of the village—had met outside and brought here.

Then Elia Waqa spoke, looking straight at me and smiling with mouth and eye and hands. A couple of hours earlier I might have been able to understand a bit of what he was saying but now a fog had entered my brain.

"He's saying," a youth who knew some English explained, "That he adopts you as his son. So now you are a member of the Waiso'i Mataqali."

The fog cleared. I turned to Elia and said "Thank you very much, Father. I am most humbly grateful."

Elia responded with a broad smile, and a friendly paternal pat on the knee.

* * *

Koleta and I had bought little notebooks, about six inches by four, that would fit into a pocket and could be used for writing down words and sentences as we heard them.

Back in Sepo's house I took down, at his dictation, the names of the four villages that make up the Boumaa Vanua. Lavena was furthest away. Then 'Orovou (sometimes just called Boumaa), where the main chief lived. Next was Viidawa, and then Waitabu. There was one more village, called Wai (the last one we had come through on the bus), but it was really an offshoot from Waitabu and went under the same chief. There was a third Mataqali—called Veiniu—all of whose members lived at Wai.

I then asked Sepo about his children, because it was going to be necessary to try to keep track of who was who. Thirteen in all, but that included the first-born, Maria, who'd died as a baby. Next was Vero who worked at the bank in Suva and had given us the introduction to Sepo. Then Peteroo, with the army in Lebanon, and Maarawa, the one who'd gone to get the suitcase I'd had to leave by the side of the road. Next came two daughters who were married to soldiers and living in Suva. Then Qito, who had met us off the bus and had been deputed by Sepo to be Koleta's—and my—language helper. Maritina, the next, would soon be returning to her school in Suva. Then two more daughters, Elena and Filo (short for Filomena), the third son, Elia, who was about eleven, then Mariana, and Vilimaina aged three (who sucked her thumb a lot of the day and had all the makings of being a spoiled youngest child).

Lunch time. Sepo got up from the floor and pulled out a chair. "We will sit at the table, this meal only. All future meals you will eat with the family, in Fijian style!" I think the others had had their lunch—while I was being adopted by Elia Waqa—so just Sepo, Koleta and I ate with forks in the European style. It was a considerate gesture by Sepo and Bogi, to ease us gently into village life.

The next thing on Sepo's agenda—were we ever, I wondered, going to have any say about what we wanted to do—was a tour of the village. It was in the shape of a square—beach on the south side, a high cliff to the east, uncleared forest at the north and a rather stagnant looking backwater over to the west. Sepo explained that only men bathed there. (It looked distinctly unhealthy so I always preferred to swim in the sea, or have a fresh-water shower under the Main Road Pipe.)

Right next to the beach was the village green, also used for rugby practice: there were large, uneven bamboo goalposts at each end. Fronting the green was a row of four houses, and the old wooden store. Then three more rows, each with houses opposite a gap in the row before, to get the sea breeze. Two houses, including that of the chief, were built in traditional style, with materials obtained entirely from the forest—thick tree trunks for the frame, bound reeds for the walls, and a rich, steep thatch of coconut fronds. The chief's house had been built just the previous year, Sepo said. All the men and youths in the village had worked together and the entire construction had taken about two weeks.

Most of the houses were like Sepo's, walls and floor of planed timber on a raised foundation of concrete blocks, and a roof of corrugated iron (not too different from most houses in the tropical parts of Australia). These houses cost money—for the planks and iron—which could be gotten by gathering coconuts and selling the dried kernels, or copra, or by money sent home by family members who worked in Suva or some other town. One house—and the new store—were made of concrete blocks. These were made at Waitabu, but money was needed for the bags of concrete, and to have a lorry (or, as Americans call it, a truck) to fetch a load of

Left: There were several places to bathe and I preferred the "main road pipe" which was high enough to accommodate me. *Right:* Since this bathing place was on the road, it was necessary to wear swimming trunks.

sand. (No one in the village owned a car, or—unlike most other villages—even a boat.)

Sepo then took us to the graveyard, at the southwestern corner of the village. There was one recent grave that had a scaffolding from which fluttered streamers of colored paper and cloth. It was Elia Waqu's wife, who had died just before Christmas.

Finally, five or six hours after we'd arrived, Sepo wondered if we'd like to see our house. (How did he guess?) It was right next to his own large house and I could have seen it through the open door during the morning, if I'd known what I was looking at.

Like a small rectangular shed, about fifteen feet by ten. Raised a foot or so off the ground on an earth foundation. The frame consisted of six stout posts, at each corner and in the middle of the longest sides, joined at the top by horizontal bars. The walls were rows of reeds (looking like thin bamboo), finished off on the outside with plaited coconut leaves. The front and side doors were the sides of old packing cases that had to be just lifted into place. For a roof, we had six pieces of corrugated iron, set at a very slight angle—about six inches difference in height between front and back—for the rain to run off. It was perhaps six feet high—three inches less than me and I had to stoop quite a bit to go through the doorway. But I was used to that.

Inside there was just floor. Woven mats were laid over a bed of dry coconut fronds which had a springy feel. Oh—and there was a curtain that could be pulled across, about two thirds of the way back, to close off the private, sleeping area. Aqela Bogi had tied a rope across one of the back corners, as a wardrobe, with half-a-dozen metal coat hangers. Someone had put our bags and boxes just inside the front door—save for the groceries, which Sepo had accepted with a formal speech of gratitude.

I was taken with the house, the village, the people, the location. Who needs anything more to live on than soft mats? We had a sandy beach. The deep blue Pacific Ocean. I had an adopted father. The chief appeared to forgive my faux pas. Outside there was the melodic sound of talk in Boumaa Fijian, full of glottal stops. (The only English we'd heard had been what Sepo and Pelasio addressed to us.) We couldn't fail to learn to speak the language in such an environment.

"This is paradise," I told Koleta. "It's going to be a marvelous six months. We shan't need to go to Suva in April, or anything like that."

Paradise isn't a lonely place. As we unpacked, placing three or four shirts or dresses on a single hanger, there was an open-mouthed audience. Young children, home from school, just came in by the front door and sat there watching, chattering to themselves about all the things we had. Cassette recorder. Books and notebooks to go into a cardboard carton that took on a new function as bookcase. I had a blue rucksack with lots of compartments. Great for storage in a house that has no drawers or shelves. Handkerchiefs on the left-hand side, underpants on the right.

Some adults and teenagers came in too; others sat outside (I'm sure we exceeded all overcrowding statutes, although all the visitors did stay on the public side of the house). There were a number of T-shirts which bore messages in English, the most priceless being FIGHTING FOR PEACE IS LIKE F**KING FOR VIRGINITY. It was plain that most people, including the chief, had no conception of the meaning of the words they wore. (However, our reaction to the FIGHTING FOR PEACE ... one may have registered, for we never saw it again.)

Finally, most of our belongings were distributed. The kerosene lamp was hung on a nail in the roof frame. Koleta put a red cloth over my half-empty suitcase, to serve as a table. The children were still chattering at what they'd seen. What was essentially a Spartan camping kit to us plainly seemed like riches to them.

I'd finished but Koleta was arranging her lotions, as much as one can with just a couple of cardboard boxes. There were still a dozen kids in the room. What better time than the present to begin fieldwork?

During the afternoons in Suva I'd organized a large notebook with some of the most basic words in standard Fijian, arranged by semantic fields. Body parts, animals, birds, cooking, gardens, then types of adjectives and verbs. I started to go through these, checking whether the Boumaa dialect had the same term or a different one.

Body parts are a good place to begin because you can point to them. *Ulu* "head." *Tautauvata*, I was told, which meant "the same." *Mata* "eye," *ucu* "nose," *bati* "tooth"—all the same. "Mouth" was different—*gusu* in the standard dialect but *dra'a* in Boumaa. If there was a *k* it got replaced by the glottal stop, which I wrote as '. *Kumi* "beard" becomes *'umi*, *kolii* "dog" is *'olii*. Standard Fijian doesn't have the sound *p* but Boumaa does, so Boumaa can have *pusi* "cat" where the standard dialect has *vusi* (this is plainly a loan word from the English *pussy*). Most words are the same, as would be expected between mutually intelligible dialects of one language, but there were some important differences. Sepo came in and took over. The Boumaa word for "road" or "track" was *wa'olo*, corresponding to *gaunisala* in standard Fijian. "Main road" is *wa'olo levu* (literally: "road big").

Now Aqela Bogi, Koleta's mother came and joined us. Nei (or "aunt") as I called her was born in Vuna, had married Sepo when she was in her mid-teens and borne him those thirteen children over a period of about twenty-seven years. During the next six months, we came to value Bogi as one of the finest people in the world—kind, sensible, compassionate, incredibly hard-working (in Fiji, as in many parts of the world, women do at least three-quarters of the work) and a fine organizer. She was concerned that everything was all right for us: the house, the mats—which she had woven.

Sepo lifted down the lamp. "I've bought you a half bottle of kerosene from the store." I'd need to learn how to light it. What was the verb for that—*waqa*? No, no, that was in Bauan (as Sepo referred to the standard dialect). In Boumaa we say *udre*.

Swish! A bucketful of water came in through the front door, all over our new mats. It is a Fijian New Year's custom to throw water over your friends and neighbors. We'd seen it happen outside Kaba's Guest House, from the back of a lorry. Surely this was a good sign, and a mark that the people of Waitabu were accepting us. Sepo didn't think so. He went outside and berated the miscreants. (Everyone loved and respected Sepo, but he did tend to go on a bit sometimes, and no one paid too much attention.) Bogi just started mopping it up, with some of the rags she had brought in, and we helped. As I was to learn in the months ahead,—months of torrential cyclonic rain— mats must *not* be allowed to remain damp, or they will rot away.

Did Koleta want to bathe before supper? She certainly did. (I said I'd wait until the morning.) Most of the women went to the pipe at *Vatu Loa* or "Black Rock." There was a path through a patch of forest at the southeast corner of the village, just under the cliff, to a bamboo pipe only about two feet above a shallow rock pool.

Aqela Bogi (my Nei, "mother-in-law," or "aunt"), kind and caring.

The Fijians had once lived in a natural way, wearing whatever clothes seemed appropriate to their climate and customs, and certainly bathing naked. Then the missionaries arrived, bringing in their baggage the doctrine of original sin. They so pushed the idea of clothes that today all Fijian women keep breasts and shoulders and legs and knees out of view. The Fijians tend to be offended nowadays by foreign tourists who wear skimpy shorts or swim-suits or off-the-shoulder dresses (that is, who dress in a manner not dissimilar to that in which the Fijians did, before the men of God came among them).

All bathing places in Waitabu were essentially public, so you could never be fully naked (except after dark). I had to wear swimming trunks, which was a minor inconvenience. But when Koleta got to the Black Rock

Pipe, she had to change into a bathing *isulu*, which went from neck down to shins, and wash herself through and under it.

She brought back our bucket full of water, for washing at night and morning, and the screw-top bottle with drinking water. (The water was lovely, even if one did have to go quarter-of-a-mile to fetch it.) *Ta'i-wai*, that's "fetch water," Sepo explained. I could see that it was a compound verb, incorporating the noun *wai* "water."

Then it was time for supper. The eating mat (really a long tablecloth) began at the door and went down the center of the house for as far as the number of participants demanded. As head of the family, Sepo sat on the end at the right, furthest from the door. As honored guest, I sat opposite him. All the men are supposed to sit at the top of the mat, and then the women, but Koleta was given a place next to me, ahead of her brother Maarawa (as a concession to foreigner customs). We sat with legs crossed and back straight which can, after half-an-hour or so, be a bit of a strain on knee muscles if you haven't been brought up doing it.

First of all, grace. Waitabu was a Catholic village, so we had a more ornate invocation than the simple Wesleyan formula Jone had taught us. Sepo said four or five sentences, everyone responded *moni masulaki keimami* then another sentence from Sepo and the communal "*Ameni.*"

The food was lovely. Fish, greens, taro. All cooked in coconut milk. The family chattered around us; I didn't even try to understand what they were saying. It was enough just to eat, with our fingers, the delicious dishes Bogi had placed all along the eating mat.

"There's a dance tonight." My reverie was broken by Sepo speaking in English. With *mata qiriqiri livaliva*, or "electric band." (The old word *livaliva* "lightning" is now used for "electricity.")

"But where...?"

"They bring their own electric generator, and fuel for it. On a lorry from Wairi'i."

The chief, having finished supper in his own house, came in through a side door and sat with that benevolent grin, watching us eat.

"You'd be too tired—?"

"Yes, Father," Koleta replied, in Fijian. "We are both very tired, and humbly beg that you excuse us from attending the dance tonight."

"Next time then." I assume that's what the chief said, because Sepo added, in both Fijian and English: "Next time you can attend, when you have recovered from the journey."

We'd finished the meal. There was, however, no such thing as just leaving the mat. Got to get it right the first day, if you're ever going to. Sepo told us what to say in Fijian, to be excused. "Nei, thank you for a fine meal. I am now quite full. May I please be excused to now go and rest."

The electric band started about nine. We had no idea what time it finished—having long before collapsed onto the floor and into sleep.

3

Our Village

When you wake on the first morning in a new place, it's often hard to realize where you are.

Boom. Boom. Boom.

"Hey," I sat up quickly. "What's that?"

Boom. Boom. Boom. Then a pause. Boom-boom. Boom-boom. Boom-boom.

"It's the drums," Koleta explained.

"Yes." I'd managed to work that out. "But why, it's only—" I looked at the clock, "—only twenty to six."

"For church. It starts at six o'clock. Quick, we'd better get dressed to be there on time. Our first morning, it'll make a bad impression if we don't attend."

Well, I had been prepared for it, but it was still a bit of a shock! Most Fijians belong to the Wesleyan church (the local name for Methodist) which has church several times a week and several times on Sunday. Waitabu was a Catholic village with church held twice each day. At 6 a.m. and 6 p.m. on weekdays, and at 10 a.m. and 6 p.m. on Sundays. I still did plan to declare that I was an atheist (although the intention was growing weaker by the hour). But whatever I might tell people in the future it was definitely a polite thing to go to church on that first morning.

One of the questions Koleta had been asked the previous week was about our religion. She'd said Church of England. A nice, respectable sounding sect that isn't much represented in Fiji. Now if we really *had* been devout C. of E. we might have objected quite strongly to attending Catholic services. (No one appeared to consider this, and smell a rat!) We started to get dressed. I had to make sure not to lift arms above stooped head when donning shirt.

Boom-bum-bum. Boom-bum-bum.

3. Our Village

Top and bottom: In days of yore, slit-drums, "lali," were a call to battle. Now they announce that a church service is imminent.

The second drums, at ten to six, were quicker, more insistent. Time to leave your house and start toward the church.

Most villages do have a central building that is used just as a church. Not Waitabu (which was one of the poorest villages in Fiji, in terms of material goods). Church simply rotated between the people's houses. There were twenty, so after twenty days the circuit began again.

I was wearing long trousers, shirt, sandals. Koleta had on a Fijian *isulu* that she'd bought in Suva. We just followed everyone toward a house in the row in front.

Dum-ti-dum-ti. Dum-ti-dum-ti.

The third set of drums, indicating that church was now about to begin, were quicker still, a rhythm that was almost syncopated. I stopped for a moment to watch two youths as they bent over the drums, called *lali*. Each was a thick tree trunk with a hollow carved slit, a bit reminiscent of a pig trough. The lali were on a high earth foundation, just like a house, protected from rain by a thatched cover, something like what you'd find over a churchyard gate in nineteenth century England.

"Come on," Koleta urged. "We should be sitting down inside by the time the drums finish. You go to the front, with the men, and I'll stay here at the back."

The back was the wall next to the front door, against which Koleta was able to lean, as a couple of old ladies willingly edged along to make room for her. I stationed myself just behind Sepo.

He and Bogi had told us not to bother about the evening service, which included many prayers and could be rather drawn out (what they didn't say but clearly implied was: unbearably tedious). The morning ones were shorter and brighter.

Suddenly, Sepo burst into song. It was so loud and unexpected that I almost jumped back—as much as one can, from a cross-legged position. Within four bars everyone else in the room had joined in. Only Sepo had a hymn book, I saw. But if you've been to church twice a day for the whole of your life, I suppose you would know every hymn in the book off by heart.

It was a European-style tune, but sung with more verve and style than I'd ever heard in an English church in my youth. Then Felise, the village catechist or church leader, called for the blessing of God the father, Him the Son and Him the Holy Ghost—I recognized that much—and began intoning a prayer. Everyone joined in that too. It was a mindless communal mumble into which came a periodic rasp of throat-clearing from the chief, stationed just in front of Sepo.

I just sat there and stole quick glances around the room. Some photographs on the wall of family members. Right in the middle of the center curtain, which had been pulled back, was a framed picture of Jesus on the cross.

Someone was gently thumping me in the ribs. A round-faced boy with a vacant expression. He moved closer, jabbing with elbow and trying to look intensely into my eyes. Then a man behind cuffed him on the side of the head, at which he whimpered and desisted.

There must have been seventy or eighty people on the floor of the house—not everyone from the village but certainly most of them. Little children sat in front of the men, going up into the private part of the house. Felise now read a lesson—something about St Paul—from a large octavo book, punctuated by random babbling from the smallest children. I noticed that an eight-year-old girl might be in charge of her little baby brother; if he made too much noise she'd quietly slip out through the side door.

Then another hymn. Part-singing this time, contraltos responding to the call of the basses. It was great sitting listening to the music, I decided, even at six o'clock in the morning. The actual sitting wasn't too wonderful, though. I was trying discretely to rub the cramp out of my right knee. Another muttered communal prayer. Then a final "God the father, Him the Son and Him the Holy Ghost" and it was all over. Not too bad. Couldn't have been more than half-an-hour.

"You mustn't mind Pio," Sepo said, as we were walking back.

"Who?"

"The youth sitting next to you," Koleta explained, "the one who was punching you half-way through."

"He's not all there in the head," Sepo said. "but he means no harm."

"I think he likes you," Koleta added, with a wink.

Breakfast was like supper. The same routine—grace, how to be excused at the end of the meal. We had a slice of *weleti*, what is called paw-paw in Australia and papaya in the rest of the world, followed by a plate-full of deep-fried pancakes—well, they are called *panikeke* but look and taste and a bit like doughnuts without the sugar. We were able to chat a bit in Fijian when people addressed us, speaking slowly and using simple language. But when they just talked among themselves we were lost.

Sepo continued to organize our time. That morning, a trip to the waterfall at Tavoro. Qito was busy so we'd be escorted by her just-younger sister Maritina. (Sepo even instructed her the exact route to follow!)

We left the village by the graveyard and walked along the beach. (I was just dying to come down on my own to swim, and then lie on the sand and read a book.) Then, to avoid a circuitous promontory ahead, we turned off to the right, through Viidawa. I remembered to take off my hat as we entered the village. This took us back to the main road—the one the bus traveled on—which then came down to the beach as it skirted 'Orovou, capital village of Boumaa. This looked big—there were houses rising up a hillside, as well as a school, a big Catholic church and a smaller Wesleyan one. I asked Maritina how many people might live there. Oh, maybe, a hundred—or five hundred. (People in Fiji don't think in terms of numbers in the way we do.)

Maritina was sixteen, and going back to school in Suva at the end of the week; she stayed with one of Sepo's sisters who lived in the city. It was the same school that Qito had been to, but Qito hadn't worked and had failed the school-leaving examination. Then she'd had a job in Suva but had lost that. Sepo heard she had got into bad company so he'd gone across to bring her back to the village—just about a month before we arrived. Oh, so that might explain why Qito seemed happy and radiant one moment but sulky the next.

About two miles from Waitabu we turned off the main road onto a track to Tavoro, one of the major tourist attractions in Taveuni. A medium-sized waterfall, with a cool, inviting pool at its base. But we hadn't brought swimming togs, so couldn't bathe. What a shame!

The afternoon was our own, it seemed. Koleta went off to talk to some of the ladies. She wanted to become accepted as just another member of the village—weaving and fishing and cooking and so on. I knew what I wanted—the beach and a swim and Plato.

It was all right for an hour. Then a realization gradually dawned. That we were here, really here, for at least three months. The first page of my small notebook was filling up with words and phrases in Fijian. But there was room at the back for some thoughts on the situation we were in.

At least it had happened gradually:

STAGE I—SUVA. No Australian papers, little world news, little English on the radio. We tried Fijian food. We spoke Fijian a bit. Lots of mosquitoes.

STAGE II—KABA'S GUEST HOUSE. We could still buy the *Fiji Times* each day. No radio (my tiny portable couldn't pick up Suva). Mostly Fijian–like food available which we had to cook for ourselves. Washing clothes and selves in cold water but at least there was a primitive shower. To communicate with Fijians we had to speak Fijian.

3. *Our Village*

STAGE III—WAITABU. No newspapers of any sort available. Only Fijian food. No electricity or running water. Except for the occasional snatch of English from Sepo, Qito, or Maritina only Fijian was available.

We were now almost entirely cut off from our own culture. For better or for worse? It was going to be for the best!

I changed behind a tree into my swimming clothes and went in for a bath. The water was about three feet deep. A great place to ruminate. There were children coming along the beach on the way home from school in 'Orovou. I had my back turned and was watching a boat go by, far out.

Suddenly I wasn't alone. Seventeen children had dropped school bags on the beach and come to join me in the water, girls still in their dresses, boys in underpants. Literally join me. I had two tiny children hanging on each arm and three pulling at my back. Babbling with laughter and Fijian. Hey, they warned, watch out for *daku-daku-laci*. "What's that?," I asked. A snake in the sea, I was told, with black and white stripes, very poisonous.

Later on, I realized that none of the adults at Waitabu ever bathed in the sea for pleasure. The women would wade out at night to catch fish. If anyone had a skin disorder they might immerse themselves rather solemnly, since sea water was believed to be good medicine for a rash. Just going for a dip—swimming and floating and relaxing—was strictly children's play. Well, it might set me apart from the rest of the village, which my skin color and work habits would anyway, so there was really no point in pretending, but I was certainly planning to have a swim at least once a day.

I later discovered that *daku-daku-laci* isn't at all dangerous. The kids were just trying to scare me. (They hadn't succeeded; I don't scare easily.) There really aren't any dangerous animals on Fiji, except for the occasional wild pig. That's because there hardly are any animals in Fiji. The rat and the bat and a few little lizards. The most dangerous animals were the olden-day cannibal Fijians.

* * *

The next day, Wednesday, we decided to miss church. About three morning services each week and then the main one on Sunday would be enough, Koleta decided (and I most definitely agreed). I'd been awakened about four o'clock by the roosters crowing as they wandered around between the houses. Then I'd half-dozed but had heard some of the women moving about and talking quite a bit before the first slow Boom. Boom. Boom from the lali.

We got up when the second drums sounded, and went off to wash just as the first hymn wafted out. We'd just got back, and opened the front door, by the time the service had ended.

Someone came through the door and plonked himself down just inside. We looked around. Oh lordy, it was the chief. Then he gave a slightly sheepish grin and relaxed. It plainly wasn't a mission of complaint—that we'd skipped church—but simply a friendly, chiefly call to ensure everything was satisfactory.

I get tongue-tied in situations like that and—in any case—Koleta was a much more natural and fluent language learner. "Any problems?" the chief inquired. "No," Koleta assured him, "none at all. This is a lovely house, in a lovely village and we have a lovely family." The chief now grinned broadly.

We wondered, what should we offer him? We must try some gesture of hospitality. "Er, how about a glass of water, Big Uncle," I suggested, recovering my tongue.

"Oh yes, that would be most acceptable."

I got out the plastic cup we had purchased in Kaba's supermarket and poured a generous draught, which he downed in one. Would he like another? A gracious nod that he would. (Must have been all that hymn singing.)

By this time several more of Sepo's children, including Qito, had come in and sat cross-legged on the floor.

The chief chatted at us in his own inimitable way, and we understood virtually nothing of it. How I looked forward to the time—surely only a month or so off—when I would be able to follow what he was saying. Some things were clearly statements. We nodded and he seemed satisfied. Others were questions. (In Fijian the voice does rise at the end of a question, but much less than in English, and it takes a while to become attuned to this.) Then he'd wait for a response. But making allowance for our lack of understanding, he'd usually supply this: "*io?*" (which means "yes"), he'd say, looking at me, "*Io*," Koleta would say, catching on first, and I'd echo it.

Then there came a question that plainly did demand an answer. The chief sat there waiting for one with growing impatience. Luckily, Qito came to the rescue. "He says, you want to record stories?" she translated. We nodded. "Well, he's offering to tell you one. The history of the Fijian people." We nodded again. "He wants to tell it *now*."

"Ah, how kind of you, Big Uncle," I became effusiveness itself (it soon percolates to one, from the society around). "You would be the best person in the world to tell a story about the old days." The chief nodded in agreement and pleasure, smiling that our temporary lack of communication had been resolved. (We hadn't understood any of the earlier things he'd said either, in the preceding ten minutes but that hadn't mattered.)

I dove into the private part of the house for recorder, microphone, and cassette. I assembled them in front of the chief, who drew himself up into a properly raconteur pose, and cleared his throat.

I made an announcement into the microphone, to lend a bit of dignity (and make sure everything was working). *A italanoa i Viti* (The story of Fiji). Then the chief gave a quick ten-minute summary of the history of his people, although the full content didn't become clear until I'd got the text properly translated and transcribed, which took a few days (with the help of Qito and others).

"Thank you, Roopate," he said. "I come to greet you this morning. This is a little story I want to tell the two of you, on your arrival here in our Vanua." Then he explained that his ancestor had come from the island of Na'auvodra and landed in the western part of Taveuni. He was referring to a traditional god called Waqalabalaba (the Fijian gods are all deified ancestors) who came to live with his brother at Natinatina, a place perhaps five miles away from Waitabu, in the forest. That was in the "days of darkness" (meaning before Christianity came). The chief described a war against the people of Ravi Ravi in Macuata, on the northern coast of Vanua Levu. Then another war, against the Tongans. His ancestors moved to Nasau (a place on the opposite side of the main road from where the bus had dropped us), then to Na'ade on the coast near Viidawa, then to the present village of Waitabu. There was quite a lot of detail about the wars, and the Catholic church and the great chief Tui Ca'an. Finally, he said: "This is the end of my story for the two of you. I ask of you to allow my story to end at this point." (One should always ask permission to finish something, in Fiji.)

This was exactly the kind of thing I wanted. The way to work on the grammar of any language is not to ask questions from another language, but rather to record texts (stories, conversation, announcements) in the language and then analyze the internal grammatical structure of these texts. If you want to study relative clauses, for instance, it is not sufficient to take a few English sentences that include a relative clause and get them translated into Fijian; as likely as not the Fijian equivalent won't include relative clauses. The only sound way to do linguistic fieldwork is to analyze texts in the language. Eventually I would see whether there was any construction type in Fijian that could be referred to as "relative clauses," and see what its grammatical properties were. Then, at a later stage, I might construct a few Fijian sentences that included relative clauses—according to the hypothesis I had formulated—and see whether I had generated them correctly.

So my thanks were doubly genuine. "We are most sincerely grateful, Big Uncle. That is a fine story, which everyone will admire when I take it back to Australia." I rewound the tape and played the story back to a happy chief, who smiled and drummed his knuckles on the floor as he nodded in agreement with what he was recounting in the recorder.

A few more things were said, and nodded to. Then there was something that was obviously a question and the chief wasn't telling me how to answer.

Once more Qito came to the rescue. "He's inviting you to breakfast in his house."

Oh no. I was getting used to the routine at Sepo's, where at least two or three people around the eating mat knew a little English, which we could revert to in case of emergency. The chief spoke nothing but Fijian, and a very fast, gabbling sort of Fijian at that.

There was no alternative but to go along. Koleta said she'd just pop over to see if her mother (meaning Bogi) needed any help in the kitchen. I pleaded with my eyes for her to come and help with the chief, just as soon as she could.

The chief's wife, Nana Vero, was a lovely person. Kind and very shy. (They'd never had children, which was sad, especially in a Fijian village where great value is placed on female fecundity.) There were just the three of us. Conversation wasn't too bad at all. Mainly a monologue from the chief. I could understand some of it and apparently said "yes" in appropriate places.

But the food! We had cold boiled cassava. Now the central component of any full Fijian meal—such as lunch or supper—is what they call *'aa'ana dina* (literally "real food"), the starch component. This can be taro or yam or breadfruit, all of which are quite excellent. Or it can be cassava, which is—in my opinion—rather inferior. It's long and thin, with an insipid pasty taste, and often full of long pieces of fiber (similar to what can be found in a poor-quality mango), which get caught between your teeth. Cassava is not too bad while it's hot, and you can dip it in the gravy from a plate of fish or greens.

Fijians often eat leavings from the previous night's supper for breakfast. This cassava was stone-cold and some of it stuck to the top of my mouth. Even a cup of hot tea didn't disturb it—just swirled around and left it still in place, like a false palate. Well I was hungry and ate the first piece quickly to get it over with. Tui Nasau offered a benign smile and another portion.

What I did enjoy was looking around the chief's traditional-style house. The steeply sloping roof, the way all the unplaned beams were lashed together, using materials found in the forest (there wasn't a nail in the whole structure). Later on, I tried to choose my church mornings so that I'd be there when it was held in one of the two traditional houses in the village. (But that didn't always work, since one house in the sequence might get skipped, perhaps because the occupants were away on a visit, or for some other reason. I found that however neat things might be in theory, they were seldom properly predictable in practice.)

The chief's wife, Nana Vero, was friendly but rather shy.

Koleta did come to join us, but after the eating was over. A little bit of chatter and then Sepo's daughter Filo came over to tell Koleta that her breakfast was ready. Tui Nasau and I went along as well.

Sepo and Bogi and Koleta and the rest of the family had slices of ripe, juicy paw-paw and then hot *roti*, a type of unleavened bread that the Fijians have borrowed (recipe and name) from the Indian immigrants. I was offered both but of course had to refuse, saying that I had already had a lovely breakfast with Big Uncle. He also declined the paw-paw and roti—how chewy they looked!—and sat there smiling at me all through the meal.

* * *

Koleta and I decided that, in order to be accepted by the village, we ought to join in a bit of communal work, at least in the early days. She went off into the house directly in front of us to learn mat-weaving from an old lady who liked to be called *Nau* (a word which really means "grandmother"). I accompanied Sepo to the new store.

Back in Australia I had been a reasonable handyman, and had built a wall or two. Here, however, I was regarded as a "lame," someone who *might* just be able to manage very simple tasks. One of the difficulties, of course, was that I didn't fully speak the language and thus couldn't properly interrelate with other workers. (A prime motivation for mankind having developed language, a few hundred thousand years ago, was surely the need to organize group interaction.)

Sepo kept my language instruction going all the time. I first wrote down a few sentences describing how cement blocks are made (that task had already been completed) and then how to say, "I'm not experienced at building houses, I just want to help" and also "I'm just admiring what you're doing."

What they got me to do was straighten lengths of twisted metal. These were rods to be inserted into the building structure at intervals, to strengthen it. They must have left a factory somewhere, sometime, in a fairly straight condition. But now they were rather rusty and considerably *ta'elo*, which means "crooked." My job was to get them *dodonu* "straight." The verb was *va'a-dodonu* "straighten."

I was given a hammer, and there were a few old concrete blocks to bang the metal against. I'd try and anchor one end with a foot, get the metal bump in the air and deliver it a substantial wham. The only trouble was that it often caused the rod just to rotate through 90 degrees and lie flat on the ground still in its crooked condition.

Eventually I evolved a method that brought some results. After every two or three rods (there were dozens in need of help) I'd have a bit of a spell and write down a few more words. How to say, "put a layer of plaster on"—Sepo explained this as he went past—and "how high will the building be?"

Almost all the men from the village were there with the oldest ones doing simple back-up tasks similar to mine (things like mixing the cement).

3. Our Village

One of them introduced himself as Suliano, making sure I understood, and could repeat it back. Just then a gentle waft of breeze came in just off the ocean. "*E mudre a cagi*," he told me how to describe it. The verb generally comes first in a Fijian sentence together with a preposed pronoun—so *e* is here "it" and *mudre* "gently blow." It is followed by the noun which is subject of the sentence, *cagi* "wind" and this is preceded by *a* which is a little like the definite article in English. Literally, one says "it blows, the wind."

After straightening about twenty iron bars my soft academic hands were raw and aching. (Gloves would have been a good idea, if there'd been any around. Instead, I wrapped my handkerchief around the hammer to avoid getting blisters.) Someone blew a conch shell to announce lunch and Sepo took me up to the Main Road Pipe. "Let's go and wash our hands at the pipe." "Now that we have finished washing, our hands are clean." We did it and said it and I wrote it down. These sentences are actually more significant than you might imagine. In Fijian, there are a number of words for different sorts of washing: *vuluvulu* is "wash hands" and *taavoi* "wash the face" while *sava* is used for many sorts of washing, including washing the body and also washing clothes.

I went back to the building site for a short while in the afternoon. There were less people there—it seemed that the villagers would come and work whenever they felt like it. Sepo told me they'd been at it for three months and that people worked one or two days each week whenever they could "find the time." (It could have been better phrased "whenever the spirit moved them" since most people didn't seem to do too much else the rest of the time.)

In view of this, I didn't feel at all bad about slipping away around three o'clock. There was that story the chief had recorded before breakfast and I just couldn't wait to get my teeth into it. For text transcription, I generally use a large spiral-bound notebook. The Fijian would go on the top line, then a word-by-word gloss and below that a translation of a complete sentence. Only right-hand pages are filled in this way, the left side being kept for comments on grammatical patterns, new words, and queries about whether I had things down correctly—things that would have to be checked again with a native speaker.

Sepo had said that Qito would help both Koleta and I with our linguistic work. She had nothing really to do in the village—well she was *supposed* to assist her mother but Qito wasn't too keen on that sort of thing. The idea of helping me write down the chief's story appealed to Qito—at least before we'd actually started on it. I played it back, phrase by phrase, asked her to articulate slowly what he'd said, then I repeated that to make sure I had it exactly right, and wrote it down. Some bits had to be listened to quite carefully—where he'd blurred a word or else stopped in the middle of a sentence and started again. But I had to take down *exactly* what had been said as the basis for linguistic study.

Qito didn't think so. "Move on a bit," she gestured at the finger that held down the "pause" button. "He's just saying the same thing as before. Let's get onto something new." I explained that I wanted to transcribe the *whole* text, and not miss out the bits that bored Qito. She continued grumpily. Then Bogi called out "Qito," simply to find out where she was, and it was an excuse to take off.

But Sepo was proving himself to be more and more valuable in every way. There was the house he'd lent us, meals with the family, which saved us—or rather Koleta, for in Fiji this must be women's work—having to cook. We planned to take the bus around the island to Somosomo sometime in the following week to get a few things we needed, some presents for Sepo and Bogi, and a supply of groceries for them. (We thought we'd buy all the "foreign" food the family used that couldn't be grown in their own garden—flour, sugar, rice, tea, cooking oil as well as soap.) "Would Qito like to come with us?," Koleta asked at supper that night. "It'll be up to her," Sepo replied—and we wrote down how to say that in Fijian. But it was plain that a visit to the shops was something Qito did rather fancy.

Almost every evening during the first couple of weeks we were in Waitabu, Sepo would come over to our house after supper and explain some linguistic topic. One night it was demonstratives, how to say "this" and "that," "here" and "there." It was one major point on which the dialects differed and we wrote the parallel forms in Bau (standard Fijian), Boumaa, and in the Ca'audrove dialect spoken on the other side of Taveuni, around Somosomo. "Here" for instance, is *kee* in Bau, *qee* in Ca'audrove but *yai* in Boumaa. One evening he went systematically through the pronouns, comparing Bau with Boumaa. Another time we wrote down a whole list of "opposites" that occurred to him—"kind" and "cruel," "modest" and "boasting," "happy" and "sad."

Sepo Cookanacagi had been born in Waitabu in 1934. He was a boarder at the Catholic school in Wairi'i from 1942 until 1950. (A school hadn't been opened in the Vanua of Boumaa until 1945.) Then Sepo was trained as a bookkeeper by Morris Hedstrom, a company that runs a chain of grocery and hardware stores through the islands. He had worked for some years at the Morris Hedstrom store just outside Somosomo. And then he and Bogi had decided that they liked village life best of all, and had come back home.

Now, besides looking after his garden—as every other man in the village did—Sepo ran the store, did the accounts for the village copra cooperative, was secretary of the Christian Fellowship group, and made himself available to anyone in the village requiring help in dealing with the outside world, such as writing a letter in Bau (or in English, although there'd be little demand for that).

He and Koleta started talking about the varieties of language. Fijian has a rather wonderful verb, *gato* which means "use a glottal stop." Boumaa—and also the Ca'audrove variety—are Gato dialects. Of course, there are other differences between Bau and Boumaa, demonstratives and verbs like "run" which is *cici* in Bau but *'ada* in Boumaa.

Josefa Cookanacagi (my Moomoo, "father-in law," or "uncle") had a large family and many responsibilities but still found time to look after us in every way. Here he returns from his garden with a shoulder yoke bearing vegetables and scales for weighing copra.

"The trouble," Sepo explained, "is that our children go to school, where all the instruction is in Bau." They come home and just pop in a glottal stop in place of *k* in a Bau word, instead of using the proper Boumaa form—saying *'ama* (where Bau has *kama*) in place of Boumaa, *udre* for "be burning." "You can say they're talking Bau Gato," Sepo concluded. Bau with a glottal stop, instead of the proper Boumaa dialect.

Now on the first day we'd arrived Sepo had insisted that *the* person to help with our studies was Sakinsa Basaa, who lived in the village of Wai. He was an educated man, a trained teacher. We'd suggested several times going over but Sepo had demurred, saying he understood that Basaa was busy that day. Would he be free the next day?, we asked. "It's not clear," was the only response. And then Sepo said there was a yaqona party in the chief's house. I should certainly come along as well. Koleta, to her relief, was excused. (Women have their own yaqona parties, usually in the late mornings or afternoons.)

Suliano, my teacher from the morning, was present with more kindly instruction. How to hold my hands out together, in cupped fashion, to accept the bowl of yaqona. Drink it down in one, smack my lips, utter an appreciative "*aah*," say "the bowl is now dry," and hand it back to the server with a profuse thank you. It wasn't hard to learn and Suliano watched carefully to see that each time the cup reached me, as it moved inexorably around the circle of drinkers, I made the right response. The odd thing was that nobody else went through the whole rigmarole—often just a simple "thanks." The same point struck home on several other occasions. People taught me how to behave but didn't feel that they had to behave in that way themselves. They taught me the ideal mode of behavior to which I must conform but from which they were free to deviate.

Luckily Sepo had taught me how to say, "Just a small portion please," so I received tiny helpings of this potent narcotic-like drink and was able to retain a reasonably clear head. At first, they asked about how much it cost to stay in Kaba's guest house (Fijians always want to know the price of everything). Then the conversation went off in other directions and I retreated into my own thoughts. It came around to the UN Peacekeeping force in Lebanon; that I could follow thanks to a fair infusion of loan words from English.

Sepo had also taught me how to say, "Please may I be excused in order to now go off and rest," which could be used at any time. After an hour, I felt I'd done my bit of socializing for that day. (A yaqona party typically goes on for five or six hours, until well past midnight.)

Then for some reason—I can't think what—someone asked who the cleverest man in the world was. Everyone looked at me. "Why, Einstein," I said. "Most people would say Albert Einstein. Although he's dead now." No one had heard of him, and I don't suppose anyone remembered his name by next morning. Why should they?

* * *

The next morning Sepo said that he believed Basaa to be rather busy that day, so we'd better not go and see him. (It is unclear how he got this

3. Our Village

It was a thirty-minute walk to the Postal Agency in 'Orovou, but a most pleasant one, along the beach.

information, but at that time we just accepted everything we were told.) I did another couple of pages of the chief's text with Qito before she remembered a pressing task elsewhere. Then I decided to do something original, to explore a bit.

My eldest daughter Eelsha would have her 21st birthday in two days time—on Saturday, January 12, 1985. I'd already sent a card and present from Suva but I thought it might be rather nice for her to receive a telegram from an obscure island in the South Pacific.

Sepo approved the plan (I wouldn't have dared go off alone without telling him) and he told me how to ask, very politely, "Where might the post office be?," once I got to the village of 'Orovou.

In Waitabu everyone watched what we were doing the whole time. (It's considered antisocial to have the doors to your house—or at least the front door—closed during the day.) So it was great just to stroll along the beach, ignore the turn-off to Viidawa, go right around a rocky promontory onto the beach in front of 'Orovou. Then I went straight past that village, and on to Tavoro for a deliciously cool swim in the pool under the waterfall.

Everyone has a number of funny things—often silly things—they have always wanted to do. Having recently deserted my marriage I was in the mood to try some of them. Such as walking down a small stream—in the middle of the flow—until it meets the sea. The Tavoro stream was mostly about two feet deep but there were lots of sharp rocks, some patches of reeds and mud and the odd deep bit. Also, it wound back and forth, back and forth. I went along for a mile or so and then jumped up onto the bank (still a long way from the sea). But I felt satisfied that I had sufficiently fulfilled that wish.

Back on the main road, just on the bridge that crosses the Tavoro stream, I was accosted by a youth from 'Orovou who demanded $2. Now I knew that was the normal fee charged to tourists from the Castaway International Hotel who take a day-trip around the island (by taxi or hotel limousine) to see the falls. But I wasn't a tourist. Speaking nothing but Fijian—although the youth must have known English, if he was deputed to collect money from tourists—I said that I was living as a guest of Josefa Cookanacagi, in the village of Waitabu. It made no impression. Two dollars was demanded and eventually I paid him. (We made many further visits to Tavoro and were never again charged. Before too long, everyone did recognize us as bona fide residents of the Vanua.)

That set me off thinking about the difference between doing fieldwork in Australia and in Fiji. The Aborigines are a proud and noble people but today they are most emphatically a minority. In the early years of white settlement, Aboriginal tribes fought fiercely to protect their traditional lands and their way of life. As several Aborigines have told me: "We only had spears while the invaders had guns, so we lost the war."

White settlers poured into Australia and spread out all over the continent with their herds of sheep and cattle. Aboriginal tribes in an area would be decimated before there was ever a police presence there (and often when police did arrive they helped in the slaughter). Most particularly, all the Aborigines identified as "troublemakers"—meaning political and military leaders—were gotten rid of. Those Aborigines that have survived into modern-day Australia owe this survival to a realization that it is best to defer to a white man.

I had made friends with Aboriginal people, and this had been the basis of my linguistic work—people were genuinely interested in what I was doing and helped me because of this interest. (You can't buy the time or skills of an Aborigine, just as you can't with a Fijian.) But there had always been an implicit understanding that I was a member of the majority group, the ones who made all important decisions and ran the country.

This realization didn't strike me until I came to Fiji. There it was definitely *not* the case. Fiji was a Fijian land, ruled by Fijians for the benefit of Fijians. A few white specialists might be employed, if they had skills which were needed. Tourists could be tolerated—provided they behaved themselves—for the foreign currency they brought. But all white people were there at the Fijians' pleasure, and could be asked to leave at whim.

It was a great feeling, and only then did I truly see the magnitude of what Aborigines had lost—control of their own lands, and their own identity.

I was now on the edge of the village and hastily removed my hat before putting the politely-phrased question about the whereabouts of the Boumaa Postal Agency to a lady. She responded in typical Fijian fashion, by leading me across the village, right up to it. It was just as well she did for it turned out to be just a normal plank house bearing no mark of any special function.

The postmaster introduced himself as Iowani. He accepted an aerogram I'd written to my secretary in Canberra—giving the address for sending on mail—looked at the front, turned it over, weighed it carefully in one hand, and said "tst, tst, tst." Then I wrote down my name and Koleta's on a card, gave it to him and said that mail would be arriving for us in due course; we'd come across perhaps twice a week to collect it. He went through the same pantomime with this, right down to the "tst, tst, tst."

Then I said that I'd like to send a telegram, which arrested Iowani's smiling demeanor. Surely it was a post office, or at least a postal agency? Yes, but there was no telephone. Iowani shook his head and said "tst, tst, tst" in a quite different and sorrowful tone. Oh dear!

Then he brightened up. There was one telephone in the village. At the house of the government Agricultural Officer, right over on the other side. Iowani even led me across to it. The Agricultural Officer—an Indian, the only one in the whole of Boumaa—was out but his brother was there, on a visit from Labasa. I was able to phone through the telegram and paid to the brother the sum the operator specified.

When I got back Koleta was working with Qito on transcribing some of the materials she had gathered on the various styles of language used among different groups in the village, and in different circumstances. I sensed Qito brighten up when I entered, and she kept looking over at the corner toward me. When she left I asked Koleta how it had gone.

"Oh," she shook her head. "Qito's attention span is about ten minutes. She keeps telling me what I should be doing and then sulks when I don't do that but keep on with my own plan."

"Yes," I agreed, "same with me. Do you think we should take her with us to Somosomo next week?"

"Let's see how it goes between now and then, shall we?"

Koleta mentioned that she had been talking to an intelligent young man called Inoke—a nephew of Sepo's—who wanted to improve his English and was ready to help her in learning and working with Fijian. Sepo had also mentioned a villager called Iowani Waqairapua who had been away at teacher's training college for three years (although he never had qualified) and he should also be able to help us. Maybe we wouldn't need Qito.

Although Sepo was totally supportive, many people in the village had considerable doubts about our value. Sitting writing in a book all day wasn't considered any occupation for an adult; it was what children did at school. I should be gardening, or building, or cutting copra. And as for Koleta, her place was to look after the house, wash the clothes, prepare food, go fishing.

Even Sepo's son Maarawa didn't hide his scepticism. That evening I was plainly enjoying a really tasty supper, and saying so. (In Fijian, it is important to keep on saying, during a meal, how good it is.) Maarawa chipped in with "Do you know the names of all those kinds of food you're eating, Roopate?" I didn't. I knew the name of a couple but not the rest. Faced with that question, I became tongue-tied. Maarawa smiled, almost in pity.

I'd have to really learn all the relevant details of Fijian culture, as soon as possible. And also temporarily forget about my own.

* * *

On Friday, church was held in Sepo's house. As members of the family we had to attend at least the morning service. Then on Saturday both services would be in our little house, next in order of rotation. And the Sunday morning service is the one you can't miss. We were going to have church coming out of our ears.

The "official" hour for breakfast is eight o'clock so there's quite a bit of time to do something before then. The chief had taken to popping in to see us after church each morning. It was a kindly gesture to make sure everything was okay. He'd say, "Any problem?" and we'd say "No, not at all, everything is fine." And I think he liked chatting to us. Or rather at us, since we only understood some of the more straightforward things he was saying. He appeared not to know a single word of English.

Sepo popped in as well, on the Friday, and I got him to tell me the names of all the sorts of vegetables Fijians used. Those grown in the garden were *manioke* "cassava" (the one I'd eaten cold at that breakfast in the chief's house), *dalo* "taro" a bit like a potato but with a good, nutty flavor; *vudi* "plantain," a sort of large banana but cooked like a vegetable; *uvi* "yam"; *'umala* "sweet potato"; *varasa* "stringy onion"; *bele*, a hibiscus-type plant that has edible leaves a bit like spinach, and of course *yaqona* "kava," used for the ceremonial drink. Then there were other foods that grew wild in the forest (although they may also be planted, in plots): *tiivoli* "a wild yam"; *uto* "breadfruit"; *weleti* "paw-paw"; and, of course, *niu* "coconut." I wrote all these down and resolved to note carefully what we were given to eat at each meal. Next time Maarawa asked that question I was aiming to be ready with an answer.

After breakfast we didn't inquire whether Basaa would be available that day. We simply announced that we were going to see him and if he wasn't free to talk—well it would be a nice walk anyway. Sepo accepted this (we should perhaps have tried it earlier) and sent Qito along as guide.

We followed the winding track up to the main road. It seemed more like four months, rather than four days, since we'd arrived on the bus with all those bags and cartons and Qito—lovely Qito!—had been there to meet us.

Ten minutes walk up to the main road then turn right and ten minutes gentle slope down to Wai. Over to the left we could see land that had been cleared, with cattle on green pastures next to the meandering stream. Qito explained that it was part of a plantation belonging to Jim Henning, a white man who was married to Sepo's sister Elena. The road then crossed the stream over a concrete bridge, women washing on the rocks below called out a greeting, and we were in Wai, half-a-dozen houses on each side of the road.

Basaa said he'd been expecting us. (This was something Koleta and I became used to, and referred to as the "coconut telegraph." People always seemed to know exactly where we'd been, who we'd spoken to, and what we'd said to them, even when we'd been the other side of the island. It was sometimes uncanny.) He invited us into his study, to sit on chairs at a table. There were shelves of books—classical authors, reference works, teaching manuals. (I don't think I ever saw a book in Waitabu, except for the Bible.)

Basaa was a stately gentleman. Thoughtful, educated, happy to pass on the results of his research. There was a blackboard on the wall and he stood by it for two or three hours, providing a marvelous lesson on the system of social organization. We did know a bit about this, from anthropological texts by Bill Geddes, Marshal Sahlins and others. Basaa explained the system as it applied to the Vanua of Boumaa.

A Vanua is divided into a number of Yavusas, each of which is associated with one or more villages. There are four Yavusas in the Boumaa Vanua and ours was Naisaqai, at Waitabu and Wai. The members of a Yavusa are all descended from a single ancestor god. For Naisaqai the god is Latia, who was originally a tall, blind man. Each Yavusa also has an animal, a fish and a species of tree associated with it; those for Naisaqai are *totii* "fan-tailed cuckoo," the *nuqa* fish that is found in great numbers just before Christmas, and *vesi*, a hardwood tree.

We wrote down all these details for Naisaqai and for the other three Yavusas, associated with the villages of Lavena, 'Orovou and Viidawa. Then Basaa explained that each Yavusa is divided into a number of Mataqalis (or clans). We already knew something of this—there was Vuunivesi (to which Sepo and Koleta belonged), Waiso'i (my Mataqali, since I was the adopted son of Elia Waqa) and Veiniu, to which all the men of Wai belonged, together with their children.

There was one further unit. A Mataqali was divided into a number of Ito'ato'as, each of which was like an extended family. We copied off the board all the Ito'ato'as in Boumaa, including some which had recently died out. The Vuunivesi Mataqali had two Ito'ato'as—Vuunivesi and Nasolo. As you'd expect from its name Vuunivesi was the senior Ito'ato'a; it was the one to which the chief and Sepo and Koleta belonged and from which would be chosen the next head of the Vuunivesi Mataqali, who would also be chief of the whole Naisaqai Yavusa.

Phew! Our heads were racing with all this detail. But it was so clear, so expertly presented. What had been learned in a morning could have taken months to work out on our own. Basaa also talked about modern administrative units. There were fourteen Yasanas—or provinces—in Fiji (ours being Ca'audrove), each divided into a number of Ti'inas, or districts, the local one being Waini'eli, which in turn consisted of a grouping of Vanuas. The Waini'eli district consisted of the Waine'eli Vanua—the senior one, which we had passed through on the bus, between the airport and Boumaa—the Boumaa Vanua and also the Laucala Vanua, situated on the island of Qamea, just off to the east.

Qito had long since returned home, and then been sent back by Bogi to find out from Basaa's wife if we'd be staying there for lunch. This was taken sitting at a table, although it was all Fijian food—taro, yams, greens and fish. Basaa explained that he'd taught at high schools in many different parts of Fiji so his own speech was an amalgam of many dialects. Because of this, we agreed, he wouldn't be the best person to provide us with language data. (In fact, the following week Basaa got a call to come out of retirement and teach at the government high school on the other side of Taveuni, so we didn't see him again.) Then we walked back to our village.

Later in the afternoon I sneaked off to do a bit more local exploring, really searching for some quiet and peaceful spot to which I could retire in order to write a novel. When I returned, Koleta was working—or trying to work—with Qito. "Oh Roopate!" Qito flashed her eyes and gave a strong intake of breath as I came in. So, I picked up Plato, swimming trunks and towel and hurriedly departed for the beach.

Bathing was getting to be a regular daily pleasure, but you had to know the time of the tides. A couple of hundred yards out there was the edge of the reef with a steep drop of tens of feet. The Waitabu women used to stand near the edge to fish, and they certainly needed sandals or sandshoes to protect their feet from the sharp coral. Between reef and shore the water was shallow—only a foot or two deep at low tide but four feet when it was high. So one could only really bathe about two hours either side of high tide, which of course came twice a day.

Qito's sister Maritina was shyer and more serious. Just before supper that night she was sitting in our house (there were almost always some children—from Sepo's family or other families—sitting there, chatting to us or to each other or just watching us). There was a book lying there, which Koleta had read and I'd almost finished, as my bedtime novel—*The Voyage Out* by Virginia Woolf. "Oh I do love stories," Maritina exclaimed. "What sort do you like?" She had picked up the book. "Like this," she started reading the blurb on the back. "Yes, just like this." I knew that Maritina was catching the plane back to Suva on Sunday, for the new school term, so I said I'd finish it that night and then she could take it.

It was dance night! Every Friday, we were told, there was a dance. But why Friday, when in most places Saturday is the main social evening? The explanation was perfectly straightforward. Any sort of dancing—as well as any sort of work or almost anything—was taboo on Sunday. If the dance were on Saturday night it would have to cease at midnight, whereas a Friday function could perfectly well go on into the early hours. (This reminded me of someone I'd known at Oxford who was a terrific student and also, like the Fijians, a literal-minded Christian. He boasted of how he dealt with the prohibition against working on a Sunday—he'd study until midnight on Saturday. On Sunday he'd go to church and do any nonwork tasks which were permitted. Then he'd go to bed very early, in order to get up and start working about 4 a.m. on Monday!)

The dance was held in a Tunuloa-style building on the beach side of the village, right next to the village green. This is a long shed consisting of just a frame, mainly of bamboo, with a few sheets of corrugated iron for a roof and low walls (two or three feet high) of quickly woven coconut fronds. It was called a Va'a-Tunuloa, Paul Geraghty later told me, because at one important Great Council of Chiefs meeting a building was urgently needed, and the delegation from Tunuloa put up one of this type in record time.

Admission was twenty cents, which included one free cup of yaqona. I paid a dollar for the two of us and said not to worry about the change; it all went into the communal fund of one of the Ito'ato'a from Waitabu. Music was provided by a couple of local youths and their guitars, with the dancing a blend of traditional and Western style. Koleta was asked to dance and so was I—it seemed by every flower-bedecked girl and woman from the Yavusa.

Being so much in demand was a novel experience. (In Australia, and in Suva, it was Koleta who'd been the center of attention for the opposite sex.) Added to Qito's hungry looks it made me feel a little flattered, but also rather uneasy. I needn't have worried though, since none of it lasted. Once my staid nature had been ascertained, the female interest dropped off. Even Qito was regarding me with moody disdain within a week.

Dancing was good fun but also rather exhausting. So, for a rest we went and sat on a square of matting at the side with the chief, Elia Waqa, and a few other of the older people. A cup of yaqona was ten cents and I contributed two dollars, which I was assured would provide a drink for everyone in the dance-shed (although there were many more than twenty of them).

We took up our cross-legged stance at the opposite corner from the chief, and next to Suliano. He was great at chatting with us, speaking slowly and carefully and explaining whatever was going on around. Most people were smoking, generally cigarettes they rolled themselves (often using a sliver of newspaper), which was the cheapest way of doing it.

While talking with Suliano we kept watching the chief. Just because he was an interesting and somewhat amazing man. More yaqona was needed. He fiddled with his pocket, pulled out a scatter of small change, most of it falling onto the mat. Trying to retrieve it, his cigarette fell onto his foot.

At this he said, "Shit."

Koleta and I sat bolt upright. We'd been certain that the chief knew absolutely no English. And now he'd burned his foot and said "shit." There was no mistaking. It was perhaps the most surprising thing I've ever heard anyone say.

We had an overpowering need to laugh. But, of course, it had to be controlled.

Another quarter-cup of yaqona. Some more conversation with kindly Suliano. And then, leaving the people of Waitabu to dance past midnight, we retired to the floor of our hut.

4

"No cyclone today!"

Church in our house today! This came around every twenty days during the months we spent at Waitabu. Koleta's alarm was set to go off well in advance of the first lali drum. We needed time to wash and then the house had to be prepared. All our cartons and cases were moved to the back wall to provide as much room as possible for the congregation. Koleta swept the floor clean with her *saasaa*, a broom made from the husks of coconut leaves.

Bogi came in and nodded at the preparations. Then she came back with the picture of Jesus on the cross, from her house, and a blue plastic chair to support it, something like an altar in the middle of our back wall.

While all this was going on I was trying to get rid of toads. These little friends tended to make a home under the mats in the corner of the house. We sometimes spent hours clearing them out, but then they'd return. Not so much through the doors, which could be patrolled. The trouble was that we had gaps at the bottom of the reed wall of the house. During the week I brought back a bag of stones every time I went to the beach, to fill in the gaps. Then I worked out that it would probably take more than the six months we planned to be there in order to complete the job, so gave up. (It would have been possible I suppose to borrow the village wheelbarrow, which was kept locked in the store, and do the job in one day. But I didn't really want to attract that sort of attention.)

Anyway, we didn't want toads jumping out onto the congregation in church. Just as I'd completed evictions people started to arrive. Lots of people, perhaps more than usual because it was in our house. The little children went at the front, right next to Jesus. Then the chief and Sepo and other men, with the women at the back. I stationed myself by a side door and was able to swat away one devout toad when he tried to join us.

Felise, the catechist, arrived with his huge volume, giving directions for prayers and lessons for every day of the year. Sepo began to sing, and we were off. I was getting used to church by now, and the singing was rather fine. Even the prayers and lesson had a certain linguistic interest—they were entirely in Standard Fijian (what is called Bau or Bauan, although it isn't exactly the Bau dialect).

As mentioned before, the early missionaries, in the 1840s, had started translating the Bible into local dialects. Then they realized this would be a huge task—there are so many dialects (and the Bible isn't short). So they decided on a form of language based on Bauan—which was something of a lingua franca—as the medium for all evangelical work.

And there it stood. You weren't allowed to pray in the Boumaa dialect. It wasn't considered proper—not the dialect that the Lord wanted used. The following week Sepo suggested that Koleta might say grace (I had to follow, a little later on, although I never did volunteer). She wrote it down from Qito and then, since we were living in Boumaa, substituted a glottal stop for every *k*, saying *'Alou* rather than *Kalou* for God. Sepo was horrified—grace can't be said in *gato* (with a glottal stop), please address the Lord only in Bauan. (This was of course exactly the sort of thing Koleta had come to Waitabu to study—the different styles of language, and the circumstances in which they were used.) In the Sunday morning service, we did have a sermon, preached by Felise or by a visiting catechist from another village. This was extemporary and although it would begin in Bauan there were usually quite a few glottal stops toward the end (which nobody ever complained about—perhaps they didn't notice).

Then it was all over. All the ladies and gentlemen of Waitabu thanked us most politely and went out through the front door. The chief stayed, since this was his regular time for a morning call and a drink of water. Sepo also stayed and he was in a workmanlike mood. "Right," he told his elder brother. "Roopate and Koleta want to know all about ceremonies." (We hadn't expressed any such wish, but it did seem like a good idea.) "The arrangements that would be made for receiving a visiting high chief."

Our chief knew more about such things than Sepo, since he was older and had lived in the village all his life. "Shall we do it right now?" he asked, just sipping on a second glass of water. Sepo nodded, so he indulged in a fit of rasping coughing, as if to get that out of the way, and then began. A high chief would come by boat, of course, and anchor offshore. Local chiefs will then go out to him and present a whale's tooth in a ceremony called "Pulling the Anchor." Then he'd come down to shore and they'd present yaqona in a ceremony called Qaloqalivi (literally: "Wading

Toward"); each ceremony would of course be a most serious affair, with lots of speeches on both sides.

So it went on. When the high chief came onto land there'd be the "Stepping Ashore" ceremony. Then "Pulling Down the Flag," to signify safe arrival. Then the Rova ceremony, then "Making Dry," with the presentation of mats. Following this came "Pulling of Leaves," involving presentation of a yaqona plant. Sepo listened carefully to all this and asked questions to clarify appropriate points. How many whale's teeth would be needed? Well, the chief considered, one for "Pulling the Anchor," one for "Stepping Ashore," one for "Pulling Down the Flag," one for the Rova; and of course lots of mats and painted *masi* cloth would also be given to the visiting dignitary, as well as a splendid feast.

The Rova ceremony fascinated me most of all. A woman of high status in the community—say, a chief's wife—would run with a whale's tooth to the next village and back again, before presenting it. The idea of a highborn Fijian woman—most of whom were of ample build—running with a tabua struck me as appealing. "Was it only a woman that would run in the Rova," Sepo asked. "No, usually a woman, but a man *could* do it instead."

That was another text in the bag, and a most interesting one. Now I'd have to get someone to help transcribe it. Later in the day Iowani (the one who had failed his teacher training course) popped in for a short while and we did about one page. Although he had offered to help it didn't turn out terribly well. The text began "If a high chief such as *Kovana Levu* came to Taveuni..." "What does that mean," I asked, "*Kovana Levu*"? Iowani became quite patronizing. "I'm not going to tell you that. I shouldn't have to." "Well," I said, "*Levu* is big, but what about *Kovana*?" Since Iowani would say no more I started looking in Capell's dictionary. "No," he grimaced, "it's the English word. *Governor—Kovana Levu* is 'Governor General.'" Then someone came by and Iowani remembered he had to speak to them. He'd be back the next day, he said. A week later Iowani apologized that he'd not been able to find the time, but said he would come and help soon. In fact, he never did, and I didn't miss him at all.

Sepo was not only supportive. He also apologized for village life being so dull. "Oh no, father," Koleta exclaimed, "it is anything but dull." And then he told us, with pleasure, how to say, "There are always lots of things happening in this village."

And there were! In mid-morning, a screaming row broke out between Qito and Maritina. (I'd given Maritina *The Voyage Out* before breakfast and that may have contributed, but it was probably that she was off to Suva the next day while Qito had to stay in Waitabu.) We heard an approaching fray and then Maritina came into our house, trying to hide just inside the doorway. Qito found her there and began to attack her with fists and nails. Maritina escaped through the side door, only to be pursued with more blows and curses. The fight passed through our hut three times and then Qito stopped, picked up my desert boots, which were lying just inside the door, and tore off outside, hurling them at Maritina.

We just sat there bemused. A few minutes later Bogi retrieved the boots and brought them back, with apologies. Later on, Sepo said that Qito hadn't been quite herself, and we must excuse her.

People were always coming in to see us. They'd just walk in with never a by-your-leave, and sit down cross-legged. We didn't even have to talk to them. "Just get on with your writing," they'd say. After ten or twenty minutes, they might want to leave. Then we did have a performance. "Roopate and Koleta," they'd say, "I kindly ask that you permit me to leave and return to my own house where I have many jobs waiting for me." We would solemnly grant permission.

One person who came to visit quite often was the half-wit, Pio. He was about sixteen, but with a very low mental age. Poor Pio had a very small tongue, which may have been the main reason he couldn't speak—except for labial sounds *"papapapa-."* He also had just four toes on each foot.

Anyway, soon after the Qito-Maritina affair, Pio came in and lay on our floor. We ignored him, continuing with what we were doing—until we noticed that Pio was having a happy time starting to masturbate!

Then it was church again. Bogi hadn't been wrong. The evening service was drawn out. It wasn't so much the unending boredom of mumbled prayers—not really any worse than having to sit through interminable meetings as a university administrator—but the posture. Sitting cross-legged, hands in lap, back kept straight can be okay for twenty minutes, a bit of a pain after thirty, and sheer agony as the clock ticks around to forty or fifty minutes.

It was now quite clear to me that Koleta had been right. I could never tell the people of Waitabu that I didn't believe in any god—that I didn't feel the need for a god in my life. If I did they'd doubtless consider me some sort of devil and fieldwork would become impossible.

All living in Fiji is highly stylized. There's the social hierarchy. And very definite and repetitive vocal responses (like what Suliano had taught me to say when offered a cup of yaqona). They loved ritual and ceremony. It wasn't at all hard to see why the early missionaries had such success—they were essentially offering a familiar package, with new labels. (Compare this with Aboriginal Australia where Christianity presented a totally alien worldview, and for the first hundred years or so of missionary endeavor there were very few converts.)

Well, when in Rome... I'd have to keep my liking for innovation and variety and free choice firmly fettered for the next six months.

* * *

In precontact days Fijians cooked in the front part of their houses, next to the front door. Smoke helped to seal the thatched roof, and it helped to keep away mosquitoes. But the missionaries told them not to. Now each household had a separate little kitchen on the edge of the village. Sepo's was a very rudimentary sort of structure, a few bits of corrugated iron put together, with a number of jagged, rusty edges. Cooking was done in a pot supported by stones over an open fire, with the cook sitting cross-legged beside it.

There was a toilet. A tiny corrugated iron house that had an enameled pedestal emptying into a pit below (but no seat or lid). You took along your own toilet paper. There was a wooden door and a couple of bits of wire to fasten it on the inside but it was hard to bring them together. And of course, there were plenty of toads jumping around inside. It wasn't the most salubrious of places, but I used it. Koleta preferred to follow the lead of some of the villagers and find a quiet spot in the forest nearby; she considered that less of a health hazard. Often people used the beach, perhaps covering their excretion with a bit of sand, which could easily get washed away. After one mucky experience during the first week I learned a cardinal rule: don't sit anywhere on the sand in front of the village.

On Sunday morning church wasn't until ten (on that day it was always held in the house of Felise the catechist since it held the most people, and on Sunday everyone had to attend). Koleta went across about seven to ask Bogi if she could help prepare breakfast. The offer was politely declined. Probably because the kitchen was so grotty (one of the worst in the village)—they were a bit ashamed of it, and it was a bit of a knack working in those surroundings.

Sepo was again in an organizing mood. "Come on," he said, immediately after church, "we'll go across to 'Orovou to record a traditional tale from an old lady who is the best storyteller in Boumaa."

Walking along the beach I picked up a piece of broken glass with a jagged edge. "Someone could step on it," I said (bare feet being the norm in a Fijian village), "and cut themselves."

Sepo simply took the glass from me and sent it skimming out to sea.

4. "No cyclone today!"

Koleta and I looked at each other in horror. "The action of the sea and sand will soon smooth it off," he said impatiently.

I was still convinced that Waitabu was close to paradise and had so far been able to perceive just one flaw. After a couple of days there we'd asked Sepo's thirteen-year-old daughter Filo how people dispose of their rubbish. "We throw it into the sea," she replied, matter-of-factly.

This we couldn't accept. We let all our rubbish—used paper, cotton wool, old batteries—accumulate in a plastic bag and every time we went to the other side of the island we popped it into a big rubbish container outside Kaba's supermarket. Then after a while it occurred to us that Kaba probably emptied that into the sea. So, we finished up behaving like everyone else in Waitabu.

The word that Sepo had used for "smoothed it off" was interesting, *va'a-tautauvata-ta'i*, literally "make it all the same." I scribbled it into my notebook and then hurried to catch up.

Now I am pretty experienced at fieldwork in Australia. There's a right way and a wrong way to go about it. You don't just go into a new community, encounter a good storyteller and expect them to record something for you the first day. It takes a while to build up a rapport, for them to get to know you, size up the situation, and decide whether they do want to help.

I tried to put this point of view to Sepo, in my half-formed Fijian, as he was striding up the path toward Viidawa. Sepo stopped. Looked at me. "Have you got the tape recorder with you," I nodded. "Don't you worry, she'll tell us a story today." And he was off again.

Going through Viidawa was a shortcut but you shouldn't just wander through a Fijian village, as you might do through an English one. Well, people generally did, but Sepo was a stickler for the olden-days etiquette. He halted briefly in front of the chief's house, called out a respectful salutation and asked permission to pass on.

Sepo slowed down on the outskirts of 'Orovou. He'd bought some yaqona root from the Waitabu store (which of course we'd paid for), and that must be presented to the chief of 'Orovou, who was also head of the whole Vanua of Boumaa. His title was the Vuunisaa (we wrote it down). People were not very happy with the Vuunisaa, Sepo said, because he'd converted to Jehovah's Witness and they forbade the consumption not only of alcohol but also of yaqona. So at all the chiefly ceremonies he'd preside over the yaqona bowl but not partake of any himself.

And we were still going to present the yaqona root to him? It seemed a bit like giving a bottle of whisky as a Christmas gift to a teetotaller. But

I suppose it wasn't really. Fijian society demands the presentation of certain commodities at certain times, even to a chief who has joined a sect that controverts one of the basic principles of the society.

As we sat cross-legged and clapped in rhythm at the appropriate spots, it became apparent that Sepo really loved making presentations. All those high-flown phrases, gracious compliments and eulogistic nothings. One thing he always lingered over was the bit about a "Professor from the Australian National University." (Hierarchy counts for an awful lot in Fiji, whereas working with Australian Aboriginals few of them had known I was a professor and wouldn't have cared a fig if they had. There I was just Bob Dixon, someone to be helped with language data because of what they thought of me as a person.)

As we climbed the hill toward the old lady's house, Sepo mentioned that the Vuunisaa also wanted to tell us a story, so we'd record that in a little while.

Falaavia Matavesi seemed to be expecting us. (Of course, the coconut telegraph!) A quiet place would be best. How about the school? There'd be no one there on a Sunday and the door wasn't locked, it seemed. We all climbed right to the top of the hill, with a marvelous view of the beach and out to sea, and over to Lavena on a promontory some miles away to the south.

Falaavia sat cross-legged on a mat on the concrete schoolroom floor, put a cushion on her lap, and she was ready to start. (Working in Australia I'd found that male informants were often too full of bombast and show-off. It was women who tended to be smart, straightforward, giving you what you wanted, straight from the hip with no unnecessary frills.) She was a most impressive woman with a face that bespoke hard work, contentment and understanding.

Caught by the occasion, Sepo provided a relatively short introduction: "Roopate and Koleta ask you to please relate the story of the political relationship between Waini'eli and Boumaa, as it was told by our ancestors. Thank you."

Then she was off. Falaavia began slowly, establishing time, place and persona. As the story unwound she spoke at a fast conversational speed. It was addressed to Sepo, who could understand. We sat and noted the intense concentration that Falaavia brought to her task, as the tension built up. A number of events were happening on successive days. She momentarily lost count. "Which day was that, the third?" "Yes, the third," Sepo quietly assented. "Well, on the fourth day…," and Falaavia was into the final denouement. I just listened to the beauty of the language, sing-song intonation leading up to a decisive statement, and then a slight pause. Church bells began to sound (we had nothing like that in Waitabu). Falaavia's story continued—a tale of traditional Fiji, now with a background of the religion brought in by Europeans.

Then she said: "The story is now finished," and it was all over. (None of that "asking for permission to conclude" that our male story-tellers indulged in.) Sepo said a few words of gratitude for "a most well-told story" and we joined in, most sincerely, for his final "thank you very much." We'd surely recorded a text of the highest quality, valuable both as a linguistic and an historical document. But it was long—seventeen minutes—and would take a fair while (and a good deal of help) to transcribe.

Falavia Matavesi, the finest storyteller in the whole of Boumaa.

Then down the hill to the Vuunisaa, for another bit of history. In the middle of Taveuni there is a huge mountain range with a lake, on the shores of which grows a unique plant, called tagimaucia, with red and white flowers (all attempts to transplant it to lower altitudes have failed). Some fifty years before, when the Vuunisaa was a youth, there had been a battle between Somosomo and Boumaa to determine who owned the lake. (You've guessed it, Boumaa won. Otherwise I suppose we'd scarcely have been told the story.) There wasn't the same emotion and excitement as had been apparent when Falaavia spoke, but it was another twelve minutes of pure Boumaa Fijian.

We didn't get back until two o'clock but Bogi had been keeping our lunch warm. Afterwards, Sepo opted for a well-deserved rest while Koleta and I sought out my father. Elia Waqa—who people said was the best storyteller in our village—had promised to record an account of the origin of yaqona. He was sitting in the shade, next to his house. "Yes, now would be an appropriate time."

Elia Waqa's story was shorter—just on four minutes—and it was very clear. He had a deep sonorous voice and articulated the words distinctly, not unlike a radio announcer. Well, he was telling the story to us—whereas Falaavia and the Vuunisaa had been essentially speaking to Sepo—and had been trying to make it intelligible to us.

Koleta went off to talk to some old ladies, and get on with her own work. I decided I didn't need any help with this text. It should surely be possible to transcribe Elia Waqa's story all by myself. I lay on the floor of our hut (no need to sit cross-legged except in church, at meals and when entertaining the chief), had the dictionary handy, opened my text notebook at a fresh page and began.

Actually, I did get a bit of help. Some small boys came in and sat watching me—as they always did—so, when in a couple of places I couldn't be quite sure whether Elia had said this word or that, I asked them. There were a couple of points that I made a note to check with Sepo sometime but I did transcribe the story that afternoon, and it gave me a good feeling of achievement.

> There was once no true yaqona in Fiji. Then came the time when there died a certain Tui Ca'au (the high chief of the Ca'audrove province): he died at Vaturova, on the other side of Natewa Bay, and was buried there. A few years later the yaqona plant began growing from the grave of Tui Ca'au from the place where his head lay. This new variety of yaqona compared very favorably with the yaqona then in existence. Its taste was so superior that the people of Ca'audrove considered it a chiefly drink, a symbol of respect which could only be consumed by chiefs.
>
> The new yaqona then spread to all places and regions of Fiji, and its use was attended with great ceremony. It didn't begin in Bau, or in any other part of Fiji, it began in Ca'audrove. And as knowledge of this yaqona spread, so did an awareness of the respect with which it must be treated. It went to Tonga and thence to Viti Levu. Some people then thought that it had its beginnings in Tonga. But that wasn't so, it had first sprung from the grave of Tui Ca'au, in Vaturova. That's why it is regarded as one of the backbones of society, as a mark of respect. So it went on for a long time but now things have changed—men who are not of chiefly rank can partake of yaqona, and even women drink it.

Elia Waqa declaimed this story in a histrionic style that would be suitable for Shakespeare. It was a little long winded (I have given an edited version in the last two paragraphs) but very clear.

And it also helped to explain one aspect of Fijian culture. Jone had told us, back in Suva, that the head was regarded as the "chief" part of the body. One should not, on any account, touch a person's head. Yaqona was originally the exclusive drink of chiefs; although anyone could now drink yaqona it was still treated with chiefly respect and reverence. And this yaqona was said to have sprung from the head (not from any other body part) of a dead chief. It did seem all to tie together.

* * *

The necessities of life are food, shelter and clothing. Although, in the Taveuni climate, clothing is scarcely essential—as the pre–Christian Fijians fully recognized.

In those days, women generally wore a blouse and an isulu, which comes down well below the knees, men a shirt and an isulu. The isulu is simply a rectangle of cloth about three feet by six feet, that is wrapped around the waist and tucked in at the top. It's not at all unusual for it to come loose and start to fall down. We used to marvel at the chief when he'd stand in the middle of the village, pull out his isulu, hold the two ends straight in front, and then wrap it around again. You'd get a clear view of underpants during this operation. (I don't think anyone but the chief behaved in this way. Maybe it was a regal prerogative—or eccentricity.)

Some of the young girls wore shorts and men could wear either long or short trousers. But for special occasions—church and ceremonies—an isulu was de rigueur. I'd worn long trousers during my first couple of days, to be properly formal, and then progressed to shorts when I saw the chief in them. Now it was time to buy an isulu.

There was a store in Waitabu, open a couple of hours each afternoon, but it was a poor thing, selling flour, sugar, rice, cigarettes, matches, kerosene and benzene for lights, and not much more. We'd need to go to the nearest "town," which was Waibula, just over four miles to the north. Now the bus went three times a day—officially at 6:45, 10:30 and 2:30, and it was supposed to come back to the road above Waitabu at 10, 1:40 and 6:15. We didn't want to spend three hours at Waibula while the bus went around the island to Wairi'i and back. So the answer was to walk there.

It took about an hour-and-a-quarter so we left at four. Up the hill to the main road, down through Wai (hats off through the village), then the road skirted Vurevure Bay, nice beaches for a swim if we had time to spare. It went straight through Cobb's coconut plantation—Cobb's cows grazing at the side of the road—up a hill and down on the other side was the Waibula river, with Indian ladies doing their washing.

Although more than half the population of Fiji is Indian, they are not

To reach the nearest store we had to walk to Waibula, five miles to the north.

evenly distributed. The greatest concentrations are on the western half of Viti Levu, around Nadi and Lautoka, and in the northern part of Vanua Levu, around Labasa. This is where the sugar fields are located, which Indians were originally brought in to work, and which they now own. Taveuni has very few Indians—perhaps ten to twenty percent of the island population. But they do have all the main shops.

Non-Fijians—whether European, Indian or whatever—can only own lands that had been sold by the native chiefs before cession in 1874. Waibula was a corner of Cobb's plantation, just south of the Vanua of Waini'eli and north of Boumaa.

And we almost missed it! There were four frail-looking wooden structures a little way off the road. The four shops of Waibula, all owned by members of the same extended Indian family. There was also a corrugated iron shack—looking a bit like a superior hen house—that had METHODIST CHURCH crudely written above the door. And three taxis, owned by the shopkeepers, which were the only non-bus transport available to the people of Boumaa and Waini'eli.

The shops sold basic foodstuffs—packets of biscuits, tins of fish, onions, curry powder—in addition to fishing lines, pails and pegs, pens and ruled pads for schoolchildren. There was one shop that had a sign that read "jelly for sale" (what is called jello in America). Koleta's heart leaped; she loved jelly and it's the last thing you'd get in a Fijian village. But—despite the sign—it wasn't easy to obtain it in Waibula. "The fridge broke down," "We've got some but it's not set yet," "Just sold out." Between January and June we must have walked to Waibula a dozen times but not once—on not one single occasion—was jelly actually available.

One shop had a dozen or so isulus. I bought one with a speckled blue background, and design of red and white leaves. Koleta already had some Fijian-style clothes, from Suva, and now she purchased a red isulu that I also liked. Men and women could perfectly well exchange clothes—which is convenient—except that men tend toward more muted colors.

We were on the main road at 6:02, which was the time quoted for Waibula in the timetable I'd obtained from the bus garage, and started walking south. The bus actually picked us up about halfway home.

I was dressed in Fijian fashion for the meal that night. The only thing was that I have rather long legs and after arranging them I had to pull the isulu firmly over my knees, to make sure that underpants weren't visible.

Meals! The central component of life in Fiji, it seemed to us. One day, during the second week we were there, our chief went off to another village for a meeting of chiefs. We asked how it had gone. "Oooh," his eyes glistened, "in mid-morning we had a baked plantain cake. Lovely food. And then for lunch"—at the thought of this he started to drool—"roasted turtle and eggplant." The chief patted his stomach, "I ate a full helping."

"But the meeting," we persisted, "did it go well?" "Oh yes, yes. Very sensible decisions. And for afternoon tea they provided flat pancakes…" As Sepo once put it: meetings in Fiji are primarily gourmet gatherings. The further up the hierarchy one goes the better the quality—and quantity?—of the food. Yaqona is also served—generally a ceremonial drink or two is necessary before the meeting can start, and there'll be several more through the day, interspersed with cups of tea.

A regular Fijian meal—such as we were given at midday and in the evening—has three components. There's the *'aa'ana dina* ("real food") which is cooked starch such as taro, yam, breadfruit, plantain, and cassava. Then come boiled leafy green vegetables such as taro leaves or *bele*, a kind of hibiscus. And finally, some kind of protein; this can be meat but at Waitabu it was generally seafood—fish or shellfish or perhaps octopus. The greens and seafood are often cooked together in coconut milk, and the vegetables rolled around a piece of fish, producing a very tasty dish.

In traditional times, there used to be only two meals a day so it is reasonable that breakfast—the one the missionaries introduced—should be largely European-type food. There could be scones or roti or pancakes—

all made with flour—or a plate of boiled rice (not the most appealing dish, all on its own). We might have leftovers from supper—last night's taro, fried on a skillet was lovely—and sometimes just dry crackers from the shop.

Taveuni has rich soil and the gardens need very little attention—about two days a week at most. Every man and youth from the village had his own garden plots, cleared from the forest; these might be anything from a few hundred yards to a mile away from his house. All the preparation and cooking of vegetables was done by the women. And almost all the fish was caught by women.

There were two main strategies. A group of half a dozen women might take out a fair-sized net, which they'd operate as a team. Or they could fish individually with hand-held lines and bait. The best time for fishing is on the incoming tide and night is superior to day. A woman—who had been working hard all day, cooking, cleaning and looking after the children—would often go off for two or three hours in the middle of the night to catch fish for the next day's meals. She'd have to use a torch (what Americans call a flashlight), with the light attracting the fish and making them easy to trap.

The day after we'd recorded Falaavia Matavesi I put in another spell straightening crooked bars of metal at the new store and Koleta joined a group of women going fishing. They first dug in the sand near the shore for bait. Then went out and stood in a row, at the edge of the reef, throwing in their lines, hauling fish in, trying to catch enough fish for lunch and supper. Koleta was inexperienced at this task. Her bait dropped off. There seemed no fish around her, although swarms came to the other women. They were too engrossed in their own endeavors to pay attention to helping her. She returned home wet and fishless and slightly fed up. I showed her the blisters that had come up on my hands from bang-bang-bang-bang with the hammer on crooked rods.

We decided we'd done our bit of helping, for a while, and could now get on with language study. Later on, Koleta went out with parties using a net and that was much more successful. We did all sorts of jobs for Sepo and Bogi, such as fetching several pails of water from the pipe morning and evening. And I tried to assist with "village work."

Every Tuesday was the day for village work. There was an elected official, the "village secretary" who organized this on Monday night and old Suliano shouted out instructions from three different places in the village (rather like a medieval town crier). All the men and youths—and sometimes also the women—were told of some communal task which was necessary for the general upkeep of the village.

4. "No cyclone today!"

The Tuesday of our second week it was clearing weeds from around the back and side of the new store, right down to a stream that wound around the back of the village. Sepo was slightly doubtful when I offered to help but he did issue me with a newly sharpened cane knife. The trick was to use it like a sickle, in long powerful sweeps parallel to the ground, and use it away from you, so as to avoid a cut foot.

I didn't think I did too badly, for a beginner. The village men seemed vaguely impressed (this was something that tourists never did). I could hear conversations going on around with Sepo proudly explaining where I was from and what I'd come there for (with the word "professor" recurring, like a refrain). Then the blisters I'd acquired the previous day really blew up. I didn't say anything but someone noticed them and I was sent back home, just a few moments before the conch shell blew for breakfast. As I left, the conversation had turned to "soft hands" and "not used to it."

We did help the other members of Sepo's family in their daily tasks in an indirect way, and without meaning to do so. Koleta had some good quality aerobics shoes (costing perhaps fifty dollars) which were stored by the side of the door. Of course people asked for a loan of them, for fishing (standing on sharp coral you do need something). Koleta asked for them back, but then they went again and were never returned. Oh, well, we *were* eating the fish they caught. (What chagrined her was that a ten-dollar pair of local sandshoes would have done just as well.) I'd brought along a pair of swimming goggles—called *suvamarini* in Fijian, a loan from *submarine*—and they too soon disappeared.

As for torches...! We had a couple and they'd get borrowed, often coming back broken or rusty after having been dropped in the sea. So we bought Sepo's family a torch of their own, and lots of batteries. That didn't last too long and they were back to borrowing ours. Finally, we took to keeping a reserve torch, hidden away, that we denied having (which was always available to read a novel by at night if all our acknowledged torchs were out of service.)

* * *

Just as in other countries, so the names of some Fijian places have a meaning, while for others the meaning is lost in antiquity. Wai-tabu is "Water-forbidden" (but I don't know why it is called that), involving the adjective *tabu*—pronounced "tamboo" in Fijian—which is cognate with the Tongan word borrowed into English as *taboo*. The tiny town where I'd bought my isulu is named after the river flowing nearby, Wai-bula "Water-healthy." The capital village of Boumaa is 'Oro-vou which is simply

"Village-new." (How many places in English-speaking countries are named Newtown?)

People tended to have two names. The first would be an English forename (generally something with Biblical overtones), cast into Fijian phonetic form—Josefa, Maria, Veronika, Jone or Iowani (alternative renderings of John), Paulo, Samuela, Mariana, Felise (from Felix), Aquela (from Angela), Vilimaina (based on Wilhelmina). This is followed by a Fijian name, which is generally descriptive. Qito is a verb, "play," and Waqa a noun, "boat." One youth from 'Orovou was called Da'ai, which is "gun" (originally "bow and arrow"). Many Fijian names can be quite long, almost a whole sentence. Sepo's is Coo-kana-cagi, literally "grass eat wind." His daughter Maritina's is Tau-tau-ni-uca "fall of the rain," while Inoka's is Soqo-o-viti, "gathering of Fiji."

Sometimes people are referred to by their English-based names, sometime by the Fijian one. Everyone used Qito for Veronika Qito and Maritina for Maritina Tau-tau-ni-uca. Sometimes both were used together, as with Elia Waqa.

Koleta's adopted father had been introduced to us as Josefa Cookanacagi. We of course called him "Father" and "Uncle" respectively. But it gradually became apparent that everyone else referred to him as Sepo, presumably a shortened from of Josefa. If we went for a stroll outside the village people would wonder where we were from. "Oh," they'd realize, "you're staying with Sepo."

The chief's name was Elia Gavidi but he was referred to by his title Tui Nasau, literally "King of Nasau." In that first text which Tui Nasau had recorded he mentioned that the people of the Naisaqai Yavusa had lived in Nasau a few generations ago, before moving to Na'ade and thence to Waitabu. Why is he called King of Nasau and not King of Waitabu? "That is a good question," Sepo said, when I put it to him, "a very good question." But he never answered it. I could have called him Tui Nasau but instead used the kin term Moomoo Levu, "Big Uncle," which he really seemed to like. He'd been chief of the village since his father died, when he was around twenty-one, Sepo said, about thirty-five years before. It had been a lengthy reign.

All the villagers called us Koleta and Roopate. Except some of the small children who couldn't yet pronounce a rolled *r* and to them I was Loopate. Actually, it was often shortened to just Pate. Our language learning was in some ways at the level of a small child and they seemed to identify with us. Koleta loved shells and when they saw she had piled up some nice ones from the beach a procession of small children came to our house with fistfuls of shells for Koleta.

4. "No cyclone today!"

Some kinds of language lessons seem a bit removed from anything you'd ever want to say. ("Where is the pen of my aunt?" and that sort of thing.) We'd been fortunate that Milner's grammar used examples that also taught a lot about Fijian culture. And so did the new sentences we wrote down each day at Waitabu. Things like "I don't mind the mosquitoes." There certainly were lots of them but we'd brought spray and roll-on deterrents and Bogi provided a net for us to sleep under. And sentences that were relevant to our endeavors. "My head is full from thinking of new words" and "We understand a little more of the Boumaa language each day."

There are two radio stations in Fiji: one is two-thirds Fijian and one-third English while the other is two-thirds Fiji Hindi and one-third English. Everyone in Waitabu would listen to the Fijian one (except that sometimes Qito, when she wanted to assert her individuality, would play Indian music at full blast).

A cyclone was coming. It was on the news on Tuesday. Two cyclones in fact, coming from different directions and both heading for Fiji. One due on Thursday night; the other on Saturday. We'd been planning to go around to the shops in Somosomo. It'd better be tomorrow, Sepo said. After the cyclones, roads might be flooded; we could be cut off for goodness knows how long.

Our original idea, hatched the previous week, had been to take Qito along, as a sort of reward for services rendered. But they hadn't been very substantial and we'd really rather have gone away just by ourselves for the day.

There was no getting out of it though. Qito appeared in her smartest outfit, suitable for going into the big town. We asked Sepo what he'd like us to buy (after all, he had provided a house, and there's no such thing as paying rent in Fijian villages). "Nothing at all," he protested. "We are happy to have you here and require nothing in exchange." Then his voice dropped almost to a whisper. "But Qito knows. She will tell you."

So there it was. We all three walked up the dusty hill to the main road, at least half-an-hour early. Early enough to catch the bus as it went down to 'Orovou (the ten o'clock service turned around there, rather than going on to Lavena) and then back past Waitabu twenty minutes later. Qito carried our umbrella (the rain storms on Taveuni are frequent and torrential) to add a bit of class to her outfit.

We went right through to Waiyevo, where there was the only real post office on the island, to buy stamps and air letters and to get money out of our bank accounts. Ten minutes after alighting Qito missed the umbrella. "Oh well," she shrugged, "the lady I was sitting next to on the bus was a distant relative and she'll have it. When we go through Somosomo I'll pick it up from her."

Down the hill from the post office was a shop called Lesuma Holdings. Two miles to the north there were Kaba's and another supermarket run by a lovely old Indian called Krishna, and then half-a-mile further on was Morris Hedstrom's. All four shops had the same sort of stock—basically, a little bit of everything. Qito told us that the family needed crockery, and the best place was Morris's. The best selection of material was at Kaba's. So let's have lunch at Lesuma—they had nice packets of curry wrapped in roti for fifty cents, and ice cream—and then catch a taxi to Kaba's.

Catch a taxi! We were looking forward to a walk. No, no. It became apparent that Qito had her best clothes on and couldn't walk in them. Well, a few hundred yards, but not two miles. I mean to say, she'd come to town with foreigners. What did we think taxis were for if not to ride in?

The kerosene lamp we'd brought out the previous week just wasn't good enough to read or write by. So we gave that to Sepo and decided to buy a benzene light which cost much more (about sixty dollars) but should enable us to work after dark. It was made in Canada, of all places.

Qito chose some nice designs of material at Kaba's, which she and Bogi would make into clothes for some of Sepo's many children. We also bought some notebooks and batteries. And then we told Qito that we were walking up to Morris's, the whole half-mile through Somosomo village.

It was nice to be back there again. Some of the children who had befriended Koleta two weeks before came and chattered away at us. There were two big new buildings going up—a church and an assembly hall, for the Great Council of Chiefs, which met in a different part of Fiji each year and would be in Somosomo next.

I wondered about the umbrella. Qito had said she'd... Oh yes. She behaved as if it were uncharitable of me to have brought the subject up again. Qito located the house of her relative and had a long, animated conversation. When at last she rejoined us I inquired gently. "The—er—umbrella" "Oh," Qito said dismissively, "it's not there now. She says she'll give it to me next time I'm in town." (Needless to say we never saw it again.)

Morris Hedstrom's was in an old building and it had an old-fashioned air. You could help yourself at the shelves but there was no cash register. The clerk wrote every item down in long-hand, added it all up, took our money, and locked it in a drawer. This took a fair while so we always had to make sure we gathered our goods together some time before the bus was due.

First of all, groceries. Four kilos of sugar, four of flour, two of rice, a big bottle of soybean oil, some salt, Chinese soy sauce, yeast, curry powder, baking powder, washing soap, ginger, onions, tea. Qito notched up a couple of heavy cartons of food before we turned to the crockery shelves. Okay, six large plates, six small plates, six cups, six saucers, six bowls, one milk jug. Wouldn't that do?, I asked.

Qito hovered in front of the sugar dishes, each with its own lid. Okay. "How many sugar bowls?" "Why—," Qito looked surprised that there should be any question about it. "Six." Actually it wasn't as silly as it may sound. Fijians consume enormous quantities of sugar—I later made observation of Sepo's household and it was about one kilo per person each week. They seem to put in as much sugar in a cup of tea as will dissolve. Anyway I suggested that two sugar bowls would be ample, and in the end we compromised at three.

Sepo himself was there, with several of his children and what seemed like half the village, when we got off the bus. Back at his house we sat cross-legged while he made a formal thank you speech for all these bounteous gifts. We could understand most of it. "You came to stay for six months," he stated, and then the rhetoric flowed over, "and are welcome to stay for seven, or even eight."

That was nice to hear. I'd have to go back to Canberra to teach after six months, but Koleta was hoping to stay on for a little longer, to finish the basic fieldwork for her Ph.D. Only, we hadn't actually mentioned that bit to Sepo yet.

* * *

Thursday, January 17, began as a normal summer day; hot and muggy without a cloud in the sky. But there was an ominous feel. A visitor was expected in the village that evening—by the name of Cyclone Eric.

Tui Nasau called in just before seven for his regular chat (or visit of inspection, depending on how one looked at it). We'd bought him a small golden folding pocket-knife (which cost all of fifty cents) from Krishna's store. I presented it in a mildly Fijian way, sitting straight up, cross-legged, facing him, and saying "Big Uncle, this is a small and paltry gift, which we beg you to accept," "Oh no, Roopate," he replied, "it is a wonderful present, of which I am entirely unworthy." And he did seem very pleased, as he sat opening and closing the blade.

In former times, a Fijian chief was treated in an exalted manner. He would have a better house than anyone else, and more wives. Nobody would dare eat until the chief tasted his food. If a commoner were walking along a path when the chief approached then he would sit until the chief had passed (it was necessary to be in an inferior position) and call out a respectful greeting, or *tama*, something like "hail!" The chief might order anyone killed, seemingly at whim, and he would then be likely to eat them.

Most of this was long in the past, but chiefs are still accorded great respect. I'd made that bad faux pas of standing—in the chief's presence—to put a photo back on its hook on the wall, on the first day. Although he was respected by everyone in Waitabu, Tui Nasau didn't live in a superior style. In fact he seemed to have simpler food, and less money than other villagers. This was partly because he was an oldish man, not terribly fit, with no children to help support him.

The chief's house was quite close to ours. Often during the day he'd sit cross-legged in the middle of the floor, so as to be able to see out of all three doors, and would periodically call out instructions to his people as they went about their daily tasks, or to children, telling them not to make too much noise, or to desist from this and do that instead. Tui Nasau had

Elia Gavidi had been Tui Nasau ("King of Nasau"), village chief, for 35 years. He liked me to call him Moomoo levu ("Big Uncle") as we were related within the kinship system into which I had been adopted.

something akin to tuberculosis and his arrival was usually heralded by a series of raw, sharp coughs. I could hear him in his house after dark, coughing through a good part of the night.

During Thursday morning, I worked with Inoke on transcribing the first part of Falaavia's text. It became apparent that Inoke was as intelligent as his uncle, Sepo, with the same intensity of concentration. Falaavia spoke very quickly. I'd play a certain sentence three or four times over to Inoke and then he'd nod, and repeat it slowly enough for me to write it down, before giving a translation into English. I'd carefully examine each word, and ask about the meaning of any I didn't already know. It was slow but satisfying work. Inoke shared my wish to write down the text exactly as it had been said. There were just a few places where Falaavia had gotten momentarily tongue-tied; he told me what she *had* said, and then what he believed it should have been, in order to be properly grammatical.

Koleta had spent the morning weaving with Nau, chatting all the time about the special language of respect that should be used to chiefs. You'd always address them using the second person plural pronoun, "you all," although referring to only one person (this seemed a bit like the use of *tu* and *vous* in French, but in a more extreme form).

By lunchtime tension was beginning to mount. A cyclone could destroy every house in the village; it could involve loss of life. Sepo wrote down the coordinates and direction of Eric, from a radio bulletin, and we placed them on a map of Fiji. It should be eighty miles off Waitabu. Could be worse. Except that the path of a cyclone can change…

The villagers had two strategies for dealing with Eric. One was just to pray. Sepo, although himself a devout Catholic, scoffed at such supplicant behavior. (I think his principle was: God helps those who help themselves.) The other was to strengthen your house. Atalemo had the only traditional Fijian house, besides the chief's, and he was up on the steeply sloping roof, reinforcing thatch with additional coconut fronds. There was banging and hammering all over Waitabu that afternoon as wooden window shutters were secured (there wasn't a pane of glass in the whole village) and weak points in walls and roofs attended to.

An old lady called to present us with a diamond-shaped fan she had woven. Koleta introduced her as Nana Maa, mother of Inoke. Oh, mother of Inoke, our wonderful linguistic helper (all the more to be valued after unsatisfactory experiences with Qito and that failed school teacher Iowani). "He is the cleverest and most helpful youth in the world," I exclaimed. Nana Maa smiled in agreement. We presented her with a packet of ten cigarettes in thanks and there were little speeches said all round. (But only little ones, since women have a better knack than men for keeping things in proportion.)

Nana Maa was the older sister of Tui Nasau and Sepo. She had, as we gradually discovered, had a most eventful life. Her eldest child, Mikaele Tauva, was begat by Atalemo before he'd married his present wife Maria. After that Nana Maa had Eroni (a name based on Aaron) by a man from Ovalau. (Sepo told us that Eroni was *gone ni wa'olo*, "a child of the road," meaning illegitimate.) Then Nana Maa had married a man from Tailevu on Viti Levu, who was the father of Inoke (based on Enoch). Normally a woman will go to live in her husband's village but the reverse can happen; then, after ten or twenty years, the Tailevu man left Waitabu.

During our language lessons in Suva Jone had warned us against any public show of affection. A couple may not hug or kiss or even hold hands where they may be seen. Jone said that we wouldn't be able to tell who was married to whom, except by observing which house they went to at night. We found even that wasn't a sure method, since so many people seemed to pack into a one-room Fijian house.

Left: Nana Maa, elder sister of the chief, had had an eventful life; here she is dressed for church. *Right:* Here Nana Maa returns home with a catch of fish, a load of firewood, and clothes she has washed.

4. "No cyclone today!"

Nana Maa lived in a small hut, the same size and construction as ours, with her eldest son Mikaele, his wife Peerina, their four children aged from nine to a couple of months old, and also Mikaele's brother Eroni. Tui Nasau had no children himself but he and Nana Vero shared their larger house with Inoke, and with Sepo's son Maarawa, Maarawa's wife Emelia and their two-year-old son Kalisito. Sepo and Bogi had in their house just their children: Qito, Elena, Filo, Elia, Mariana, Vilimaina and, when she was there, Maritina.

All this was quite complicated. But the important thing to think about was Eric. Sepo asked Tui Nasau if he could borrow two pieces of corrugated iron from the village stock. (They were in a pile near Big Uncle's house and bore a mark to show that they belonged to the village rather than to any individual.) They were put in front of each of our side doors. Two pieces of bamboo were hammered into the ground in front, to keep them in position and then a couple of loops of string attached the bamboo to part of the house frame. The same treatment couldn't be afforded the front door since we had to get in and out. But I had twine to tie it in position from the inside.

By four o'clock the sky was cloudy and a mild breeze had arisen—but nothing more than we might encounter on any day. I was keen to do a bit more linguistic work. No, everyone was far too preoccupied. Not that they had anything more to *do*. The banging had stopped and all relevant prayers had apparently been uttered. People just sat around full of foreboding. It was like a dramatic moment in a Shakespearean play, drawn out to a duration of several hours.

Koleta and I worked on our materials. A common noun in a Fijian sentence is generally preceded by the article *na*, a bit like *the* in English. In standard Fijian one would say *na koro* "the village" or *mai na koro* "from the village." The Boumaa dialect was different. The article was usually just *a*, but sometimes it was *na*. I examined occurrences in the texts so far transcribed. Then the condition became apparent. It was always *na* after a preposition, but *a* elsewhere: in Boumaa one says *a 'oro* "the village" but *mai na 'oro* "from the village."

We had supper early, so that everything would be washed up and the plates stacked away before Eric came in all his anger to attempt to break them. Now the wind was rising. "Back to your house, Roopate and Koleta, and secure the front door well!"

We'd only been doing fieldwork for ten days but the data that had been collected seemed all-important. We had a stock of plastic bags. Notebooks went into these, sealed with sticky tape. If the roof did blow off and rain came in at least our notes should be all right. We had various Fijian grammars—by Milner, Churchward, Father David Arms and the earliest missionary Hazlewood. These slipped into one bag. There was a bag left over. We also had a bulky, duplicated copy of the typescript of a new grammar of Fijian, which would be published the following year. Not of a very high linguistic standard, but it included many interesting example sentences, from a heterogeneous array of sources. I'd read it, Koleta had looked at bits of it, and planned to study the rest.

I popped it into the last plastic bag. Koleta took it out again. "No," she said, tongue in cheek, "if the cyclone wants to spoil that, then it must be God's will. Don't put it in a bag!"

When he came, at about ten o'clock, Eric *was* something to get worked up about—even though we were, as predicted, about eighty miles off his path. The wind rose to a screaming pitch. Then rain, which on our roof sounded like the sputtering of a machine gun. The wind came in gusts and lifted one piece of iron above the other, so that we could see the storm and lightning for a moment or two before it came crashing back into place.

Now for ten days I'd been living in paradise. Just marveling at the simplicity and serenity of Waitabu, and trying to learn the language. I hadn't taken everything in, like how our roof was fixed on. I hadn't really looked at the roof, hadn't thought about it. Until Eric started playing games with the roof, like a giant shuffling a pack of cards.

It seemed to us that the roof was just sheets of iron lying on the house frame. We couldn't think of how it was fastened down. There were clearly no nails, or it could scarcely have been lifted up like that by Eric.

We couldn't survive. The roof must blow away soon. We gathered plastic bags full of notebooks (but not that mediocre grammar), put rain coats over heads and went to seek shelter in Sepo and Bogi's stouter house. Then, when we got outside, it was dark in their house with everyone plainly asleep. We felt cowardly at the idea of knocking on their door so we went back to our own fragile dwelling. The wind stepped up more, tearing at the roof and making a rasping noise like a thimbled hand skating across some celestial washboard.

We dozed a bit, now and again. If the roof was going to come off it was going to come off. But by morning the cyclone was gone. The dance hall had lost its roof—pieces of iron scattered across the village green—but ours held, just. In the morning, we went out to look—oh, so there were poles across the roof, tied at the ends to a pole from the house frame. That explained why it had stayed on, but oscillated so violently.

Bogi told us she'd hardly slept a wink. "I was so worried about you,

I wanted to fetch you into our house, where it was safer. But we thought you might be sound asleep and we didn't want to disturb you." She really was the kindest, most considerate person.

We didn't say anything, except "Oh, well we were a little bit frightened."

On Friday people were sleepy and quiet. A day to relax before the next cyclone, Nigel, which was due to pass near Taveuni on Saturday night. (I didn't at first understand why Eric was followed by Nigel. Aren't they supposed to be given names beginning with consecutive letters of the alphabet? It should surely have been Fred or Frank after Eric. But then I realized that since they came from different directions they had perhaps been christened by separate cyclone naming centers, each with its own list of labels.)

"Is it usual to have two cyclones in three days?" Sepo taught us how to say this, and we wrote it down. "No, it happens *va'a-vuudua*," which means "only very seldom." Fiji has an average of about one cyclone a year; we experienced five between January and March 1985, which must be something of a record.

A dance had been planned for the Friday night, with an electric band from the other side of the island. The roads hadn't been badly flooded so it was held, and it went on after midnight. We excused ourselves, as being mildly exhausted, and grabbed a long sleep to recover from Eric and prepare for Nigel.

Church was fuller than usual on Saturday morning. Pio, the halfwit, came to sit next to me. I wasn't quite sure what the fascination was, but I got a few more jabs in the ribs before someone cuffed him. He even tried to speak to me: "*paapaa...*" Then it dawned. The word for "white skinned person" is *paapaalagi*. Pio had a mal-formed tongue and could only pronounce labial sounds. That was one word he *could* say at least half of.

I didn't try and get anyone to do linguistic work that Saturday. On a cyclone day you thought about the cyclone, or God, or the afterlife, or whatever. Eric hadn't wiped out any walls or windows but he had shaken them somewhat. More banging and hammering. Atalemo up on his roof again, weaving in a few more fronds. And I joined in too. Now that we knew our roof was tied on I put a bit more string around each of the six pairs of protruding poles.

Notebooks into plastic bags. And then lie there, shivering, not so much in fear as in uneasy anticipation. Nigel was just about the same strength as Eric. The wail of the wind, staccato pummeling of rain. The roofing iron still opened up, and snapped tight shut. (Maybe but for that extra twine it would have taken off into the night.)

Breakfast the next morning was almost light-hearted with relief. I remarked: *"E sega ni cagi-laba ni'ua"* ("No cyclone today then"). This really broke up Maarawa and everyone laughed with him.

I always know that when I can make jokes in a strange language (even if they hadn't been intended as jokes) then I am making progress. And now, with the village easing back into normalcy, we could get on with what we'd come for—linguistic fieldwork.

5

"Do you want to live or do you want to die?"

When I had worked on Australian languages some of the most intelligent and dedicated teachers would happily put in a six- or eight-hour day. And then we'd stop because I was the one who was exhausted, my head aching with the complexities of a strange and beautiful language.

Things were different with Fijians. After an hour or two their attention would tend to wander, however much I varied what we were doing, and the diminishing returns would force me to stop. Just occasionally we did go on longer. Such as the morning that Inoke and I did a bit more of Falaavia's story, and then more, and more, and it was so engrossing that we went on for four solid hours until it was finished.

Our house was small and Koleta and I couldn't both work there with helpers at the same time. She was interviewing a series of young girls that day so Inoke and I sat just outside. Then, when the sun moved around, we took up position on a couple of rocks in the shade of Sepo's toilet. The location was irrelevant. All we cared about was Falaavia's tale.

> There was once a king in this land of Boumaa, the Vuunisaa. He had a son, who was Raavouvou (the title of the king's son, which was akin to Prince). When he was grown, the Prince made his abode on the bank of the river mouth at Muanacivicivi, together with all the youth of Boumaa, from Lavena right up to Waitabu. They camped on the riverbank and all day they sang songs and had a good time.
> One day the Prince said to his main attendant: "Let's go out and spear fish. The rest of you please stay here." So the two of them took their spears and went a little way up the coast. They returned home with a full shoulder-yoke of fish, cooked and ate them, sat and chatted awhile, and then slept. The next morning Prince and attendant again went out fishing, starting at the place they had finished at the previous day, and going further north. At night they returned to Muanacivicivi with another yoke of fish. On the third day they progressed further up the coast, to Naveitala, before returning home with a yoke of fish for the supper of all the youths.
> On the fourth morning they started at Naveitala and reached Qeleni, in the Vanua

of Waini'eli, before returning home. On the fifth day they started at Qeleni and went further on, to Nagasau. There, at Nagasau, the Prince's attendant looked out to sea. "Hey, Prince, there's a group of fisherwomen out there." The Prince replied: "Light our fire here!"

The fisherwomen were the daughter of the King of Waini'eli, called the Raaluve (or Princess) and her attendants. "Look," one of the women cried, "there's a big fire blazing on the land." "We'll go ashore there," the Princess replied.

The women came ashore and found two youths sitting there, the Prince of Boumaa and his attendant. Now custom requires that the best part of a catch be presented to an important person, such as a Prince, so the biggest fish were put to one side for that purpose. The women then cooked the remaining fish and the whole group ate them. The Prince of Boumaa was sitting next to the Princess of Waini'eli. The chatted together, and then he asked her to be his wife. She agreed.

When the meal was over, the two men prepared to return to Boumaa. The choicest fish were given to them, to take home. (As a result, the women returned to their homes empty-handed.) The Princess told her suitor: "Don't let there be any delay." "I'll go and tell the King my father straightaway and next week we'll come to present tabuas (whale's teeth) in order to seal the wedding agreement," he replied.

The youths returned home to Boumaa, cooked and ate the fish they had been given and then slept. Next day they didn't go out fishing, but just lay around the camp. All that day, all week, for two weeks, they just idled their time away at Muanacivicivi. The Prince of Boumaa didn't go and inform his father of the intended marriage.

Meanwhile there was activity in the Vanua of Narova, which was situated on a hill behind Waini'eli. The people of Narova decided that they should ask for the hand in marriage of the Princess of Waini'eli, for their own Prince of Narova. This proposal was accepted. The Princess of Waini'eli had heard nothing from the Prince of Boumaa, and it wasn't clear to her whether he really did want to go ahead with the marriage plan. So a date was set for her marriage to the Prince of Narova.

Invitations were sent to Boumaa and surrounding Vanuas. Many people went to the wedding. The Prince of Boumaa heard of it, but he did not attend. Then, he traveled north on the evening of the wedding day. Let me say that this youth, the Prince of Boumaa, had exceptionally long feet; they were two finger spans in length. He was known by the unusual size of his feet.

The Prince neared Nagasau after dark. He heard two youths discussing the wedding festivities at Narova, and when he reached that village they were in full swing. The Prince of Boumaa approached the house to which the newly married couple had retired. He went around the back, where a leba tree was growing, by their window. He climbed up the tree and saw that they were both asleep.

Then he climbed in the window, grasped the bridegroom's tongue and tore it out, killing him. He pushed him toward his wife, saying: "There's the husband you love." The Prince came out through the window and returned to Boumaa. Not a single person there knew what had been done.

The Princess of Waini'eli woke early in the morning and touched her husband's body. It was cold. Then she saw that their sleeping mat was covered with blood—he was dead. She burst into tears, wailing out her grief. One of the relatives was sent to investigate. It had never been heard of, that a wife should cry like that on her wedding night. What was happening, had they had a fight? Then they found that the bridegroom was dead.

The news of his death was sent out. Many people from Boumaa went to the

5. "Do you want to live or do you want to die?"

funeral. But the Prince of Boumaa didn't attend. Then, after dark, the Prince traveled north. Once at Nagasau he whistled with his fingers. The corpse returned his whistle from 'Alele, where it was buried. The Prince of Boumaa went and opened up the grave. He carried out the corpse on his shoulder, took it to Narova and placed it on the connubial mat, next to the sleeping Princess, saying "There is the husband you love!" Then he returned to Boumaa.

When the Princess awoke and found her dead husband lying next to her again, she cried and cried. That day he was re-buried, this time in the chiefly graveyard at Naselesele, in Waini'eli. On the evening of the second burial the Prince of Boumaa again traveled north. At Nagasau he whistled, and an answering whistle came from the chiefly graveyard. He hurried there, dug up the corpse and again placed it next to the sleeping wife, saying: "There's the husband you love!" No one had seen what he had done. Then he came back to Boumaa.

When the corpse was again found lying on the sleeping mat, the people asked who could have done this thing. There was a third burial that day but no news was sent out, since the whole affair had become so shameful. He was buried at Naisogo. But the Prince of Boumaa came after dark, whistled, located the body, and put it next to the sleeping wife, saying: "There's the husband you love." Then he returned to Boumaa.

On the fourth night he was buried at the base of Viubani Island, loaded onto a boat which was sunk in the sea. But again the Prince of Boumaa went north after dark and whistled. The corpse returned his whistle from the base of Viubani. So he got a boat and paddled out to retrieve the corpse. He put it on the sleeping mat, saying once more to the Princess: "There's the husband you love." Then he returned to Boumaa.

The people of Narova decided that they wouldn't bury him again. They put the corpse inside their village and fetched from the far-away island of Naqelelevu a traditional god called Matawalu (literally "Eyes-eight"), so that he would shine and illuminate the place and they would be able to observe who came to tamper with the dead Prince.

That evening the Prince of Boumaa came north. He whistled, and it was answered from Narova. When he reached that village it was brilliantly illuminated by the eight eyes of Matawalu. The people of Narova stayed awake for long time, on watch, but eventually sleep overcame them.

Then the Prince of Boumaa tore off a leaf, rubbed and twisted it in his hand and threw it into the middle of the village where it extinguished one of the eyes of the god. He rubbed and threw a second leaf, and extinguished a second eye. He did this seven times, and seven eyes were extinguished. There remained just the biggest eye. Then he rubbed leaves again and again, threw them many times and eventually that globe was extinguished. He took the corpse, put it into the marriage bed and said to the widow: "There's the husband you love."

As the Prince was returning home, morning began to break. He reached the village of Nava'acoa just as it became light and people were fetching water from a spring. A woman from Nava'acoa met the Prince on the road.

Now the King of Waini'eli had sent a messenger, to try to find the person who had moved the corpse. The messenger saw a distinctively long footprint on the road. Then he met the woman from Nava'acoa and asked her. "Did you see anyone go by here?" "Oh yes," she replied. "The Prince of Boumaa just passed me." The messenger now knew who had done it. He returned to Waini'eli and told the news to the King.

The King of Waini'eli sent his messenger to Boumaa, to tell the King of Boumaa about the things that his son had done. The Prince of Boumaa was relaxing, doing nothing in particular, in his camp at the mouth of the river. He was summoned by his father, who said: "Because of the things you did at Narova, the King of Waini'eli has declared war on Boumaa. Because of your behavior, trouble will befall the whole Vanua."

The Prince replied: "That's all right, sir. You just take it easy. I'll fight the battle by myself. You and all the other people of Boumaa can just relax." Then the King of Boumaa told the messenger that the declaration of war was accepted. The messenger returned to his King.

The King of Waini'eli addressed his subjects and told them they were all to go and fight Boumaa. All the people of Waini'eli set forth, except for women who had very young children and those too infirm to make the journey. They camped at Waitabu that night.

A messenger was sent to the Prince that the opposing army was nearby. "That's fine," he said. "Let them come." Then he addressed the youths who were his companions. "You stay here and sing songs. I'll fight on my own." He filed his spear, making the point sharp, and then swam across the mouth of the river.

The people of Waini'eli came down from Waitabu toward the place where the Prince of Boumaa was waiting to give battle. It is said that when the first of them reached Tovutovu, people were still coming down from Waitabu, indicating that the line of warriors must have been about one mile in length.

The first person from Waini'eli came forward. The Prince speared him, so that he was dead. More came forward and he speared them. The warriors from Waini'eli advanced one by one and were each slain until there remained just a single person, the last one, the Princess of Waini'eli.

The Prince of Boumaa asked her: "What do you want? To return home or to die with your people?"

She told him, "In the place where my people died, I will die there too."

So the Prince pointed his spear at her, and ran it through her body. Then he put her on his shoulders and carried the corpse up to Waini'eli, only removing the spear when he got there. Then he told the King of Waini'eli: "The people of Waini'eli are slain. They are all lying dead at Boumaa. I asked the Princess "Do you want to live or do you want to die?" and she told me that she would die in the place where her people had perished. That's why I put my spear through her and now I've brought her body back to you. If there are any Waini'eli people remaining, tell them to come back to Boumaa with me if they want to fight."

But they told him that they begged for peace. The Prince returned to Boumaa. He camped at Muanacivicivi with the other youths. And told his father the King: "You, the people of Boumaa, can rest easy. If there is any more trouble I will fight. And if I should die, there will be no one to blame but me."

Not only was this a wonderful story, it was also a grammatical goldmine. There are more than twenty little words that can follow the verb in a Fijian sentence, and modify its meaning—for example *vata* "together," *sara* "really," *to'a* "try to do." A verb may be followed by one or two or even more of these modifiers; but they must occur in a fixed order. Falaavia's text included many verbs that were followed by two or three modifiers. Things like *dabe vata sara to'a* "really tried sitting together" (where the verb is *dabe* "sit") describing the Prince of Boumaa and the Princess of Waini'eli sitting side by side at the picnic meal, just before he proposed to her. This showed that *vata* must come before *sara* which in turn precedes *to'a*. Such was the richness of Falaavia's story that by looking at all the combinations of verb modifiers in it I could work out almost the entire set of ordering restrictions concerning modifiers.

We were also advancing our ability to speak the Boumaa dialect. Koleta is a natural and uninhibited language learner and just loves to talk in a new language. One day we were strolling along the road near 'Orovou when some ladies inquired where we were heading. "Nowhere in particular," Koleta replied without any hesitation "we're just walking up the road, and when we start to feel exhausted we'll turn and go home." The ladies responded with an open-mouthed, "Oh!" (It may have been that fairly obscure word *dagadaga*, "exhausted," which Koleta had recently acquired and was enjoying using.)

There was one time when Koleta was chatting in the village and I heard her use a word I didn't recognize. "What does that word mean?" I asked later. "I'm not sure," she mused, "but it just seemed like the right word to use in that sentence." My own approach to speaking a new language is quite different. I think everything through quite carefully first, and really plan what I am going to say.

There was more to our life than language. Living in a village, even if someone else does the cooking, there are still chores to be performed. Such as washing. In Fiji women do the washing. A man could carry the basket of dirty or clean clothes to or from the pipe. But if he helped in the job itself it would reflect badly on the woman's domestic abilities (and perhaps also on his manliness). I suggested we ignore all that and just do it together but Koleta was doubtful; she wanted to be accepted by the women of Waitabu.

The first couple of weeks she did do it by herself and it was a time-consuming, back-breaking task. Then we hit upon a solution. When the first lali sounded, at twenty to six, we'd get up, and sneak off to the washing pool while almost everybody else was at church. That way there would be no one to watch what we did!

It was a fair walk. A quarter-mile along a winding forest path to Black Rocks. A bamboo pipe diverted water into a couple of shallow rock depressions. We first soaked the clothes, then Koleta rubbed them all over with a thick bar of yellow soap. They were then piled up and slapped against a rock or else hit with a stick (Koleta's relatives had taught her how). I stood at the other side of the pool and did all the rinsing and wringing. We went to the pool about once every ten days and the whole thing took about an hour and a half (it would have taken Koleta three hours all by herself).

Different people can view a situation differently. One morning I was rinsing and wringing away, thinking of how I could quite happily wash clothes in this way for the rest of my life, in a clear spring on a warm tropical morning—when Koleta's voice said: "We're sure going to appreciate washing machines when we get back to Canberra!"

Other days we went to church at six o'clock. Three mornings a week and the big service on Sunday at ten was what we settled down to. An initial rousing hymn. Then people would pray while giving their children mild slaps to make them sit still. A three-year-old might start playing with the catechist's hymn book, be given a harder slap and then start crying. A seven-year-old sister then carried her out, the two smiling at each other at the joy of going outside where they could run and play. Then we'd have a lesson.

Felise the catechist always used a set phrase to introduce the lesson. It sounded to me like "*Cyclone qori a vosa ni Tuuraga*," which would mean "That cyclone is the voice of the Lord." (Surely not totally unreasonable? I mean, if there were a god, and he did speak, why shouldn't he sound like a cyclone?) That's what I heard. I know I must have had cyclones on the brain. (In any case the name for cyclone in Fijian is *cagi-laba* "wind-murder," literally "murdering wind.") What he actually said was "*Sa i koya qari a vosa ni Tuuraga.*" This *sa i koya* is an odd sort of construction which doesn't occur in Boumaa. (Paul Geraghty told me that it didn't really occur in any dialect. He uses the term "Old High Fijian" for church language. It was based on Bau but the early missionaries hadn't learned that dialect fully and their translations included some things that were either mistakes or inventions.) Whenever a lesson is introduced in a Fijian church I always hear that English word *cyclone*, I just can't help it.

What with church and everything we were beginning to fit into the village. But sometimes I felt really on the spot, not knowing exactly how to behave. One afternoon I was sitting outside chatting with some ladies who were weaving mats in the sunshine. They were asking simple questions that I could answer, some to satisfy their curiosity about what things were like in Australia and others to check up on my perception of their world. Suddenly one of them asked "Where's your mother?" Big pause. What should the answer be to that? I had a father, Elia Waqa, and I knew his wife had passed away before Christmas. I hesitated, but everyone was looking at me. "*E mate*" ("She's dead"), I ventured. This was met with smiles and nods; I had passed that little test more by good luck than anything. My mother had died before we'd arrived there, before she even knew that she had me as a son!

In the first few weeks at Waitabu both Koleta and I read the novel *Return to Laughter* by Elenore Smith Bowen, nom-de-plume of the anthropologist Laura Bohannan. It is based on Bohannan's experiences doing fieldwork in West Africa and there were a lot of similarities with our situation. One difference was that Bohannan worked during colonial days—she had her own "boys" to cook and wash, and a folding table and gin and tonic before dinner. (We normally loved to have a drink in the evening but there wasn't any at Waitabu, and so we did without.) Bohannan was faced with a strange culture and we could sympathize with the confusion she felt.

One thing that I couldn't agree with Bohannan on was her characterization of Africans as "savages" and her assumption that European and North American culture (things like classical music) were intrinsically superior. My opinion, at the end of January, was that African or Fijian culture is neither better nor worse than ours; it is just different. Falaavia's story was as fine an example of "literature" as anything produced in Australia (or Europe). The Fijians have a much more complex and highly articulated kinship system than we do. It is a classificatory system so that everyone in Waitabu and surrounding villages is related to everyone else (in terms of the way their fathers were related, and so on). You should choose a spouse from among the people who are in a certain relationship to you. There are plusses and minuses on both sides and the cultures are, overall, just "different."

There were, however, some things from our own culture that we couldn't do without. Koleta has double curvature of the spine, which requires regular treatment from a chiropractor and the right sort of exercise. Having to live and work on the floor was making things very difficult for her. (It wasn't easy for me, and my back is okay.) We really did need a table. Sepo offered his but he did use it for all sorts of things so we said no. But he had six chairs and we would borrow a couple of those.

So one day in the week after the cyclones we caught the ten o'clock bus around to the commercial side of Taveuni. There were two places selling furniture. (You had to know how to go around the back of a shop to find them.) We found a wooden table that would just fit at the side of our house, between the front door and a side door. I bargained them down to seventy-five dollars (I love bargaining), then we bargained a taxi driver down to thirteen dollars, for us and the table and just one box of groceries. All the taxis on Taveuni are like mini-buses, for transporting dozens of people with lots of chattels.

Everyone in the village crowded round when we got back. Tui Nasau came in and sat down to admire it (we of course sat on the floor with him when he was present). He coughed, talked a bit in Fijian, looked at the new acquisition. Then he grinned broadly at us and said: "Good tepel." They were the second and third words of English we'd heard from the chief. His principle seemed to be: use the English language for an English artifact.

* * *

When I'd passed the age of forty, a few years back, I started writing novels. First of all, genre stuff—detective stories. Victor Gollancz had published one, under the nom-de-plume Hosanna Brown, and another was due out soon. One of the things I planned to do in Fiji was write another novel.

My house in Canberra had backed onto the bush and my way of writing was to take a clipboard a few hundred yards off, into the trees, and sit on a flat rock or on the ground. That way there was no possibility of interruption from things like a telephone ringing. I'd write for two or three hours in the early morning, covering perhaps five closely written pages. That made 25–30 pages a week and the novel should be finished in six or eight weeks with another couple of weeks for revision and typing a fair copy. I'd choose a quiet time of year, in the university vacation, and then go into my office in the university during the afternoon, to deal with administration, supervise graduate students and do research. I tend to work fairly quickly and efficiently at whatever I do, and I thrive on doing several quite disparate things at the same time.

Right from the time we arrived in Waitabu I was looking around for a quiet place to write, away from it all. I hadn't planned to start my novel for a while, until we got settled in the village and started on language work. This was lucky, since it took all of three weeks to locate a suitable writing nook.

You'd think that there'd be lots of quiet spots near a village. Not so! The beach to the west, toward 'Orovou was lovely but also busy. Every half-hour or so someone would come by, and they'd expect to have a bit of a chat. The forest behind the beach was just plain unpleasant—dark, overgrown and teeming with mosquitoes.

One morning I climbed up a steep track (which went off the path leading up to the main road) onto the cliff to the east. That bit of forest seemed full of people—well, quite a few people did have gardens in the vicinity. A youth spotted me at once: "Oh, you are looking for Inoke?" I wasn't looking for anyone, just trying to explore a bit on my own. Anyway,

5. "Do you want to live or do you want to die?"

Inoke was fetched. He showed me his garden plot—taro and plantain and some yaqona plants. They took a good few years to mature, Inoke said, but when they did the crop could be most lucrative. I insisted on going on alone, following paths through the forest. I got lost for a while. Then I climbed a fence into Jim Henning's plantation—cleared ground, and it was easier to walk and navigate. I got down to the sea but there was a high cliff between me and Waitabu. Eventually I scrambled over rocks and waded waist-deep and got back to the village—rather scratched and extremely wet. It seemed to me I'd been away for ages, but it was only two or three hours in all.

The village contained only about a hundred and twenty people but there seemed to be one of them hiding behind a tree in any place I went within a mile of our house. There were pleasant grassy patches on the other side of the main road but it was a bit far and I met a group of Waitabu children who wanted to engage in conversation.

Finally, I decided on *Nu'u le'a-le'a*, which means "Short Sand," a place beyond Black Rocks. It wasn't at all easy to get to, and for that reason I could be alone. You first went to the washing pond, at the beginning of Black Rocks and then scrambled along a barely discernable path over the top of the Rocks. It was covered with moss, and a bit slippery and treacherous when it had been raining recently (it had almost always been raining recently, at Waitabu). Sometimes I went into a skid and once my pen flew away into a crack in the rocks; but I soon learned which bits to be careful over, which trees to hold onto for support. Then jump down from the rocks at the other end onto a small, calm beach. I'd settle down in a shady spot on the sand, making sure it wasn't under a coconut tree—one of the nuts falling from a height can kill—and write.

Every morning a coconut or two would fall, plop, somewhere on that Short Sand beach. Crabs walked across the beach, some of them in an amazing variety of purloined shells. I was writing a book about a middle-aged man who left his wife. Not really anyone like me, he was a businessman and very rich (the ex-wife was the one who was the academic). This man meets a young lady publisher, whose grandfather is a duke in England, a direct descendant of an illegitimate son of King Henry VIII.

Sometimes a group of women would pass by in the sea, wading out to do a morning's fishing. They knew I'd come there to be alone and work peacefully. We had to exchange greetings, of course, but these were formulaic and didn't interrupt my train of thought. "Going fishing?" I'd ask. "Yes." "Well, good luck then."

There was another way to get from Waitabu from Short Sand. At low

Top, left: For a quiet place to write I went past the washing pools at Black Rocks and then along a slight path. The rocks covered with moss could be treacherous footing. *Right:* One had to negotiate around ferns. *Left:* And over slippery roots.

tide you could just about wade around the rocks, thigh deep. I soon evolved a way of telling whether this was feasible. There was a log lying on Short Sand at right angles to the sea. When the water didn't come more than about two yards up the log I would be able to wade back; otherwise, slip and scramble over the rocks. (My indicator at the other end was how far the water came up a large rock by the washing pool.)

The only way to achieve any-

5. "Do you want to live or do you want to die?"

Onto the idyllic beach called "Short Sand," shown here at low tide.

thing, I've found, is by sticking to a pretty regular schedule. So immediately after breakfast, on five or six days of the week, I'd take my notebook and umbrella (we'd just bought a new one) and go off to Short Sand, returning by lunchtime.

You'd be amazed at how often something quite important had happened in the village while I was away. One morning, Koleta said, there'd been a tremendous shouting match between Qito and Pelasio's daughter Luisa. Apparently Luisa had suggested that Qito might be pregnant but Koleta's lovely sister had denied this, hotly. I wish I'd heard it, Koleta said that the insults which these two girls had hurled at each other across the village were fairly comprehensive.

When I went across to the toilet, Sepo, Bogi and Qito were having a serious discussion in the lea of their kitchen. Apparently, they quizzed her for two hours solid on whether she was pregnant. Qito insisted that she wasn't and convinced her parents of this.

As time passed, the lives we'd lived in Australia seemed increasingly remote. My birthday came around. Now such an anniversary is something which Fijians neither notice nor value. The literal translation is *siga ni sucu* "day of birth." But in Fiji *siga ni sucu* is the term for Christmas. Jesus's birthday is the only one which counts. Nevertheless, in the afternoon of that day Koleta came into the house with Nau, broad smiles on their faces.

Even at high tide there was enough dry sand for my "office."

"Close your eyes!" So I did and when I opened them there was my birthday present, a real Fijian gift, a large mat that Koleta had woven. There were little bits of colored wool sewn up the sides—a modern day embellishment that I could have done without—but the main thing was the mat. Nau had gathered the leaves of voivoi, a type of pandanus, dried and prepared and split these and taught Koleta how to weave them in a cross pattern, and how to finish them off at the edges. All the while she was weaving Koleta had been discussing different language styles, kinship, ritual and the like.

We were starting to think a bit in Fijian. There is one marvelous verb *'ere'ere* which means "ask" or "beg" or "supplicate." It's a very polite word, and the person you address it to can't really refuse what is requested. One morning, early in our stay, the chief was chatting at a time when I wished to go off and wash. I said "I want to wash" at which he said "Oh, I see" and left abruptly, in something of a huff. I had in fact spoken rudely. On further occasions like this I said: "Big Uncle, I *'ere'ere* that I go and wash," that is, "I humbly beg that you allow me to go and wash." He would smile, say "Certainly" and leave in a courteous manner.

Mr. Waradi, of the Fijian High Commission in Canberra, had told us about another use of *'ere'ere* (which corresponds to *kerekere* in Standard

5. "Do you want to live or do you want to die?"

Fijian). If someone comes into your house, sits down cross-legged and uses *'ere'ere* in relation to something that you own and which they want, then you must give it to them. It's no good at all saying that you need it yourself—if they *'ere'ere* it, they get it. Of course, you can go and *'ere'ere* something back from them in exchange, which is a way to stop anyone being too greedy. This principle insures that if someone in a village has more of something than other people, then it gets fairly evenly distributed through the whole community.

We didn't get any *'ere'ere* in the first couple of weeks. Then it gradually built up. People knew that although we didn't smoke (and hated the habit) we bought cigarettes to give to people who helped us. Inoke's mother Nana Maa would drop in and make inconsequential small talk. We knew what she was after from Nana Maa's slightly embarrassed air, but it might take ten minutes before she got to the point.

Tui Nasau smoked and of course we'd always give him a packet if he came to *'ere'ere*. Sometimes there were none left and we had to admit this. The chief would then be covered in embarrassment and try to pretend he hadn't said it, that he'd called for a quite different purpose.

Money wasn't used much at Waitabu, but it was needed for a few things, like buying clothes and cigarettes and "foreign" food like flour, rice and sugar. The only way people could get money was to go away to work on a plantation for a few weeks or months (some of the youths did this) or cut copra at the village. Either way the return was around five dollars for a full day's work—say sixty cents an hour. Many families had members working in Suva or other towns—earning a little more than that—who would send money home from time to time.

Tui Nasau had no children and he was old and unwell, certainly not able to cut copra for any period. So he had virtually no money. One morning he called to *'ere'ere* twenty cents from us to make a call from the village telephone, which was located in Suliano's house (and worked perhaps half the time). We gave him a dollar. A week later he called after dinner and mentioned that he was on his way to ask his brother (Sepo) if he could lend him $2 for the bus fare to attend a regional meeting of chiefs; of course we gave him the $2. In some ways Tui Nasau was a sweet, soft old man. But he was the chief, and knew how to wield power. He could certainly have banned us from the village, and there would have been no possible court of appeal.

After supper our tiny house became something like a youth club. Anything from six to fifteen children and teenagers might sit around, swapping stories about what had happened during the day, asking us things. After we'd been working hard all day it was good to relax, and this interaction was great for our Fijian. Tina, an extrovert eleven-year-old, stood up and sang a traditional Fijian *me'e* song, complete with appropriate dance movements.

Then I stood up and banged my head on the middle cross-piece of the house frame, which was only about five feet and six inches off the ground. There was a nail in it, on which we'd hang the benzene light, and I grazed that, making me wince with pain. Everyone in the house burst out laughing.

Jone had warned us of this. He'd told the story of one elderly Peace Corps lady who slipped and fell when visiting a village early in the orientation program and been so upset at the laughter that she'd wanted to go home to America at once. I got used to it (being of a reasonable height, I do tend to bang my head quite often), but it was always a little unnerving.

Laura Bohannan commented on the same thing in *Return to Laughter*, at how people teased a blind man, and laughed when he fell. "Their laughter at suffering," she wrote, " was merely one symbol of the gulf between their world and mine." Well, maybe. But it *is* funny when someone bangs their head or slips over, so long as they don't seriously hurt themselves! (No one in any society of the world—so far as I know—laughs at people dying.) Tiny children laugh at this in our world but we've trained ourselves not to. It's surely just a matter of habit.

* * *

A couple of weeks after recording texts from Falaavia Matavesi and the Vuunisaa in 'Orovou, Sepo decided that we should visit another of the district's leading story tellers. On Wednesday, January 30, we got up extra early and Bogi—bless her heart!—prepared, for all three of us, an early breakfast before we went up the hill in plenty of time for the 6:30 bus.

Sepo said we should get off at Waibula in order to buy yaqona from one of the shops. (The village store at Waitabu was out of yaqona. It was, in fact, usually out of most things.) Sepo carefully combed his hair in a mirror while I also purchased a spare pen. Then we walked up the road—about half-an-hour—to Qeleni.

As soon as we reached the first houses, Sepo cupped hands to mouth and shouted a greeting into the village. It was what visitors had to do in olden days. I never saw anyone else behave in this way in 1985 but Sepo did like to do things properly (perhaps, especially for our benefit).

Qeleni was a big village, two or three times the size of Waitabu. Quite a few of the houses were built of concrete blocks and a fair proportion were divided into several rooms, an introduced habit that had not yet spread as far as Waitabu. We climbed up to the high end right next to the forest, and the house of Siriloo Saabai.

The family was just finishing breakfast around their eating mat on the floor so Sepo, Koleta and I presented the bundle of yaqona roots and then sat off to one side and chatted among ourselves until Siriloo had finished eating, gone into the bedroom to change his clothes and then he was ready. We were to sit around the table. I tested the recorder and switched it on. Siriloo said grace before the tale.

Sepo told me that he said grace not only before meals but before commencing any job of work and then another prayer when he'd finished it. Feeling the need of a supplication to the Lord before telling a bit of history was, however, unusual. I later played the tape to Inoke and some other youths and they exclaimed "What, he didn't have to say grace then!" as if there was enough religion around anyway, without inventing new occasions for it. (Some of the young people at Waitabu were obviously a bit skeptical about the Christian religion, but they never said anything openly, and made sure they attended church often enough to avoid any criticism.)

> Let us pray, in the name of the Father, and Him the Son, and Him the Holy Ghost. Great Father in heaven, you who are most exalted over heaven and earth, you see that we are gathered here this morning, to hold a discussion, together with my friends, who are here. I look up now and beseech you for your blessing, and for the enlightenment you can give us—pour it on the top of this table, that the discussion which is being undertaken this morning can be clear and properly organized. Thus we pray to glorify your holy name, Jesus, the Saviour, Amen. In the name of the Father, and Him the Son, and Him the Holy Ghost, Amen.

What was particularly interesting about this was that Siriloo used church language, based on the Bau dialect, with a full complement of *k*s and no glottal stops. He used the Bau pronoun *kemunii* "you all" to address God (employing the plural form as a mark of respect). Then, when he began the story proper it was in the local dialect, with *'emunuu* "you all" and all the other familiar local features.

The story concerned a Tongan chief, Wainiqolo, who brought his army to Fiji in 1865–6 and conquered many provinces. Then he launched an attack on Tui Ca'au, high chief of Ca'audrove. It was partly a religious war, the Tongans being staunch Wesleyans. A French priest, Father Lorenzo, was a missionary at Solevu, on Vanua Levu and, when he heard about the coming attack, sped along the coast to warn Tui Ca'au. Then he offered the high chief a wooden cross: "Will you take this into battle as your flag of war?" Tui Ca'au accepted.

When the Tongan army—augmented by soldiers from their Fijian vassal states—came ashore near Wairi'i, Tui Ca'au and his fighting force were waiting. And, of course, the local side won hands down. Siriloo told of how the vanquished Tongan soldiers swam out toward 'Orolevu Island (which is just opposite the Castaway International Hotel) each calling out to the other "Hey, that's my island!" "No, it's mine," even though it could accommodate all of them.

Then Siriloo switched to 1874 when the chiefs of Fiji were ceding their land to Britain, represented by the commanding officer of the battleship H.M.S. *Miranda*. Ca'obau, the King of Bau, styled himself King of Fiji, but this annoyed Tui Ca'au who said that Ca'obau was no more than King of Tailevu, the eastern part of the island of Viti Levu (including Bau) while he, Tui Ca'au, was king of the whole of the island of Vanua Levu. Tui Ca'au at first refused to attend the cession conference. Several of the other chiefs, who had been freed from the Tongan invaders by Tui Ca'au's victory, said that it should not begin without him. So Ca'obau sent a group of chiefs on a mission of atonement, and the cession meeting eventually got underway three days late.

The Catholic church had a role here too. Father John Baptist had the best knowledge of Fijian of any white man and he was appointed official translator. "The translation was clear and well-done, and every aspect of it stands true today."

Siriloo Saabai was a shy, oldish man who declaimed this story in a histrionic style, with all sorts of rhetorical devices, almost as if delivering a sermon. It was in marked contrast to Falaavia's un-self-conscious, matter-of-fact narration. When he'd finished Sepo asked me to play Elia Waqa's text concerning the origin of yaqona. There was a bit of rivalry between Sepo and Elia Waqa, as members of different Mataqalis, and I don't think he was displeased when Siriloo said there were considerable errors in what we'd been told.

So the recorder went on again. Siriloo was, of course, most deferential into the microphone. He referred to his respect for Elia Waqa, mentioned the story he had just heard and stated: "It is totally correct." Then he said: "I just wish to add a little to one part." This involved saying that the chief had a different name and came from a different place to what my adopted father had stated. Yaqona did grow from his head, and also sugar-cane sprouted from his feet. If you get a bit under the influence, from too much yaqona, then drink a bit of sugar-cane juice and "drunkenness flies away."

5. "Do you want to live or do you want to die?"

Several times he kept on coming back and maintaining that everything Elia Waqa had said was absolutely true.

We'd recorded two fine texts. Walking back down the main road (because the bus wasn't due for a while) Sepo said that Siriloo had spoken in the Waini'eli dialect, but that it was very similar to Boumaa. In fact, I was never able to find any definite difference between the speech of these adjacent Vanuas. It seems that there is just one dialect of Fijian—which should properly be called Boumaa-Waini'eli Fijian—spoken in the north-east quarter of Taveuni.

There was to be an important meeting that day, with representatives from all the villages in Waini'eli and Boumaa, and it was to take place at Wai. (These meetings were held once every two months or so and rotated around the villages.) Sepo had arranged for us to attend, and to record the proceedings.

We got to Nava'acoa and waited in the bus shelter there, just by the place where the Prince of Boumaa had been seen in the early morning by the woman fetching water, and had left his distinctively long footprint. There were some officials from Naiviivi village, on the island of Qamea, who had come across by boat and were also waiting for the bus. When it came we saw that Siriloo Saabai was on board; he'd be a delegate from Qeleni. Siriloo wore a cross on his chest, hung from a wide blue ribbon; he truly was a most devout man.

Meetings always began when the bus arrived (and it often was late). None of the delegates had a car, although a couple of government officials from the other side of the island did arrive by jeep. We all sat on the floor of the largest house in Wai and began with the yaqona ritual. It was served first to the King of Waini'eli, as chairman, and then—in strict order of seniority—to every other person in the room. There was of course a prayer as well.

Once it got started the meeting was pretty businesslike. People talked about the state of the road, a few matters of health care, a report which the government had just issued on the "future of the Fijian village" and plans for the forthcoming Great Council of Chiefs in Taveuni. Attention seemed to focus most on feeding the chiefs and their advisors; this was planned to be a feast among feasts, and it would last all week. Each village should contribute two thousand taro in order to meet the eating schedule. These would have to be planted very soon. There should also be a certain number of pigs and one cow from each village. In most villages there were two or three pig pens but Waitabu had none at all. Some of the young men would have to work on plantations to earn money—thirty or forty dollars for a decent-sized pig and about two hundred for a cow.

Then Sepo spoke. "I have been asking at these meetings for the past four years why the bus cannot come into Waitabu, as it does into every other village. The manager of the bus company said that our road is not good enough. But it has been upgraded. He says there are not enough passengers; that is not so. I believe that the top manager of the bus company in Suva has given permission for buses to come to Waitabu. It is not clear to me why this has not happened." (The phrase with which Sepo concluded "*E sega ni macala*," "It is not clear," seems to recur an awful lot in the conversation of all Fijians.) The point was noted.

It was great that Sepo had taken us to the meeting. He was determined to do everything he could to assist our linguistic work, and had long sessions with Koleta, answering all her questions about the different kinds of language that are used in varying social circumstances. Now Sepo decided that he was going to help me transcribe Siriloo's long historical narrative—no on else should help, just him. We'd start the next morning (so I had to put off novel-writing, but there was plenty of time for that). The only trouble was that Sepo had so many things to do and I often had to wait and wait and wait until he did have time.

Tui Nasau popped in after breakfast to ask what we'd been doing the previous day. I explained about going to Qeleni and the long and wonderful story. Then he interrupted and said: "*Dolava, dolava, Roopate*!!"

Now *dola* is "open" and the suffix *-va* makes it into a transitive verb, "open it up!" I looked around. The front door and one side door were open but the other side door still had its packing case side in position. Was the chief asking me to open that door? Why? He'd never worried about anything like that before. I was just about to get up and open the door when I realized that *dolava* has another sense. It can be used for switching on a radio. What Tui Nasau was asking me to do was to play him the Siriloo story I'd been talking about, to "open up" the tape recorder. So I did, after a considerable pause, and my Big Uncle sat listening, nodding and smiling.

Then Sepo did come. Once he settled down to a thing Sepo really concentrated, and of course he was good. (Sepo and Inoke were well-nigh perfect as linguistic consultants, way ahead of everyone else in the village.) We did three hours that morning and transcribed almost half the text.

Sepo said he'd have a short rest after lunch and then be back at around two to finish it off. Just after three o'clock he passed by my door and said he just had to go to the toilet, but would be with me in five minutes. At four he passed by again and said he had to go to the store to attend to an urgent task but would be with me in quarter-of-an-hour. Foolishly I just stayed in the house, waiting for him (and didn't even go for a swim, although it was high tide and I was dying for one). At supper, Sepo didn't even mention the fact that he never had come that afternoon.

Well, he had been busy. He didn't say he wouldn't be able to come because I think he'd kept hoping that he could fit in a bit of time with me. We finished the text over the next five or six days, in odd bits here and there, with Bogi gently suggesting that Sepo ought not to neglect his other duties. But after that story was done he did permit Inoke to help me with other texts, which was better because Inoke had much more time.

Living in a strange culture one must just take things as they come, and not superimpose the expectations of another life style. Even with that in mind, there can still be surprises.

A Fijian man has no regular work schedule; he can go into the garden on any day he chooses (except Sunday), help his friends on any other day. Once, just after breakfast, I asked Inoke what he would be doing that day. He replied "*E sega ni macala*" ("It's not clear"), which I found surprising. But I know that Inoke lived in the chief's house. "Oh, does Tui Nasau have to tell you what to do?" "Oh no," Inoke said, "I decide."

In our society someone would reply "I haven't yet decided what I'll do today," accepting responsibility for the decision-making. But Inoke just used that favorite phrase, the impersonal, "It's not clear" as if it really was nothing whatsoever to do with him. (As Koleta commented: it takes the agency out of indecision.)

E sega ni macala is also interesting from a linguistic point of view. The only way to express negation in Fijian is by a verb *sega* which means something like "it is not the case." *Macala* is an adjective "clear, intelligible," *ni* corresponds to "that" in English while *e* is the subject pronoun "it." The sentence literally means "It is not the case that it is clear."

6

Becoming a Part of the Village

The Fijians must be the most thoroughly converted people in the world, scarcely needing any attention from the mother church. This is just as well, since those in Boumaa receive precious little. There were at least half-a-dozen Catholic priests in Taveuni, all living together at Wairi'i. One of them would visit Boumaa for a single day each month.

Otherwise it was all left in the admittedly capable hands of Felise, our catechist. He'd had two years at a church training school and conducted services twice a day as well as giving the sermon on Sunday. (If for any reason Felise couldn't be there then a younger man, Mikaele Waqa, would take over the huge volume which specified lessons and prayers for every day in the year, and lead the service.) Felise had the same responsibilities as everyone else in the village—he had to tend his garden, look after his family, help with village work—and he had to do his church duties on top of that with no kind of recompense that we were aware of. Fortunately, he was a very well-organized man, in addition to being sensible and kind.

The last Sunday of the month was mass in the church at 'Orovou, taken by a priest from Wairi'i—sometimes a Fijian priest, sometimes a European one, but the service would always be in Church Fijian. Everyone in Waitabu got dressed up. There was a king tide on the last Sunday in January, which completely covered the beach, so we all went—a hundred people in single file—along a snakey path through the edge of the forest; the bright blues, reds, yellows and purples of ankle-length dresses glowing against the dull foliage.

The priest went first to Lavena for a seven o'clock mass. Then he came to 'Orovou, which was the service for everyone from that village and from Viidawa, Waitabu and Wai. When we arrived he was hearing confessions. A few dozen people were lined up, waiting their turn. Then it was time for the service and most of them couldn't confess that day. Since Father always returned to Wairi'i immediately after the mass they'd have to wait another month and hope to get a little earlier in the line. (But I never heard anyone complain about this. They were just grateful that Father came at all, and heard any confessions.)

I used to enjoy those services because the priest would give the sermon in very clear language and I could understand every bit of it. We were the only white people in the congregation of several hundred and he'd often make some allusion to us, dwelling on the need for good relations between nations. We shouldn't go up for communion, Sepo insisted, since we weren't real Catholics. Everybody else did, though, and it took an awfully long time. We weren't exactly bored—fine, lilting hymns were sung the whole time. It's just that knee muscles and back muscles don't appreciate a straight-backed cross-legged stance for a whole hour. One was permitted to stretch one's legs for a minute or so, if it was possible to find a direction in which to stretch them in that crowded church, and then get back into proper posture. But that wasn't enough relief. The priest said "Our mass is concluded," and I staggered outside, feeling that someone had just sawn through my cartilages.

As is the case in many parts of the world, church is primarily a great social occasion. Friends and relatives reunite, gossip is exchanged. And Sepo took great delight in showing us off.

It was an opportunity to reflect on why Fijians embraced Christianity so readily (whereas Aboriginal Australia, for instance, rejected it for generations). Well, the Fijians already had a religion with many points of similarity to Christianity—priests, an afterlife, heaven. (They actually believed in a multiplicity of heavens—one for people, one for animals, and a special heaven for coconuts!)

The olden-days Fijians would pray to their gods for a good harvest. If it failed they'd berate the gods as good-for-nothing deities. Then the Christians came along with their God who was different in one important respect—he was infallible. Suppose that the harvest now failed. It wasn't God's fault—oh no. God is all-powerful. He must have made it fail deliberately. Why? Well, didn't you sin last year? Of course you did, everyone does a few bad things from time to time. (Or, if you didn't, think on it hard enough and you'll imagine you did.) That must be the reason then. God is punishing you for sinning. Confronted with the great new omnipotent God, of course the Fijians learned to fear and worship him above their own fallible deities.

Christianity, and especially Catholicism, is extremely chauvinistic (no female priests, and so on) which also suited the Fijians down to a tee. The everyday chauvinism in Waitabu was something which it had been particularly hard for us to adjust to.

Like most people in Western countries I was taught to finish up everything that was put on my plate. That is not what you do in Fiji. At least, it's not what men do in Fiji. The men are served first and their plates are piled high. After they've eaten what they want the plates are passed down the eating mat and the women and children get what the men have deigned to leave.

In other ways, though, we found Fijian eating customs appealing. If anyone should walk by outside across the open front door, when a family is squatting down eating, they must be invited in to join in the repast. People generally decline, but they must do that in a polite manner. Koleta would sometimes accept an invitation to "come and eat" when she was walking through 'Orovou or Viidawa or Wai at tea-time (Fijians have innumerable snacks, on top of the three main meals) partly because she felt like a couple of hot scones, and partly for a bit of linguistic practice with a new family. Qito often sat next to the door of Sepo's house, and she'd make sure to shout an invitation "come and eat" to any handsome youth who happened to pass by. He'd say no, but just the act of communication would please her.

Another nice habit is that people will swap food between households. If one lady has cooked more of something than can be eaten at that meal, she'll take a plateful around to another house which belongs to the same Ito'ato'a, an extended family unit. Bogi might have cooked fish and greens and taro and then Nana Vero, Tui Nasau's wife, could pop a plate of breadfruit in the door, which would add a bit more variety to our menu.

In most Fijian villages one or two people are likely to own a car and several would have boats. No one in Waitabu had either. There wasn't even a dog in the village. As a light sleeper I was heartily glad of that—it was hard enough to get a good sleep with roosters crowing at four a.m. without the chance of dogs barking. Hens and chickens ran about between the houses and we noticed that each had a bit of colored wool tied around its leg. That was how you could tell who they belonged to, Sepo's daughter Filo explained, since each household had its own color of wool.

We ate healthily in Sepo's house but we certainly lost weight. I was down from 185 pounds to about 160 (85 kilos to 73) by the time we returned to Suva in April, and Koleta had lost about 15 pounds (7 kilos). Maybe it was because we had no dairy products—cheese, butter, ice cream, eggs (Sepo's family didn't own any of the local hens) and almost no meat (which might contain fat). We were a lot leaner but still perfectly healthy.

The Fijians, though, didn't see it that way. To them fat means healthy. When we came back from Suva they told Koleta "you're looking fat" and I had to reassure her that it was just a general compliment. The difference between us and everyone else in Waitabu may have been that we ate much less starch food. Sepo or Tui Nasau or even Qito would manage four or five pieces of taro or cassava or yam, each as big as the largest potato you could imagine. Bogi would give us a special plate containing much smaller pieces. I ate what would be a normal Australian portion—perhaps the equivalent of one huge potato. Koleta never did care much for potatoes and she extended this feeling to taro and breadfruit and the rest. They didn't seem to notice that I was the only person who made inroads into our plate of "real food." And I never really did discover what happened when I returned to Australia and Koleta was left there all by herself, confronted twice a day with a plate of taro or whatever.

* * *

People in Fiji are divided into five categories. The children are *gone*, all lumped together regardless of sex. *Tuuraga* are married men, the ones who are supposed to run the village. Then there are the *marama*, the married women, the ones who do—as in most other parts of the world—exert a covert but considerable influence on decision-making. Any man who has passed through puberty but not yet settled down and married is a *cauravou*, which can roughly be translated "youth." The equivalent female category is *gone-yalewa* which can only be translated by "unmarried girl" or perhaps "maiden." Having me there put Koleta into the marama class, which gave her more status and probably more freedom to work; if she'd been gone-yalewa there would have been a certain pressure to help with the chores.

It was the cauravou who were causing trouble. Not the cauravou from Waitabu, those from other villages. Our Friday evening dance with an electric band had become quite an institution. People attended from all over Boumaa, mostly cauravou and gone-yalewa. Admission was one dollar and the takings might be close to two hundred dollars. After paying the band and a few other expenses there could be a profit of over a hundred dollars, which was a lot of money in our village. Each week the dance was organized by a different Ito'atlo'a and the proceeds went into their communal funds.

But the youths weren't just dancing. They'd broken into the local store and taken the small sum of money it contained. A bit of damage had been done to buildings. Sepo advised us not to attend the dances but to stay home to guard our belongings—we had no locks, or even doors that could be secured.

There were always lots of meetings in the village—of a whole Ito'ato'a, or the women of one Mataqali, or the rugby players, or a church fellowship group. They'd be long serious affairs, always accompanied by yaqona and ritual spoken formulas, with rhythmic clapping at the end. But during the first week in February there seemed even more than usual; at almost any time of day there was a meeting going on in one house or another. We weren't invited, and our questions about the reason for all this confabulating elicited no firm response.

We only discerned what they'd been talking about when something actually happened—the dance hall was pulled down. Apparently, Tui Nasau has become worried about the drunkenness and thievery which had accompanied the Friday evening hops. The way to avoid that was to stop the dances. And the best way to make sure no more dances were held was to pull down the dance hall.

I'm sure that the chief thought hard and came to this decision all on his own. But he didn't just issue an order. Instead, every person in the village was drawn into an overall consensus. Since every person felt that he or she had played a role in reaching the decision on this they each abided by it. First of all, Tui Nasau spoke at length with Elia Waqa, leader of the other Mataqali, and got him on his side. Then the two of them organized all those meetings. Every possible shade of opinion had been put forward, every objection considered. And finally, after tens of hours of debate, the whole village agreed to do away with the dance hall.

This wasn't a huge job. The corrugated iron roofing sheets were taken off and stored away (they belonged to the whole village). Then the low plaited coconut leaf walls and the bamboo frame were dismantled and burned. This Tunuloa-like structure could easily be erected again (and it was, less than two months later, when a faith-healing priest came to visit). But the fact that it had been pulled down was an overt gesture that the dances were over. (The actual timing of the demolition was interesting. The chief's Ito'ato'a had in fact organized the final dance, which yielded a healthy profit. It didn't seem entirely coincidental.)

Demolition was to be done on a Tuesday, as part of "village work." This was organized by the village secretary, a quiet cauravou called Sa'apo. But the announcements about village work were always made by old Suliano, who had a fine voice and a lovely turn of phrase. These were supposed to be made on Monday evening but—like everything else in Waitabu—sometimes they were late. On Tuesday, February 5, at about half past seven in the morning, Suliano blew his conch shell—to attract attention—and called out the same message from three different places in the village, in order to reach everyone's ears. One spot was directly in front of our house and, with Suliano's permission, I recorded it:

> Yes, you please listen here, our people in this part of the village, you listen carefully to the thing which has been ordered to be proclaimed. Well, I am calling out, if you please, the tasks of you women for today because it is our day for village work. Well, you women are very respectfully asked that the walls of the Tunuloa-style shed should be dismantled for them to be disposed of by being burned on the beach. Well, when this is finished, the inside of the shed is also to be swept out, together with the rubbish that is lying on the beach side of the village green. Well, you listen very carefully, our people here, and do not anyone at all mishear this. This is all the news I have for you, our people in this part of the village here.

The chief, Tui Nasau, made all important decisions, and then backed them up with a show of "democracy."

Suliano's voice rose high and plaintive on the last word *yai* "here," which was a characteristic of all village announcements. I recorded several more and found that the first sentence and the last two were always nearly identical—ritualistic formulas that flanked a central message.

We were getting accepted as a part of the village. People dropped in for a chat or an *'ere'ere* (not just out of curiosity, as they had during the first couple of weeks). There was even an invitation to a wedding at Wai (the first letter, written in Fijian, that had been addressed to us). We had to hike up to Waibula to buy a suitable wedding gift, and we also got something for Sepo and Bogi to give (a large pan, and a big casserole dish). There was a rather fine feast afterwards.

Soon it was again "church in our house." Put the shoes in a neat pile in a corner, cases and bags against the back wall. Bring in the picture of Jesus, from Sepo's house, and prop it on a chair. What about the table—should it be moved out? No, no, Bogi said, just leave it there. It was fine—children sat underneath the table during the service. Later in the day, when we were sweeping out all the dirt that had been brought in on a few dozen pairs of feet, Koleta said, just to me: "I always love the feeling when church has just been in our house." "Why?" I asked, in surprise. "Because I know it won't be back for three whole weeks!"

I rather enjoyed being divine host for a day. Eli Waqa stayed on after the morning service. The previous week I'd joined a yaqona party outside his house for an hour or so—about my threshold of tolerance for a session of aimless chatter, in any language—and Elia had promised to continue the story of the origin of yaqona. (Of course I never played him Siriloo Saabai's ever so polite list of corrections.)

Now, after church, he was ready. "In Fiji, in olden times, people's heads were regarded as chiefly, the head was the 'chief' of the body. No one could touch the head of any person," my adopted father declaimed, in his deep, resonant tone. "I do not know about the rest of the world, but in Fiji in the olden days it would not have done for me to touch Roopate's head. It was forbidden." He related this to the fact that yaqona, the chiefly drink, sprang from the head of a chief (something I had already, more-or-less worked out). Then he mentioned that if anyone did touch another's head, even by accident, they would have to fight. Finally, Elia Waqa explained how he had a responsibility to tell the story, as one of our parents, and as an elder of the Yavusa of Naisaqai.

The special status of the "head" has cultural implications. One day I put a pillow on my chair since it made it more comfortable working at our table. Bogi saw this and was horrified. A pillow is intended for the head, and should not be allowed to touch the bottom! She hurriedly brought in a cushion, something intended for bums.

Touching a head was totally out, but in fact you'd think twice about touching any part of another's body, in public. In the late afternoon, there'd often be rugby practice on the village green. I admired the skill with which the cauravau from Waitabu and Wai would run and pass and kick. But there was no tackling, they just didn't want to touch another's body even around the waist. (The Fijian national rugby team tackle well enough. But they perhaps pretend they are fighting a war. You can do

6. Becoming a Part of the Village

things to an enemy that wouldn't be proper toward a youth from the same village.)

And of course the prohibition on touching extended to us. We couldn't hold hands, or even grab an arm, where people might see. Nau's house was right in front of ours and she had a window in the back wall through which to keep a sharp look-out, directly into our little hut. We have a name in Australian for that sort of person: "sticky beak." It was accepted practice to close the doors for an hour after lunch, at siesta time. And Nau didn't have X-ray eyes (or I don't think she did!).

* * *

We were now into a regular routine. Once every two weeks there'd be a scenic bus trip to the other side of the island. After that first experience with Qito we always went alone. First to the post office at Waiyevo to buy stamps and get money from the bank. Then we used to creep into the Castaway International Hotel, hoping no Fijian saw us. (Although they undoubtedly did, and no doubt Sepo was informed over the coconut telegraph.)

First of all, a gin and tonic. There were never many guests staying in there and it took a while to rustle up the Fijian barman. Then he'd agonize over what price to charge. Consult one list, then another, then back to the first one. Then complicated sums on a pocket calculator. Finally he might say "Two dollars–thirty seven cents each." "But they were only one dollar eighty last time," I'd protest and he'd hurriedly charge us that sum. (It was quite obvious that all the Fijian staff of the hotel operated a gigantic rip-off against the white owner.)

We'd sit on the verandah—overlooking 'Orolevu island, to which the defeated Tongan soldiers had retreated in Siriloo's history—and eat something totally un–Fijian, such as fish and chips, or a toasted tomato-and-cheese sandwich. Then a forty-minute walk up the road to Kaba's and Krishna's for batteries and soap and notebooks. Finally, on to Morisi—the Fijian name for Morris Hedstrom's—for two big cartons of groceries and whatever other items Sepo and Bogi had requested, maybe six glass tumblers and a matching jug.

That evening, Sepo would ask where we'd eaten lunch. "Oh," we lied, not daring to admit that we'd escaped for an hour into something resembling our native culture (and spend what Sepo would have considered an awful lot of money doing so), "We had curry and roti at Lesuma's for fifty cents each."

The week in between a Somosomo trip we'd take a late afternoon walk to Waibula to see if there was yet any jelly for sale (there never was), and make just a few food purchases for the family. Not too much partly because we'd walk a good part of the way back, until the bus caught up with us.

Most days we just stayed in Waitabu. Two cauravou would drum out the first lali at about twenty to six. The next one was supposed to be ten minutes later and the third ten minutes after that. But time was a variable quantity in our village. There could be a twenty-minute gap to the second lali and then the third might follow just one minute later (or, just occasionally, they both ran together).

At six a.m. there was church, if we felt strong enough or if we hadn't been for a couple of days. At six-thirty I'd pop off for a dip in the sea, if the tide was right, while Koleta took a fresh-water bath—with her clothes on!—at the Black Rock Pipe. From seven to eight we'd work on our linguistic materials, either going over what had already been collected or else getting more, if Sepo or Inoke were available. Then breakfast at about eight.

At around eight-thirty I'd go off to Short Sand to write my novel, which now had a title, *The Price of Love*. A city gent leaves for work each morning, in the frantic rush hour, with bowler hat, rolled umbrella and briefcase. I went off to my "office" with a similar assortment of gear. There'd be an old rain jacket to sit on, on the beach. An umbrella to sit under if it rained (there was a short shower—lasting ten minutes or so—most mornings). My wide brimmed black leather hat, which I'd bought at about 11 p.m., from a shop in Greenwich Village a couple of years before. And the notebook on which I was writing the novel. My habit is first to read and revise the four or five pages I'd written the previous day, and then that naturally flows into today's output. I'd mull over—during the rest of the day and at night, just before going to sleep and just after waking up, and at church—what I'd write the next day.

I didn't have a watch and anyway I wouldn't have taken it with me when I went to write. (Time is a nasty distraction, which can interfere with proper creative effort.) So I'd return to the village when I felt I'd done enough—generally between eleven-thirty and twelve-thirty, which was about the time for lunch. But that wasn't fixed either—sometimes we didn't get to eat until two o'clock and we were by then fairly hungry; but there was nothing at all we could do about it.

In the afternoon, I'd work intensively on the Boumaa language, sometimes transcribing a text with Inoke—or checking earlier transcriptions with Inoke or Sepo—but often just working by myself on grammatical analysis of the growing body of text I had processed.

6. Becoming a Part of the Village

Pio the half-wit was still very much attached to us. He'd follow Koleta when she went to bathe at the Black Rock Pipe and stand a few yards off, just watching, even though she told him firmly to go back home. But then she dropped a comb into a crack between two rocks and couldn't get it out. Pio was across in a flash, and he did find a way to extract it. Then Pio was all smiles as Koleta said what a helpful boy he'd been.

I might be working on the floor—which in fact I sometimes preferred to the table—and Pio would come in to "help." He'd watch me write and rub out, and turn a page. Then he'd try to turn over the next page when I'd only written two lines on it. I'd point at the door and tell him to go off home which he would, rather crestfallen.

Verbs in Fijian have fascinating properties. Most of them can be used intransitively, with just a subject (which can be abbreviated by S): *au la'o* "I am going." Or they can take an extra syllable at the end—*la'o* becomes *la'o-va*—and are then used transitively, with subject (A) and object (O): *au la'o-va a suka* "I'm going for sugar" (here *a* is an article, used before the noun *suka*, "sugar").

About half the verbs are like *la'o/la'o-va*, with intransitive subject being the same as transitive subject (*au* "I" in the sentences just given); this verb has S = A. But with the rest of the verbs, intransitive subject is the same as transitive object, i.e., S = O. You can say *au wili' a a ilavo* "I'm counting the money," where the verb *wili* has its transitive ending, *'-a*. But using *wili* with no ending, just taking subject but no object, one would say *e wili a ilavo* "the money is being counted"—literally it (*e*) is being counted (*wili*) the (*a*) *ilavo* (money). (You can say *au wili* but it means "I am being counted, not I am counting [money]").

I'd be sitting at the table, in front of a side door, wrestling with what sort of verbs were of one grammatical type and what sort of the other type. A small child would walk by and call out "*Bula Pate*." *Bula* (literally "health") is the regular greeting "good day" and *Pate* was the young children's shortening of *Roopate*. I sometimes didn't notice such a salutation, being engrossed in grammatical cogitation. But the infant was insistent. "*Pate*," he'd call, in loud and impatient tones, "*Pate*." Eventually I would look up and respond—"*Oh—bula*." And he'd wander off, satisfied, to some other part of the village.

At about four o'clock I might go for a swim, if the tide was high, and then perhaps rest on the beach for half-an-hour. After finishing Plato's *Republic* I went on to another classic that I'd always meant to read but never previously got around to, *The Wealth of Nations* by Adam Smith.

Some days Koleta and I would walk to 'Orovou in the late afternoon to see if there was any mail come to Iowani, at the Postal Agency, or to give him cards and letters to dispatch. Iowani was supposed to be in the Postal Agency during the morning and afternoon but he seldom was. Sometimes he'd go off to the garden and it wouldn't be possible to transact any postal business that day; but generally we did find him in his house nearby.

Each day the bus driver delivered a thin packet of mail, sent on from the Post Office at Waiyevo (if a parcel should arrive, you'd have to go to Waiyevo in person to pick it up, a total of three hours on the bus and three dollars in fares). The whole Vanua of Boumaa—with getting on for a thousand people—might receive 20 or 25 letters a day. If there was anything else for people in Waitabu, Iowani would ask us to take it across. That was how postal delivery worked—everyone who happened to be walking to another village, Iowani would give them mail to take along (a haphazard system, but I don't think much went astray).

If we had anything to go, Iowani would accept it carefully, inspect both sides of the envelope and make his characteristic "tst, tst, tst." Postcards were particularly welcome. They'd be passed around everyone sitting on the floor in Iowani's house, and the picture admired, before finally gaining acceptance as outgoing mail. (Incoming postcards received the same treatment.)

Postage was quite cheap from Fiji—about 25 cents for an airmail letter overseas. I was sending a fair bit to foreign countries and

Iowani was in charge of the Postal Agency at 'Orovou. He once left a postcard in its pigeon hole for a year.

generally bought plenty of stamps in Waiyevo. But one week I did run out. Surely Iowani sold stamps? He did, but he only had three-cent and two-cent denominations and not many of those—a couple of dollars worth at the most. He had a handbook quoting the postal rates to different countries, but no scales on which to weigh letters. And he wasn't at all keen to sell us all his stamps. We got enough for the urgent letters and kept the rest back for our next trip to Waiyevo.

One time, toward the end of our trip, I went to check for mail in the afternoon. "Sorry, Iowani must be at his garden and goodness knows when he'll be back." So I went across again after supper (it was a good half-hour walk each way) and found Iowani sitting around drinking yaqona with friends. "The post office is closed," he told me. I pointed out it had been closed that afternoon, when Iowani was paid to have it open, so he grudgingly went and fetched our mail.

After I returned to Canberra in July 1985 I sent some letters and cards to Koleta, who was staying on longer. Then she left Waitabu a little earlier than planned and some of my mail arrived after she'd gone. Iowani forwarded on a letter but not a postcard (probably since there wasn't enough room to cross out the address and write in a new one). The following June Koleta returned before me for another spell of fieldwork and I again wrote to her. On the first two occasions that she went to 'Orovou to ask for mail Iowani gave her cards I'd sent, things posted the previous week. The third time she went, in June 1986, he also gave her a postcard. Koleta found the message on it most puzzling. Only later did she work out that this was a card I'd sent in July 1985. Iowani hadn't given it to Koleta when she first called the next year. Perhaps he kept it back purposely for a day when there was no new mail, so that she wouldn't be disappointed. But there was no comment at all that this postcard (although not the two previous ones) had been sitting in one of his pigeon holes for eleven months!

* * *

Just walking along the road in Fiji—as when we went to and from 'Orovou for the mail—one had to be ready to speak Fijian. In Australia one traveler would say "G'day" to another and the response would be the same. But in Fiji people ask a definite question "Where are you going to?" or—if you're just outside a village and obviously headed there—"Where are you coming from?" These were generally said very elliptically: *i vei* "where to?" or *mai vei* "where from?"

Such questions have to be answered explicitly and exactly. On occasion, we gave one answer to the first group of people we met and a slightly different answer to another group half-a-mile further on. When we got back to Waitabu Sepo appeared to have heard (by the coconut telegraph) about this inconsistency of our response and questioned us about it. We said, trying to think quickly, that we'd changed our minds about where we were headed to, and he accepted this, grudgingly.

I often felt like supplying a joking response to questions like this. Only once did I do so, replying to the "where from?" of a group of youths, "Oh, I've just swum across from the island of Qamea." They seemed so insulted that I never again tried to utter anything but the solemn truth. People's persistence about knowing exactly what you were doing and where you were going could be wearying. Several times I walked away from the front door of our house and Sepo, sitting just inside the side door of his, shouted out "*Roopate, i vei*?" "I'm just going to the toilet, Uncle," I'd reply, in the tone of a martyr.

For the first couple of months we were so new and shy we just let people say *i vei* to us and tried to explain where we were going and what for and so on. Then we decided that we too could play the game. Meeting a group of Fijians on the road we'd shout out "*'i vei*?" or "*mai vei*" before they had time to, and nod approvingly as they told us. (If someone asked it of you, it seemed that you wouldn't normally ask it back of them.)

Getting back from our mail-checking trip at about five o'clock, there would still be an hour or two before supper. I'd usually do a bit more language work and Koleta might go and join the gone-yalewa in a netball game. This would be strictly for linguistic—rather than sporting—reasons. She'd discovered that girls who spoke the Boumaa dialect all day switched to Standard Fijian (which they refer to as Bau) when playing netball; there was a special use of language to mark this particular sport and the social interaction involved. Why associate the Bau dialect with netball? Maybe because they'd learned the game at school, some years before, and at school all the teachers used Bau.

About six o'clock a cry would be likely to rebound around the village: "*Teliva*." This marked the arrival of one of the taxis from Waibula, which was fitted out as a mobile shop, with racks of food and other items. The name came from English *deliver*, although it wasn't really any sort of delivery (nothing had been ordered in advance). Teliva was scheduled to come to Waitabu—and the other Boumaa villages—at about six o'clock Monday to Saturday but sometimes it just didn't come, so you couldn't rely on buying anything there.

A dozen ladies and a few men would line up as the driver moved into the back of the van, buying some sugar or a tin of fish or a fishing line or

6. Becoming a Part of the Village

a large bar of yellow washing soap. Other people came up just to gawp. One evening Sepo's son Maarawa stood by and it wasn't clear whether or not he was in the queue. I was and I asked him "Do you want to buy anything, cousin?" Maarawa muttered and moved away a bit. "He just wants to buy the van," said one of the women in line, and everyone laughed.

Teliva had fresh bread from a bakery at Naselesele in Waini'eli (if it hadn't broken down). We evolved the habit that each Saturday evening I'd buy bread and butter, for Sunday breakfast in Sepo's house. Five or six loaves—there were a lot of people in the household, and they had big appetites—and one half-pound of butter. Next morning we'd have two or three slices of bread with very thick streaks of butter. No jam. (They did make jam. We had it with scones at wedding feasts. But there was never any available with regular meals.)

Teliva wasn't cheap. A half-pound of butter might cost ninety cents at Kaba's supermarket, a dollar-ten if you walked to Waibula and a dollar-thirty on our mobile shop. The Teliva driver was an Indian, of course. He worked long hours and expected to amass a fair profit.

We found it interesting to observe the interaction between Fiji's two major races. Each expressed total disdain for the other. The Indians considered the Fijians lazy and worthless while the Fijians called the Indians *mata-ilavo* "money face." They said there was more to life than work, work, work and filthy lucre; but if the Indians wanted to provide a service like Teliva, they would tolerate—and patronize—it.

In the years after independence from Britain, in 1970, the two races were nicely balanced. The Fijians owned most of the land: some of it was leased to Indians who'd work hard at growing sugar, yaqona or other crops. (Fijian owners sometimes charged rent, but other times they'd just let the Indians use their land for free.) Almost all the shops and other economic activities were dominated by Indians. They also drove the majority of the buses and taxis. But the army and government (and boats) were the province of Fijians.

The traditional Fijian political system had more-or-less continued under the guise of democratic rule. The prime minister was one of the most respected chiefs, and the governor-general another; they exercised patronage among their noble kinspeople much as in pre-colonial days. Then at the 1987 election an Indian-dominated party gained power; they put a Fijian in as prime minister but he wasn't of a noble family or even from a prestigious district. The balance of power had shifted; this could be the thin edges of a wedge that would lead to Indians controlling all aspects of life, including—eventually—ownership of land.

The only area in which Fijians were still in control was the army. And the army moved in, to put the government back into Fijian hands, trying to return to the balance of power that had been relatively successful between 1970 and 1987. There was a coup, in fact two coups, in 1987. And then a couple more coups in later years. But life in Fiji—in villages and in towns—continued pretty much the same.

None of this was even thought about while we were at Waitabu. People prided themselves that there had never been any fighting or race riots in the country. Each ethnic group kept to itself (there was very little in the way of mixed marriage) but each needed the other, just as plants need bees for pollination and the bees need the plants as a food source.

Quite soon after Teliva we'd be called across for the evening meal (it could be any time between 6 and 7:30). Sepo, if he was there, would pick out one of his children or one of us to say grace. I had it typed on a card, in my pocket (although eventually even I knew it by heart!). "In the name of God the Father, and Him the Son and Him the Holy Ghost. Amen. We are praying concerning this food. Lord, bless this our food. In the name of Holy Mary, of unsullied soul." Then everyone present would join in on the chorus. "Please bless us all. Amen." And the grace-saying would conclude with "In the name of God the Father and Him the Son and Him the Holy Ghost. Amen."

What I found bizarre about this was that it had to be in Bau (the dialect that God had directed the people of Fiji to pray to him in, was how Sepo put it). Imagine a Scots family chattering away with their rolled *r*s before and during the meal but insisting that grace be said in a posh London accent, with ne'er an *r* in sight. It's a very similar circumstance (just substitute glottal stop for rolled *r*).

Bogi was always trying to give us new and interesting meals—and she succeeded. We might have curry, but very mild. Or fried *baigani*. It took a few minutes to identify this—it's what is called aubergine in England and eggplant in Australia. That Fijian name? It's taken over from Hindi *baigan*, another small example of cultural percolation.

After the meal, we'd say a profuse thank you. This appeared to be one place where inventiveness was permitted; Koleta and I would vie with each other to find new ways of saying "That was a lovely meal." "Heavenly," "delicious," "delightful," "scrumptious"—there were quite a few appropriate adjectives and they could be combined in all sorts of ways. Then we'd ask to be excused and say goodnight to everyone, looking around the table and naming them individually. Little Mariana, the second youngest child would always wait, with a worried look on her face, to see whether she'd

6. Becoming a Part of the Village

Bogi always provided a fine repast. She is here preparing vegetables with help from seven-year old Mariana.

be forgotten, and then burst into a big smile when she did hear her own name.

Sometimes Sepo wouldn't be there for supper. Perhaps once or twice a week he'd attend a yaqona party in one of the other houses with other tuuraga and cauravou. For some reason people don't like to eat much before partaking of yaqona. When he did come home—often at eleven o'clock or later—Bogi would have kept some cold supper. (Even if she was already asleep, Bogi—good and caring wife—would wake and feed her man.) Sepo didn't drink as much yaqona as many Fijians. Real over-indulgence can lead to a sort of scaly skin rash, there was even a special ointment to put on it, on the shelves of Kaba's supermarket.

We discovered that yaqona is actually the Bau name. In the Boumaa dialect it is properly waqona, although a lot of people do say yaqona instead.

After we'd been excused from the supper table there'd be time for another hour's linguistic work before fatigue took over. But often there was no chance—children and other visitors would call to chat about what had happened in the village that day. One day a certain man complained about some aspect of a meal and his wife emptied the whole lot over him, and then he set about her with a piece of wood. Nothing of this nature could possibly be kept secret in Waitabu, and there'd be speculation about what might happen next.

One thing people didn't like to talk about too much was their traditional religion. *'Alou* (*Kalou* in Bau) was the term for "spirit" or "god"— an important ancestor who after death had become a god. *'Alou* was taken over for Jehovah, the God with a capital G and traditional gods were called either *'Alou vuu* "original gods" or else *Teevoro*, from English *devil*, a term the missionaries introduced and encouraged, to turn the people away from their indigenous religion. (But this word didn't have any bad connotations for the Fijians.)

The missionaries did a few funny things with Fijian. Take the word *tabu*, which originally had the meaning "forbidden" just like our *taboo* (which is actually a loan from a cognate word in Tongan). Sunday was called *siga tabu* (*siga* is day), perhaps because work and fishing and gardening—about everything, except prayer—were forbidden on the Sabbath. Then the missionaries started using *tabu* to mean "holy"; the Bible is *A ivola tabu*, which is supposed to be "holy book" but is literally "forbidden book." It seemed an odd shift of meaning.

One evening we were sitting there chatting with a group of young people, the front door open to a pitch black night. Suddenly a figure jumped in through the door making a *"hoooo"* noise. It was just Inoke, providing a light-hearted scare. "Oh," I cried, in mock alarm, "*teevoro!*" Everyone looked to make sure it *was* Inoke, and then laughed.

At breakfast next morning, Bogi said she'd been really worried. "I heard Roopate call out *teevoro*," she said. We assured her it had been said as a joke, at Inoke's prank. Bogi said she had heard laughter and been partially reassured. But I got the impression that this was a topic it would be best not to joke about any more.

People would drift off home about nine o'clock, or else we'd send them away, with a polite *'ere'ere*: "We beg *'ere'ere* that we might now retire to bed." Koleta always did exercises for twenty minutes or so, to alleviate the demands which village life made on her curved spine.

I'd read for a few minutes, with a torch. There were always ants in our house and they were particularly attracted to this after-hours glare. So, after finishing my read, I'd first put the book down and then shine the beam of light onto the sheet, squashing with the flat of my hand a few score—or a few hundred—of tiny black ants, before settling down to slumber.

7

A Divine Visitor

Sepo still tried to organize and control our lives. I remember one morning he told me that it was definitely going to rain—heavily—and very strongly advised that I shouldn't go off to Short Sand. I simply said "Yes, Uncle" and slipped away two minutes later. (As I've mentioned before, it's necessary to have a regular schedule to achieve anything.) I was used to a short, sharp daily shower but in fact it didn't rain at all that morning. In the afternoon Sepo went off to his garden and then it really did pelt down, for more than an hour.

But he was also tremendously helpful to us. Sepo sat down one day and we went through every house in the village, entering the full names of all the occupants, their ages, relationships, etc. This kind of census information was something that Koleta needed for her study, and it interested me. Other things Sepo told us because he considered it important, like the Fijian name for steps in the church hierarchy. I rather liked *Tui Tabu* for "Pope": this is literally "Sacred King." Then there is *karadinale* "cardinal" and *epikopo* "bishop," loan words from European languages (some of the early Catholic missionaries were French and Spanish).

There were just a couple of people in the village who didn't seem to like us—Iowani, the failed school teacher and his brother Elia Gasaiwai. No one in Waitabu really liked Elia Gasaiwai, who tended to strut and posture and do very little work. They called him *Tamata Do'ado'a* "Show-off Person." Sometimes he acted a little bit friendly, as when he promised to assist Koleta in her linguistic survey and told her to come and interview him on Sunday afternoon. When she did turn up, with tape recorder and notebook, Show-off Person looked her up and down and inquired, with malice, "Well, what seems to be your problem?" I provoked some amusement by calling Show-off Person *Tamata Yalo Vuni-Vuni*, which means

"Modest Person" (*yalo* is "soul" and *vuni-wuni* "hide a lot," the combination meaning "modest").

One morning just before breakfast Sepo was sitting doing linguistic work with me when there were signs of trouble from the direction of Show-off Person's house. Sepo's eleven-year-old son Elia had said something out of order and Show-off Person cuffed him on the side of his head. Sepo saw this through our side door and was off like a shot. Voices were raised. Fists were raised. A couple of dozen people hovered nearby, watching to see who would deliver the first blow. But then Elia Waqa—the leader of Show-off Person's Mataqali—walked with slow and judicial gait from his own house and told the two protagonists not to be foolish, like an old schoolmaster addressing boys who had been scrapping in the schoolyard. (Tui Nasau was away at the time, or else he would have diffused the situation just as effectively.)

Sepo himself was the best educated person in the village and at first, we were impressed by the varied opportunities he had provided for his children. The eldest, Vero, had a responsible job with the bank in Suva, and the next, Peteroo, was with the army in Lebanon. Qito had been to high school in Suva and Maritina was there currently. But the youngest children seemed to be treated differently. Thirteen-year-old Filo desperately wanted to learn but she wasn't allowed to attend school in Boumaa that year, being told instead to stay at home and help her mother.

Elia and Mariana did still go to school—but only spasmodically. Some children from Waitabu would walk along the beach to 'Orovou every day but after a while we noticed that Sepo's two children—and quite a few others from the village—attended school only two or three days each week. Koleta became friendly with Silipa, one of the teachers, who said it was almost impossible to teach a class where a third of the children weren't there yesterday and a different third would be absent tomorrow.

Just as a man would have a choice of activities each day, so would a child, and school was just one of them. Now what should we do today— go with father to the garden, help mother with her chores, or play, or go to school? But how surprising that Sepo didn't insist that his children go to school regularly, as did some of the Waitabu parents.

Koleta put forward a possible explanation. He'd provided every educational advantage for his elder children and what had happened? They'd left the village. Sepo valued village life so his attitude had changed. He wanted to ensure that the younger children remained part of a traditional way of living.

There is a special kind of party in Fiji called *Unu-sede* (drink-cents),

7. A Divine Visitor

"Money-drink." This is a fund-raising event, with every participant making a small donation, perhaps twenty cents, and drinking yaqona provided by the host. (It reminded me of "rent parties" among the black population of Chicago and Harlem between the wars.) Sometimes a Money-drink can be a really organized affair, effectively a levy on every member of a community.

At about seven in the evening of Monday, February 14, I recorded another village announcement from Suliano with details of the following day's "village work." Then he said: "One more thing. There is also a request from our school committee concerning a Money-drink at three in the afternoon on Thursday. It is asked of all of you, married men and married women, youths and girls. It applies to all those young people who have left school, and is one dollar for each person."

Thursday was a day marked on the calendar "Church in our house," and the service went off as usual at six in the morning. Then Bogi asked if we would go to the Money-drink at 'Orovou on behalf of the whole family. What she meant was would we please pay a dollar for everyone in that large household, as the obligatory contribution to school funds.

Sure, we didn't mind about the money. But we had to be back well before six, "Church is in our house." Better go promptly at three, the time Suliano had mentioned. Well, no—Sepo advised—nothing would happen at three, neither perhaps at four. We could—he supposed, without too much confidence—get there at four and we might then be able to leave by five.

We were there by four. No sign whatsoever of anyone to pay the levy to. Anyway one couldn't just hand a sum of money over, in Fiji; it had to be a bit of a ceremony, with yaqona and so on.

At about quarter to five the Vuunisaa arrived with other village dignitaries and sat cross-legged at the end of the largest schoolroom. Since we'd been so anxious about the Money-drink, someone hustled us into that room. Then the yaqona party arrived—five youths with a large carved wooden bowl.

Nothing is ever hurried in Fiji, least of all the preparation of yaqona. Water was poured into the bowl. Powdered yaqona root was placed in a cloth strainer and this was squeezed, time and again, until all the juice was extracted. The residue was lifted above the bowl and squeezed three more times. Then it was discarded and a further batch of yaqona treated in the same way. The whole thing seemed interminable. The cloth had to be passed in a fixed way, in a set direction. Then again, and again. Time was passing. "Church is in our house tonight." Finally, the solemn process of preparation was complete. Now of course the dignitaries must drink. Not the Vuunisaa because of his religion, although he presided over everything. All the lesser chiefs drank. And not just once. The coconut shell cup went around and around.

Finally it was all over. We had a chance to escape. (There had been no one else but us in the schoolroom with the chiefs and the yaqona party.) The youths stood, again with full solemnity. Those bearing the wooden bowl went first. We were nearer the door so we slipped through ahead of them. Even while doing this I realized it was an error of etiquette. The Vuunisaa passed a hand in front of his eyes. (But who was he to criticize? He hadn't even drunk any yaqona.)

We stood outside, stretching our cramped legs. Other people started going in for a cup of yaqona, having seemingly avoided the opening ceremony. It was now five-thirty. Church was to be in our house at six. Who to pay the levy to?

Eventually someone admitted responsibility. He hadn't planned to accept the dollars until quite a bit later but we talked him into getting out his register, with the names of all the people who were supposed to contribute. (It wasn't at all accurate. We wouldn't have expected it to be.) He ticked off Sepo, Bogi, Maarawa, Emelia, Qito, Elena, Filo. It's not done to run within a village. We walked very smartly down the hill from the school and then onto the beach.

All along the way we met groups of people from Waitabu on their way to the Money-drink. Why were we going in the wrong direction? "Well, we had to go early," Koleta explained, "and get back. Because church is in our house tonight."

We must have said this to half-a-dozen groups, each of whom nodded in appreciation of our level of commitment and organization. Then, two-thirds of the way home, we met a group that included Felise, the catechist. We didn't say it to him. (I'm not at all sure why not.) We did say it to the next group, following on a hundred yards behind. We were used to saying it, but now it had a slightly hollow ring.

"Oh, you're back early," Bogi exclaimed. "Church is in our house," we told her. It had been so that morning, thus it must also be in the evening. "So it is," she agreed. "But we saw Felise walking along the beach toward 'Orovou." "He'll be on his way to the Money-drink," Bogi said.

So we actually asked an explicit question. "Is there going to be any church tonight?" We could have predicted Bogi's response: *E sega ni macala*, "It's not clear." She sent a child to ask around the village and see what other people thought. It came back with the same message: "It's not clear."

7. A Divine Visitor

"Well, we got out of it," Koleta said, as we lay on the mats on the floor, quite exhausted.

"But if all those people we met along the beach knew there wouldn't be a service tonight, why didn't they tell us?" I wondered.

"They were just being polite," Koleta explained. Which was true. We were so proud of running home for "church in our house" that it would have been quite cruel to disillusion us at that point in time.

* * *

Two more cyclones came and went during February. Again, they were a few score miles off Waitabu so no major damage was done to our village. Still, they were just as frightening as before. We sealed notebooks into plastic bags, watched the roof bend and buckle, and cringed at that eerie celestial scraping noise of wind on iron.

Then there were the mats. Mats are everything in a Fijian house, the whole furnishing, and they mustn't be allowed to get wet. I could understand it. If a mat got ruined you couldn't just take money out of the bank and pop around to the shop to buy a new one, as we would in Australia. You searched in the forest for voivoi plants. Gathered lots and lots of leaves. Dried them, cut them with a sharp blade into strips of the right width and then wove these—carefully and laboriously—into a mat, often working in a pattern by alternating voivoi dyed in different colors.

Now in a place where the rainfall is getting on for two hundred inches a year, mats need a lot of attention if they are not to get damp, and start rotting. Bogi showed us how—whenever there was a really heavy storm—the mats should be rolled back from the doors, and covered with pieces of plastic. That wasn't always enough and if a mat did get wet it should be put out to dry in the sun the next day. Koleta entered into this activity with gusto and became the main "protector of mats" in our minute household.

Tui Nasau, on his regular visits, would nod with approval that Koleta was turning into such a good housewife, in the Fijian way. Our chief was what you could call an individualist. One day when it was absolutely pouring with rain he turned up to church dressed in long trousers, with a loud check pattern, and sunglasses!

There can be fashions in language, quite as much as in anything else. One word then in vogue was *waananavu* "wonderful." Koleta picked this up from the young girls and women. One morning I was half-listening as she told Tui Nasau: "Waitabu is a *waananavu* village and you are a *waananavu* chief." This was, I thought, laying it on a bit thick. But Tui

Nasau didn't share my opinion. He gave a wide and genuine grin and replied, coyly to Koleta "Oh yes, and you are *waananavu*."

The chief would often sit there and just chatter. Sometimes about the old days, before he was born. "Did you know," he said one day, "that we used to eat people?" This was a topic we hadn't considered polite to bring up. But now Tui Nasau had introduced it himself. "Oh really?," we responded, in an intonation loaded with tell-us-more. "Oh yes," he went on, "we'd use special wooden forks, with four prongs set in a square." Tui Nasau's face now bore that happy, contented slightly-drooling look, as when he told us of the eel and turtle served at a meeting of local dignitaries. "The chiefs would eat their enemies. Roast them in the fire and then..." He smacked tongue around lips and moved jaw into chewing motion. Just at that moment one of Sepo's children came to say the breakfast was ready. (But it was only paw paw and pancakes!)

We once asked Tui Nasau why they'd stopped eating people. Oh, he said, the Christian priests told his ancestors that God didn't like it—the new God, Jehovah. In other words, the Fijians didn't desist from their cannibalistic practices because they realized it was not a good thing to do. They'd have carried on—Tui Nasau seemed to imply—except that they took up with the powerful new God who had an odd quirk, that he didn't approve of people eating people.

The chief's cough seemed to be getting worse. It was quite useful in some ways—in providing advance notice of his approach, so that if anyone were doing anything they shouldn't, it was possible to stop in time. But he did cough an awful lot in the night, sometimes for two or three hours at a time.

On one of our trips to the shops on the other side of the island both Sepo and Inoke had asked for new knife blades (they'd make handles and attach them themselves). Tui Nasau never asked for anything but we decided to buy him a large bottle of cough medicine.

The next morning, he called around and asked to see Inoke's new knife blade—shining and sharp and about two feet long. I presented the cough syrup. My Big Uncle clapped his hands in delighted acceptance. Then he sat very straight and made a long and solemn speech, just to me, full of reference to God and church and responsibilities properly discharged, ending in a rising *e dina* "that is true" and clap, clap-clap, clap clap-clap, clap, clap, clap.

Now that the ritual was over, down to business. "Spoon?" he queried. We had one which I found and wiped. "Open it up," the chief instructed. So I unscrewed the top, poured out a spoonful which Tui Nasau emptied

7. A Divine Visitor

into his mouth, rolled around a few times and then swallowed. "How often?" he said. "What?" "Look at the bottle," the chief told me, "how often should I take it? Once each day? Twice each day?" Oh, I hastily read all the small print on the label. There were no instructions of that sort. "Well," he suggested, "take it as required." Yes, I agreed, that was the best plan.

He then accepted the bottle, asked permission to leave and went off to his own house. Within ten minutes I could hear Tui Nasau having the most terrible coughing fit, worse than anything we'd ever heard before. He sounded on the point of choking to death! Oh dear! I wasn't sure whether to laugh or cry.

After the first couple of weeks all pretense of Qito helping us in linguistic work was dropped. She was still, of course, a member of the household and had to do a certain number of chores. On a couple of occasions Koleta insisted on helping to cook breakfast with Qito. But that lady was in no mood to be cooperative and after a couple of the roti were seen to be slightly burned it was emphatically Koleta's fault.

One of the items we always brought back from our shopping trip was soybean oil. Surely a two-liter bottle should be enough for two weeks? But often Bogi asked for four liters. And the following week, when we walked to Waibula, there was a request for more! It was Qito. She refused to pour back any oil that hadn't been used up, just chucked it away. We overheard Bogi remonstrating about the waste and Qito's response "Ah, the *paapaalagi* (white skinned people) eat some of the pancakes. They've got plenty of money and can buy all the oil we need!" After that we bought just two liters each trip, and Qito's cooking habits had to become more restrained.

The big question in our minds remained—was she pregnant? Koleta had more opportunities than me for close observation and she couldn't quite decide. She might well be, although Bogi and Sepo still accepted Qito's word that she was not. Most of the other people in the village had no doubts at all.

Not only were our resources being drained by buying cooking oil, but the level of *'ere'ere* began to escalate. We always kept a good supply of Panadol headache tablets and plastic-strip medicated dressings—not for us, but to supply the other hundred-odd people in Waitabu. There'd also be requests for batteries, paper, matches, cigarettes and money. Only small sums but it did mount up. "I felt like a piggy bank," Koleta complained, "everyone wants to get a few coins out of me." And Sepo noticed that his fellow-villagers were becoming more demanding: "They think you're a cigarette factory." In the end, it was a matter of supply and demand.

They really did clean us out and we had to say, truthfully, that there were no more cigarettes, no more money. All we had left was the bus fare to Waiyevo and we weren't going until the next week.

Koleta was carrying out a comprehensive series of sociolinguistic interviews—with children, young adults and old people—getting them to give short texts, translate sentences from Standard Fijian into Boumaa, and also finding out what their attitudes were toward different varieties of language. I'd completed transcription of the texts recorded by Tui Nasau, Falaavia Matavesi, the Vuunisaa of 'Orovou, Elia Waqa and Siriloo Saobai, and was well advanced with examining the grammatical constructions they showed. Another task that had been begun was to investigate each one of a sample of about 450 of the most commonly used verbs, asking about its meaning and grammatical properties—whether it was S = O or S = A type—with a few illustrative sentences. The aim was to check each verb with two people. I used a blue pen for information obtained from Inoke and a red one for what Sepo said.

You'd think it might be quiet and peaceful in a village. Not at all! There were no motor cars or pneumatic drills, that is true. But other noises can be just as annoying. Things like hens scratching at the outside of the house walls, radios blaring, and children crying. Bogi and Sepo's youngest child Vilimaina was rather spoiled. If she wanted something Vilimaina would just cry. And cry and cry. It wasn't unusual for her to wail for three hours solidly, not far from our door.

There was grass between the houses in Waitabu. Not that it was any real use—I mean you couldn't sit on it, as you would sit on the grass in a European-style garden, simply because often children and adults would stand anywhere on the grass and pee. And it did have to be cut. There was one village lawnmower and of course it was the noisiest thing you could imagine. So, for a couple of hours each Tuesday—the day for "village work"—we had that cacophony as well to try and work through.

My father, Elia Waqa, was unfailingly courteous. Yes, of course, he'd tell more stories. First of all, a long account of all the different kinds of native food, with full instructions for their planting, care, and harvesting. *Uvi*, a species of yam, should be planted in June, July, August or September. It can be planted in October or November, but these times are less propitious. If *uvi* is planted in June it can be harvested in December, in time for the special Christmas dinner. *Vudi*, or plantain, would be planted in November, just before the cyclone season, so that its fruit do not appear until the possibility of high winds has passed. But taro (called *dalo* in Fijian) can be planted any time of the year. In the olden days it was given twelve months to mature, but nowadays—Elia lamented—people don't follow the proper procedures for its care, and harvest it too early.

Then he explained that the first fruits of any crop must be presented—with solemnity—to an older brother, or to one's father, and he will then make an offering to the chief. This is called a *sevusevu*. (I could appreciate the custom. Home gardeners know how exciting it is when the first fruit appear. How appropriate that this should be marked by a ceremony.)

There were a lot more fruits, for which my father provided a manual of instruction. Then, with scarcely a break, he told another long story about the coming of white-skinned people to Fiji. First of all, Europeans avoided the islands, Elia Waqa told me, because they'd heard of cannibalism and how they'd be clubbed to death and eaten. Then the church arrived. A lot of missionaries died but they persevered and the people then realized they'd been doing wrong, because it is in fact forbidden by the new God to kill people and to eat them.

Then other white men came and they tricked the native chiefs—often making them drunk with whisky—into selling the best tracts of land for some paltry price such as a pipe and tobacco and a musket. Those white men cultivated the land and employed Fijians as laborers, paying them nine pence a day, or twelve pounds for a year's work; some only paid sixpence a day, which is equivalent to six cents today. They had to work all year, through rain and hurricanes; if they didn't work the white man might kill them. Later on, when a government was established, if you didn't work you could be sent to jail for two months; and after that you'd have to return and finish up the year's work contract.

"We had no schooling, no education," Elia explained. "So we let the white man swindle us out of our land and exploit our labor. Today we are better off. But the suffering of our ancestors was terrible, and that is what I wanted to tell you about."

We made a short speech of thanks for these stories, and everyone present clapped in rhythm. Elia Waqa smiled—that he had discharged what he considered a parental duty by recording these tales.

People like Sepo, Tui Nasau and Elia Waqa couldn't have been more welcoming. But nothing could alter the fact that we were aliens in Fiji. Koleta's aim was to assimilate into the village and she was able to succeed at one level. But at another level she could never change her white skin, blond hair, education, and Australian background.

One incident kept recurring at the end of February and it made us realize how vulnerable we were. It always happened after nine o'clock at night. Koleta would be doing exercises to help her back cope with village life. I'd be reading, often by our benzene light—put on the floor near the sleeping mat—or else by torch.

Suddenly someone put their mouth right up against our reed wall and shouted out a word. Then we heard the patter of several people running away. It was pitch dark outside and, although there were other houses all around, this incident really scared us. Who was it? What were they saying? Why? Did they mean any evil toward us? Did they want us to leave the village?

The first night this happened we just got a fright. Then the same thing the next night, which made it more sinister. And the call was repeated on the next two nights. We didn't tell Sepo, hoping to deal with it by ourselves. What was the word they called out each night (it was always the same thing)? Nothing recognizable. It sounded to me something like *wujabulu*.

On the fifth night, I switched on the recorder, with a blank tape. Nothing happened—no shout, no running footsteps. On the sixth night, we didn't bother with the recorder and that shout came again, right next to the wall and then they all ran away. It was like being surrounded by enemy warriors under cover of dark. Then they didn't attack, not tonight, just a cry of warning. But tomorrow?

On the seventh day, I again switched on the recorder to try and at least catch the word. Nothing happened. On the eighth night, there was no recorder on and the shout came, once. Then they grew bolder. On the ninth night, we received this treatment no less than five times. There'd be the shout, then running footsteps, and then the same thing ten minutes later after they'd stealthily returned. But with what intent?

It was both worrying and frightening. But still we didn't tell Sepo. Then, on the tenth night I happened to go out of one side door at about nine-thirty to the toilet. I returned on the other side of our hut. There were three small figures crouched against the wall. Then I heard the word. They started to run and so did I.

It was three boys, about eleven years old. I probably could have caught at least one of them. But that would have created a real incident and we had no wish to make trouble. On the other hand, we did want these after-dark assaults on our privacy to cease. There wasn't much time to think. I chased the three boys for a few yards and then let out a blood-curdling howl (a cry I'd learned from an old Aboriginal man in Queensland, as a way of cowering fierce dogs). I just wanted to scare them—and it certainly did.

Of course, everyone in the houses nearby heard the noise. Koleta thought it was the half-wit; one neighbor thought it was a dog. Bogi knew it was me and thought I must be feeling ill. Anyway, Bogi came around and we told her the story. Sepo wasn't anywhere around; he was off drinking yaqona at a far house. He should have been here, Bogi complained, to protect you from whoever it was.

The story passed around the village that night. We could hear it gradually diffusing, from house to house, since at a certain point the storyteller would have to imitate my "*hu-hu, hu-hu*" in a suitably loud voice, and at twenty-minute intervals this sound would come from a new direction.

The next morning—as I was coming back from bathing at Main Road Pipe—I passed a boy and it was plain from the look on his face that he'd been one of the culprits. We had no wish for anyone to be punished; all we wanted was peace at night. Later, I went off to write at Short Sand and a group of women at the washing pool demanded to know the whole story, right from my lips. On the way back there were different ladies washing and I had to tell it all over again.

Everyone soon knew the identity of the boys and one of the women told Koleta. The ringleader had been Sepo's son Elia! That afternoon Sepo came across and made a ceremonial apology, on behalf of the whole village. He said the miscreants had been caught and punished but he didn't say who they were. He also said he'd like to build a proper house for us with none-see-through walls. What amused us most was Bogi's impassioned cry that Sepo should have been there protecting us. Protecting us from his own son?

I finally had heard the word properly (it had been called out so many times)—*va'ajaabolo*. This wasn't in Capell's dictionary but Inoke said that it meant "naked." Later, Paul Geraghty provided a full etymology. It involves the Fijian prefix *va'a*- and a loan from Spanish *diablo* "devil." The word *va'a jaabolo* means both "heathen" and "naked," and was used by the early missionaries to describe the Fijians who had not embraced both the European God and European-style clothing (which went together, as a package deal).

Koleta didn't of course wear clothes to do her exercises and there was some light in our house since I was reading. What could be more natural than for young boys to peep through gaps in the reed wall. Of course, when we put the recorder on, they could see it and didn't call out on those nights.

* * *

Things were never quiet in our village. Elia Waqa had stopped Sepo and Show-off Person from coming to blows over Show-off having cuffed young Elia. But this set off a low-key feud between the two Mataqalis. It was realized in a curious way—by attendance at church. Each day church would be held in a house belonging to one Mataqali, and few or no people from the other Mataqali would come (except Felise the Catechist, who was too sensible and responsible to get involved in such hostility).

There was also trouble outside the village. A number of Waitabu men worked during the week as laborers on Mua plantation, on the other side of the island, and it seemed that employment conditions weren't too good there. Sepo helped them phrase a letter—in Standard Fijian—to the plantation management with what seemed to me perfectly reasonable demands—things like a pay-as-you-earn tax deduction scheme, and membership of the Fijian National Provident Fund. I agreed to type it out on my tiny battery-powered electronic machine. It had to be done in a hurry, during Sunday lunch, for the men to catch the last bus back to Mua. Qito was sent to sit beside me, answering queries about bits of handwriting I couldn't quite read (except that she changed a few things, as you'd expect). I said it was a good idea to write to the management in the first place but if that didn't bring results they should address a letter to their local member of parliament. What actually came of it was that all the Waitabu people working at Mua got the sack a couple of weeks later. No one wrote to an M.P.

Around that time I made a notation at the back of the small pocketbook in which I recorded new words and phrases: "This is definitely *the* most intellectually stimulating period of my life." There were two great things to fill most of my time—and all of my thoughts when doing things like walking along the beach or sitting in church—my novel, *The Price of Love*, and the study of Boumaa Fijian.

The structure of the language was becoming clear to me. First of all, the sound system. Fijian has five vowels—*i, e, a, o, u* (similar to the sounds in the English words *bean, Ben, barn, born* and *boon*, respectively). Now a word can involve a sequence of vowels with no consonant intervening—in words like *lailai*, "small," and *lialia*, "stupid." But I noticed—just by keeping my ears open—that some combinations of vowels are said as a single sound (a diphthong) and make up just one syllable whereas other combinations are pronounced as two distinct sounds and make up two syllables. *Lai* is pronounced rather like the English word *lie*, whereas a *lia* is something like *lee-a*.

I found that combinations *ai, au, ei, eu, oi, ou*, and *iu* are pronounced as diphthongs, whereas *io, ua, ie*, and in fact all other vowel combinations are pronounced as two syllables. Later on, I discovered that the first early missionary David Hazlewood had noticed exactly the same thing in 1850 and it had been repeated by Churchward in his 1941 book. But Milner's grammar, published in 1956, hadn't mentioned this important distinction. Then I remembered how—back in Canberra—I'd grumbled that *cauravou* was too long a word to remember in Lesson 5. Now I saw that it didn't have five syllables but really just three, with *au* and *ou* being diphthongs (it is pronounced *caw-ra-vow*). If only Milner had explained this it would have made his admittedly good textbook even better!

The great thing about living in Waitabu was that there were few real distractions. In Canberra, I attended meetings, made small talk, read newspapers—not activities that could be described as intellectually stimulating. I did have to make small talk in Fiji, but here it was exciting—seeing if I could use the language adequately and notice how people responded.

Of course, other things beside the mind have to be considered. There are feet. People in Fiji seldom wear shoes or sandals, except when going to town. At first, walking along the road was sheer agony for us—lots of tiny sharp stones. But after a couple of months our soles became as tough as they come. Sometimes a Fijian might put on a pair of sandals and we'd prefer to go barefoot.

Then there is that other important body part, the stomach. Fijian food was tasty and healthy but we sometimes missed little things from our own lifestyle. Also, we were entirely reliant on Sepo's family calling us to meals. There was no refrigerator or cookie jar to raid if one felt like a snack. So what we did was semi-secretly buy an odd packet of Twisties (a type of potato chip) or a few lollies—from Teliva or from Waibula or from the Waitabu store if it had any in stock. Just something to nibble on in the back corner of our house if we felt peckish or simply in need of a change.

Suliano called one day with the offer of a story about an incident in his youth. Yes please. I enthusiastically switched on the recorder. "Thank you very much Roopate and Koleta," he began. "One day, on a Saturday—just like today—I met up in the forest with a friend of mine from 'Orovou, called Tainayau."

They had heard that there was a large wild pig rampaging through the forest at the back of Qeleni. On that Saturday they caught just one tiny pig. They stayed the night at the house belonging to the elder brother of Suliano's friend and next morning called for directions at a village nearby, of Solomon Islanders (people who had been, like the Indians, brought over under indenture to work in the plantations, and then stayed). They were shown which trail to follow and set off along it, together with the fifteen dogs they'd brought. Eventually, the dogs cornered a gigantic pig. Suliano's friend slit its throat and the two youths set off for home, each carrying a piece of the carcass.

Near Wai they met a search party, coming out to look for them since they hadn't returned on Saturday night. It was thought they might be injured or lost in the bush. What nobody had thought of was that they'd do what they had done—break all taboos and go hunting on the Sabbath. "We repented of it," Suliano said, "and never again would I do any work on a Sunday. And now I ask of you—Roopate and Koleta—that my story may be allowed to end here."

This was an illuminating tale and also one full of interesting grammatical constructions. I now had as many texts as were needed for a full grammatical study, and was keen to check up on some of the generalizations I was coming up with, as well as continue going through my list of 450 verbs.

Inoke was unfailingly helpful when he had time and felt in the mood. So too was Sepo. But Sepo liked to be the judge of what we should work on together. And now he had an idea. There was in his house a mimeographed booklet telling the history of the Ca'audrove Cooperative Association, written in Standard Fijian. Sepo planned to read this into the tape recorder for us, translating into the Boumaa dialect as he went.

Both Koleta and I were interested in spontaneous texts in spoken Boumaa, not the translation of a written document in another dialect. But Sepo was not to be deterred. On the morning of Tuesday, March 12, he came in with the booklet, told me to switch on my recorder, and began a laborious translation. An hour in the morning and another hour in the evening, Sepo felt the story of the Ca'audrove Cooperative Association was important and his family should listen to it. He'd already heard a playback in our house and this was now repeated during and after the meal while everyone just sat and listened, no talking allowed. He lent us the booklet between reading sessions and we checked up on differences between the Bau original and Sepo's Boumaa version. They were quite minor, things like a transitive ending *-ta'ina* in place of Bau *-taka*, all things of which we were already aware.

The booklet had fifty pages, of which Sepo had done eight that day. Not only did we have no wish to make the recording but Sepo had no further time available to answer any of the questions that were building up in Koleta's file and in mine. Not until the history was finished. On Wednesday morning, he turned up as usual but decided to précis it a bit. Sepo would sit and read several pages to himself and then tell me to switch on the machine. He'd essentially translate a couple of crucial paragraphs, with an impromptu sentence or two on the side. There was only time for one session on Wednesday (Sepo had lots of things to do in his garden, in the store and in the copra shed) and we covered about the same number of pages as the previous day. Again it was played back at meal time for the whole family to hear.

On Thursday, the history of the Ca'audrove Cooperative Association was completely forgotten, for two quite different reasons. First, and most important, Sepo's eldest son Peteroo was flying in from Suva. He was due to go back to the Middle East in a couple of weeks and Sepo had put through a telephone call to Pete's commanding officer in Suva asking for his son to be given a week's leave in order to visit his home village. Sepo had talked about the importance of maintaining village life and said Pete might be the chief someday—surely he should come home for a visit before flying off overseas. The C.O. had agreed.

When the present Tui Nasau died a new one would be chosen by and from the adult men of the Vunivesi Ito'ato'a which was one division of the Vunivesi Mataqali. It was very likely—although not absolutely certain—that Sepo would succeed his elder brother. But after him? Pete was the eldest son and would make a great chief. But he had a wife from Rotuma who didn't care for village life (and wouldn't even accompany him on this short trip). Otherwise it could be Maarawa... Or things might change. The Waiso'i Mataqali—of which Elia Waqa was head—had more members and they sometimes muttered that they should supply the next chief.

Pete (both vowels are pronounced, *Pe-te*) was great. Strong and well-built with an easy assurance and sunny disposition. It was good to have him there at that time, to help with the preparations for another visitor, one less welcome. The radio announced that cyclone Vina should be down toward us on Saturday night. And that time it was definitely going to be coming our way. Plotting present position and direction of movement on the map gave a course going right over Waitabu.

The two or three days before a cyclone are spent in steady preparation. Young Elia really loved going with his glamorous elder brother up the hill to the east for sturdy lengths of bamboo. They just threw them over the steep hillside, piled them up at the bottom, then Pete and Sepo put these pieces over our roof, tying them down at each end. (And then I went and put a few more loops of twine around.)

Some people in the village just prayed. Others scoffed at Pete's careful preparation. "It won't come here," they opined, not believing our exercise in course plotting. "You'll see, tomorrow," Sepo admonished, "when your houses have no roof, maybe no walls."

Our old house on a fine day. The chief's traditional-style house is to the left.

We were told of a pre-radio way of telling when a cyclone is due. There's a species of bird (called "cyclone bird") that flies low at the first hint of a high wind. Some people in the village said they'd seen the bird but others denied this, saying it was a case of mistaken identification, a quite different bird.

All preparations were complete by midday. Sepo had done no linguistic work since that interminable translation on Tuesday and Wednesday. There was nothing to stop him sparing us an hour on Saturday afternoon. Except that Vina was on his (her?) way. When a cyclone is in the offing you concentrate all your energies on just waiting for it. (We got the impression that to do otherwise would be disrespectful to that "murdering wind.")

Bogi provided an early supper. At six o'clock the wind grew stronger. Both our side doors were barricaded with sheets of corrugated iron. We were about to close up the front door when there appeared an apparition. We looked again. No, it was Tui Nasau. Dressed in that green PHANTOM CLUB CALIFORNIA T-shirt and a green isulu. And carrying a green palm frond. Holding it above his head in the light rain. He said a word and grinned broadly, like a clown at the circus. Then again. We strained to hear. It was an English word. Tui Nasau was posing with the palm frond

7. A Divine Visitor

The house battened down ready to receive the fifth cyclone of the season.

and saying *umbrella* (the fourth English word we'd heard from him). Just then Sepo came up in a hard hat (the sort people wear on construction sites) in case a branch fell on him. They made a strange pair. The powerful old chief acting like a goat and his workmanlike brother, who shook his head in disbelief.

We put up the barricades, sealed notebooks and tapes into plastic bags. Wind and storm increased. It was then that the knock came on the door—"Tui Nasau here," wanting a pack of cigarettes—which put me in mind of the Queen of England popping in to borrow a cup of sugar.

In the end Vina was no worse than her (his?) four predecessors. What had happened was that the cyclone suddenly changed course by ninety degrees and went straight over Kadavu Island, to the south of Viti Levu—which had not been prepared—destroying scores of houses there. People in the village said to Sepo: "There, I told you so, all that preparation was quite unnecessary." We knew better, of course, but we felt too superior to offer any reply.

There's always a light-hearted feeling on the morning after a cyclone. As we sat eating breakfast Nana Vero, the chief's wife, brought in a dish of cassava that she had left over. "It's like the Duke of Edinburgh calling with a plate of chips," I whispered to Koleta, continuing the analogy of the previous night.

On Sunday Sepo was too tired for linguistic work. Then, on Monday morning, he appeared in our house, fresh and lively. We jumped up eagerly, until we saw what he had in his hand. The history of the Ca'audrove Cooperative Association. "We must finish it," said Sepo, defensively. I could see his point. I always like to complete any job I start. Anyway, Sepo stepped up the pace of his précis and finished the last thirty-odd pages in a single day. On the Tuesday—exactly a week after he'd started on that history—Sepo had time to help us in our work.

* * *

Not for long though. Waitabu was to receive several more visitors before the end of March.

First of all came Ralph, a young German tourist, who was traveling around the world for the minimum of financial outlay. Sepo got talking to him outside Lesuma's in Waiyevo, and invited Ralph to come and stay in Waitabu for a day or two. "Or stay for four or five days if you want," Sepo added, with a characteristic Fijian generosity that is mostly said out of politeness. Ralph took him at his word. After all, he had to buy some yaqona roots to be presented to the chief on the first day, and after that it was all free.

Koleta recorded the presentation, a part of her study of the language of ceremonies. But, apart from that, Ralph's visit was a real hindrance to us. He was a novelty, who both Sepo and Inoke favored, practicing their English. Neither showed overmuch interest in doing linguistic work with us.

Sepo did, however, pop in one morning with a surprising piece of news. Pelasio—the man with a limp and a facial tic who'd been at our first presentation—had gone to Suva to consult an Indonesian priest, newly arrived from the Philippines, who had semi-divine power of diagnosis and cure. There were only two priests in the whole world who were recognized by the Pope to be "faith healers," Sepo said, and he was one of them.

Pelasio had been most impressed. The village elders met together. There was lots and lots of illness in Waitabu, Sepo explained. (We hadn't noticed anything of the sort, but were prepared to take his word for it.) Father Hendricks—let that be the magical priest's name—was to be invited across to cure the whole village.

That wasn't the real surprise. It gradually became clear that Sepo was using "illness" in a way quite different from the one we were used to. It was not a sense of physical disorder. He explained that there were devils, which were put inside people to adversely affect their minds and bodies. This was done by the traditional priests in the village (practitioners who would no doubt be called witch-doctors by some).

For two and a half months we'd been totally unaware of this. We'd thought it a nice Catholic village, all that church twice a day. But Christianity was only the surface dressing. Every single person still believed in traditional gods and feared much more what they might do than they trembled at the wrath of Jehovah.

Really it should have been obvious. The traditional gods were believed to be the Fijian's ancestors. You can't make a people stop believing in their ancestors. The missionaries had just superimposed another layer of religion and driven the older one underground, so that it was not spoken of to outsiders. But traditional beliefs were all the more powerful because of that.

"I didn't tell you about native Fijian religion before," Sepo explained "because I didn't think you'd believe in it when you first arrived here." I didn't like to say we didn't even believe in the Catholic God. "Now that you're part of the village you will believe in our traditional gods?" he continued, anxiously. "Oh yes, Father," Koleta said, with indrawn breath. "Yes, Uncle," I echoed.

So Father Hendricks was to be fetched from Suva to exorcize evil spirits, which had been implanted by the local traditional priests. Pelasio was said to have had a stroke—but that was actually a devil entering his body. Nau's arthritis had a similar cause.

We had to proceed cautiously. Just who were the traditional priests in Waitabu? Well, no one could be absolutely certain, Sepo said, but there were thought to be three. Show-off Person was one; that we could thoroughly believe. And old Atalemo, who had the fine traditional style house. Well, he was a rather old-fashioned kind of person but Atalemo seemed so nice and friendly. "Aha," Sepo smiled, "that's to fool people." The third suspect was another man, but someone we scarcely knew. Were traditional priests always men? No. Sepo replied. Usually men but not always. Elia Waqa's second wife (my mother)—who had died before Christmas—had been thought to be one.

Wait a minute—Show-off Person and Atalemo went to church, at least as often as anyone else. Surely if they were avid practitioners of the traditional religion… Sepo shook his head at our naiveté. Of course they go to church, to allay suspicion, so that people won't guess they are traditional priests. (Well, Koleta and I were attending for our own, non–

Christian, reasons. Why shouldn't the traditional priests do the same thing?)

Pio the half-wit, Sepo continued, had had a terrible devil put in him directly by a god. Apparently Pio's first cousin (his father's brother's son) was also a bit deranged. Where we would attribute this to a genetic defect, the Fijians said that Pio's grandfather must have mortally offended a traditional god, and he had taken his revenge on two of the grandchildren.

The whole village was in ferment. Each Ito'ato'a had contributed something to Father Hendricks's fare, and he'd be coming very soon. The word spread throughout Taveuni: and people from other villages proposed to make a pilgrimage to Waitabu. (For a short while what had been one of the most insignificant villages on the island became the center of all attention.)

Ralph the tourist stayed on, wandering across the village taking photographs. He learned to reply *bula* "hello" and that was all. Our German tourist ate all the food given to him. A plate with four slices of paw-paw and Ralph would scoff the lot. We had to take him on one side and explain that he should eat one slice only—well, two if he must but no more—however much they pressed him. Otherwise the women and children got nothing. Ralph was very dubious about this. "They want me to eat, and I do." "Yes," we countered, "but the custom is that men are offered all the food and only consume *some* of it."

Ralph shrugged his shoulders, got out a novel and sat in the sun on the top step of Sepo's house, leaning against the doorpost. Koleta happened to walk past the next-door house where Elia Waqa and other elders were discussing Father Hendricks's visit. Atalemo called her over to the group for an urgent whispered consultation. "Tell that white-man not to sit in the doorway." He appeared quite agitated. "It will anger the god of the house, who lives above the door. He has been sitting there for an hour. The god must be livid."

So Koleta told Ralph. This he wasn't going to accept. "I'll sit where I want." There was no easy chair and he had to sit somewhere. "You mustn't," Koleta cajoled. "Please respect the beliefs of the villagers. You are a guest here." Ralph still objected: "No one's said anything to me about it." (He hadn't noticed the worried looks from Elia Waqa's house, just a few yards away.) Eventually he did move, but just to please Koleta, giving the impression that he considered her slightly bonkers.

Inoke did pop in that evening. For once my questions weren't about matters linguistic. How do traditional priests work? Well, Inoke explained, there were several methods. A traditional priest can call up a devil by going to the beach when a full moon is just rising and dancing naked before it. (Should you happen to see a traditional priest actually doing this all you have to do is throw a stone or call their name and it kills them.) When drinking yaqona in a house a traditional priest will throw two bowls of the liquid out of a window; the devils outside will fight for it, and you can harness them this way. Or it is possible to go to a high priest and ask for a devil; but you must remember to pray to him three times a day or else he'll kill you. Anyone can be a traditional priest—it's just a matter of inclination and practice.

Inoke also explained that the Christian God offers long-term promises. But Fijian gods—or devils (the word doesn't have the negative overtones for Fijians that it does for us)—provide quick results and are preferred for that reason. He said that Indians have their own devils, which is why they make money. If an Indian goes bust then his devil has let him down.

Sepo came in after supper. Father Hendricks was coming the next day. He'd called to *'ere'ere* a whale's tooth from us, which his Mataqali would present to the priest. It would be our contribution to the welcoming ceremony. We grudgingly produced one of the small tabua from the pawn shop in Suva and said it was our last.

I tried to take the opportunity to find out a bit more about this item of traditional wealth. How many tabuas might there be in the whole village? How many might each person have? Ah, Sepo fell back on that familiar response. *E sega ni macala*, "it is not clear." No one would say. Each man had a store of whale's teeth. He'd have to present some at certain ceremonies and would receive some at others. But the actual number he had hidden away in suitcases or nooks and crannies of his house was kept a close secret. Certainly Sepo wasn't letting on about how many he owned. One thing I did know, though, and that is you can *'ere'ere* most things, but *not* a tabua. Sepo insisted on keeping to the letter of Fijian law with us most of the time but was quite capable of deviating when it suited him. After all, we were only foreigners.

Tomorrow promised to be an interesting day. In readiness for it we were both asleep by nine o'clock. At ten there came a knock on our door and the call "Roopate, Roopate." I wearily rose. "Yes, what is it Uncle?" Sepo had come to *'ere'ere* a mosquito coil, a spiral of compressed chemicals you burn to keep those biting insects at bay. "But I was asleep, Uncle." "I am so sorry, Roopate, I would not have knocked if I had known." Of course he knew we were asleep; there wasn't any sort of light showing through the many chinks in our wall.

* * *

Tomorrow began very early. Ralph was being sent off before Father Hendricks arrived. The pretext was that he should go down to the other end of Taveuni and visit one of Bogi's relatives in Vuna. He must catch the six-thirty bus, Sepo insisted. There would be a bit of a wait outside Lesuma's, then he could get on the twelve-thirty to Vuna. Now, this was totally untrue. Ralph could have had a leisurely breakfast, got on the ten o'clock bus from Waitabu and been at Lesuma's by eleven-thirty, which allowed an hour before the Vuna bus, a sufficient interval even given the haphazard schedules on Taveuni. Sepo just wanted him out of the way as soon as possible.

(Ralph later came to stay with me in Canberra. He said that the men at Vuna had made him go to the store each day and buy a certain quantity of food, quite unlike Sepo. In Canberra Ralph ate my food and slept on my bed with only the mildest thanks. And when I asked for his address in Germany and said we might come and stay with him there he was quite nonplussed!)

Felise had borrowed a car from another village with which to meet Father Hendricks off the morning plane which was due at Matei at 9:50. The car journey would take perhaps twenty minutes. Everyone was in welcoming posture well before ten.

The previous day a Tunuloa-style shed had been erected, on the exact spot where it had been before as a dance hall. Fijians don't work very much but when they put their mind to it a great deal can be achieved in a short while. A dozen youths, armed with sharp knives, could cut and trim and erect and tie together a bamboo frame, weave coconut fronds for low walls, and put some pieces of iron on for a roof—all in a matter of hours. There were mats laid on the floor and a single chair at the far end, in case Father required it.

Everyone was dressed in their very best clothes, the women looking like a flower-bed of colored isulus and bangles. Each man wore an isulu below the waist topped by his choicest shirt. Atalemo's bore on the back a legend WINDSURFING, against a red and yellow sail. Tui Nasau wore his sunglasses, simply because they were the smartest thing he had.

The chief and other elders sat in state about two-thirds of the way up the shed, Tui Nasau slightly further forward of Elia Waqa, with Sepo, Suliano, Pelasio and Atalemo a short way behind him. Then came the rest of the men, packed in quite tightly, and at the back the women and children. Every single person in the village was there, sitting cross-legged in the Tunuloa-style shed, waiting.

We sat behind Sepo, but several yards further back (Koleta, just

7. A Divine Visitor

behind me, to accord with Fijian chauvinistic principles). He turned and motioned us closer. When Sepo says a thing he's generally fairly insistent and the simplest thing is just to do it. But then, when Sepo became engaged in discussion with Tui Nasau and Elia Waqa, we moved back a yard or two. Many of the villagers murmured their approbation of this attempt at self-effacement.

What I found incongruous about the scene was that washing was hanging on the line at several spots in Waitabu. My mother—the real English one—was a very mild Christian, the sort who goes to church just at Christmas and Easter. But the one thing she wouldn't do was have washing on the line on a Sunday, in case it offended people who might be more devout. Now this wasn't a Sunday, true, but the sight of every inhabitant of the village looking so clean and neat, while the village itself fluttered with washing seemed somehow comical.

We waited. I had a recorder ready. Sepo checked the microphones and—speaking quite close to it—recorded an introduction to the ceremony much in the manner of a radio commentator. "This is to be a traditional chiefly welcoming ceremony for a priest from Suva, in this church in the village of Waitabu. We are very happy for this chiefly ceremony to be recorded. We are happy that it is to be recorded by Roopate and Koleta, here in the village of Waitabu. I'm just recording a short introduction to the traditional chiefly presentation before the priest arrives. That's the end of it." Then we waited some more. Children cried. Ladies fanned themselves and whispered together. Waiting, waiting, waiting. Someone passed me a fan. They were always doing this, especially in church. Neither the heat nor the flies worried me particularly and I couldn't really be bothered using a fan. But of course I had to.

Finally, at 11:32 youths stationed at the *lali* began beating a slow rhythm. Dum-dum dum-dum dum-dum dum-dum dum. Dum-dum dum. Dum. Di-dum-ti. Dum-dum dum... Before the priest's car had stopped, Tui Nasau called out a traditional greeting and all his subjects gave the response.

The car door opened and a youngish man jumped out, wearing an open-necked Hawaiian-style shirt and a toothy grin with hand outstretched. Goodness, he was even more gauche than I'd been on our first day. The elders and people of Waitabu continued to sit cross-legged, stern and solemn. No one shook anyone's hand. A priest was expected to wear clerical collar and bear a vague look of divine satisfaction. But I could sense surprise being replaced by adjustment. This was a special priest, one of only two in the whole world—with no medical training at all—

authorized by the Pope to cure people. He should be different. Yes, that might explain the dress and grin.

Felise conducted Father to the chair, which he sat on without a moment's thought even though everyone else, including Felise, was on the floor, and it would have been both humble and polite to do likewise.

Now for the presentations. Tui Nasau had decided in advance that they'd have just four of the welcoming ceremonies traditionally accorded a high chief, who in the olden days arrived by boat. These would be Wading Toward, Pulling Down the Flag, Making Dry and Pulling of Leaves. Tui Nasau shuffled forward and displayed a whale's tooth. "*Aaah, oi, oi, oi,*" the Waitabu people exclaimed. Felise—who was acting as spokesman for Father—exclaimed (as he had to) "*Aaah, oi, oi, oi,* this is a big tabua!" Then Tui Nasau made his speech for the Wading Toward ceremony, saying he hoped the visitor had experienced good weather (I suppose that's as important for plane travel nowadays as it was for boat travel in days gone by) and extending a warm and humble welcome, Felise replied on behalf of the visitor.

Elia Waqa was supposed to have presented his tabua as a Pulling Down the Flag ceremony, but he forgot and did a second Wading Toward. (Sepo later drew attention to this, as a black mark against the rival Mataqali. I said I had noticed it at the time. But really, did it matter—all four ceremonies were pretty well identical except for the name, performed in the same place and at the same time. In the old days they'd have been enacted at different stages of coming ashore.) Anyway, my adopted father gave a notable speech, as he always did, that sonorous voice lauding both village and visitor in poetic vein. Felise again replied.

Then it was the turn of Sepo, second representative of Vunivesi and after him Suliano, second from the Waiso'i Mataqali. Each time Felise replied on behalf of Father and I marveled at his ability to say the same thing in four different ways. The ceremonies were impressive. This ancient culture was putting on its very best show for a valued visitor who sat in his chair, grinning from time to time and not understanding a single word of what was being said. Tui Nasau coughed and loudly cleared his throat at fairly regular intervals and there was an odd snoring sound. I peered around to see who could possibly have fallen asleep at such a moment. It was only Pio the half-wit being witty; his father slapped him every minute or two, to try and stop the noise.

Next followed the yaqona ceremony. Five youths brought in a large carved bowl and went through the ritual of presentation. Nothing is said during this. Finally the cups are offered around, in order of seniority, with the assembly clapping in time as each one is quaffed. Sepo turned to me: "You are recording this?" "Yes, all the speeches Uncle." "And the clapping?" Of course I wasn't. Who wants the same clapping repeated twenty times? "On it!," he said in English, as the clapping started again. And I had to.

When this was over Father Hendricks made his own speech of thanks, in English. "I am *feeling happy* that I could come here. I feel that I am close to you, because my place in Indonesia is the same as your place." Felise translated this. "*Tarayi tu-*." Father Hendricks stopped himself, having chosen the wrong language. Begin again: "Therefore I am very happy to be with you because I feel close to you and we thank the Lord because we *could* pray together, not feeling only close to you, feeling at home, but we feel also how God loves us so that I *could* do good things for everyone of us here and for that also I am very happy to come here." Felise rendered this more briefly, just mentioning how happy the Father was to be here at this time.

The priest continued: "And at least thank you very much to everyone who prepared this meeting, this ceremony. I am very happy because with this I feel also I could do what God *ask* from me, to serve you, as a priest in Suva but now also—." He plainly didn't remember the name of our village, but there was only momentary hesitation. "He *give* me things that I could do more for you so that we know him as the one who *care us*." Felise rendered into Fijian Father's thanks for the welcoming ceremony. "And *last* I came here to *helep* any one of you." (Father Hendricks's native tongue plainly didn't allow *l* and *p* together at the end of a word. He inserted a very clear *e* between them.) "I pray for you and I hope, with God's help, I *could* give you also happiness by health that maybe you can have in this place. Thank you." Here Felise's translation was much more imaginative, offering Father's profuse thanks to the people of Waitabu and generally inventing a few sentiments that he might have been expected to say but hadn't.

It couldn't rest there. Every speaker must receive a reply and, at a nod from Tui Nasau, Elia Waqa shuffled forward once more and expressed the profound gratitude of the whole community. "*Mana*," he concluded and everyone responded "*E dina*," it is true. Then more clapping and the welcoming ceremonies were finished.

We suddenly became important people. Father Hendricks knew no Fijian (he'd only been in Suva a short while) and scarcely anyone at Waitabu spoke English. So he was brought over to our corner of the Tunuloa shed, for someone to talk to.

This did serve one purpose. Sepo had asked me which languages

Fijian was related to and I'd tried to explain that it was a member of the vast Austronesian language family, covering Malaysia, Indonesia, the Philippines, parts of New Guinea, New Zealand Maori and all of the Pacific, over to Hawaii and Easter Island. "And Africa," Sepo had added. "No," I said, "not Africa." But he wouldn't have it.

It seems that for the last hundred years there had been a prevalent belief in Fiji that their ancestors had come from Tanganyika (now Tanzania) on the east coast of Africa. This idea was ingrained, and Sepo wasn't receptive to anything I might venture to the contrary.

I'd told Sepo that the original Austronesian language—from which the eight hundred or so modern tongues are descended—is believed to have been spoken somewhere in the South China/Philippines/Indonesian area. This had met with disbelief until the good father arrived. The first thing I asked for was the numbers in his native language from Indonesia. This is an area where it's almost always possible to find cognates between any two Austronesian languages, and I was able to point these out—words like *lima* "five." "Do you think we came from Indonesia?" Sepo inquired. "Oh yes," replied the priest, his ethnocentrism flattered. In such a way was I finally believed!

We were intrigued about what would happen to the tabuas and mats that had been presented. Perhaps they'd be left in the village, since clearly a priest had little use for tabuas. Not at all, Sepo said. Father would take them back to Suva with him. But what happened to them there? No one seemed to know. Later we heard that the church has a big warehouse full of whale's teeth. And another story is that they dribble them out to the pawn shops...

Father Hendricks must have been the first priest to actually set foot in Waitabu for goodness knows how long. Every bus brought people from other villages and there were also several tightly jammed lorries. Where was he going to conduct a mass? Oh dear, this was something the Father hadn't come prepared for. He could do it? Certainly, he could—and would—but one must have the proper impedimenta, you know. So a hasty phone call was made to Wairi'i and a man from Waitabu set off by bus— four hours round trip—to fetch the chalice without which mass could not take place.

Whatever else Father Hendricks might have been, he was no slouch and started immediately on the healing. "You've told him about the devils, that traditional priests put into people?" I asked Sepo, "so that he'll know to exorcize them?" "Oh no," he replied. "Father wouldn't understand at all about such matters. We didn't tell you until you'd been here for two months."

7. A Divine Visitor

So the whole exercise was at cross-purposes. The people wanted the priest to pit the power of Christianity against the magic of their native gods (on the principle that Jehovah is supposed to be infallible). Father Hendricks was attempting to divine the cause of some ache or pain—without any medical methods—and then produce a way of curing it. They were in two different worlds, just like Ralph and the villagers a few days before.

Stories buzzed around us of the miracles Father was working. Of course there were limits to his power, people warned. He'd never be able to make Pio fully normal, although there could be some improvement. And no cure would be instantaneous, rather a gradual thing. Old Nau—who could scarcely stand or walk—was already reporting a noticeable improvement. In a week or two, Father said, she'd be trotting around the village again.

Our turn came late that first afternoon. As members of Sepo's family we had to go into the house and watch. Father Hendricks sat his patient on a chair in quite un–Fijian pose and then stood over them, passing one hand—with a finger of the other hidden behind it—a couple of inches off the body part that was said to be faulty, this finger would quiver in a certain manner as if receiving a bolt of electricity. (It seemed a bit like what a water diviner is supposed to do.) From the way it moved, Father Hendricks diagnosed what was wrong and then prescribed a remedy. He might specify a certain kind of exercise or manipulation and show how it should be done. And then an elixir. The only trouble was that the ingredients were things readily obtainable in a big city but not in Waitabu. Some of the things he mentioned no one had even heard of. Try again. "Honey? Can you get that here?" They could have gone to buy it in a shop if they had enough money, but no one ever did. Sepo didn't like to say no. (Later, in Suva, I saw a book called *Secrets of Fijian Medicine* by Dr. M.A. Weiner, and thought of purchasing a copy for the good father.)

We had to take part as well. First Koleta. I'd be interested to see how he undid that horrible curvature of the spine. Then me. "No, Uncle, there is nothing wrong with me." "Oh yes," Sepo said "there is—that cramp in the knee." I didn't like to say that I'd never had it before (and in fact I've never had it since). If one hasn't been brought up to sit cross-legged for lengthy periods and then suddenly has to do it at the age of 45, of course knee muscle might complain. So I sat on the chair, had the magic hand click in discovery and then was shown how to massage it, exactly what I did anyway.

When we'd read *Return to Laughter*, in January, Laura Bohannan's superior attitude to the "savage civilization" of Africa had seemed gratuitous.

Fijian life was just different—neither better nor worse. Only very gradually did our attitude change, with Father Hendricks's visit providing the final push. They really were all a little bit naive. Once an attitude to one thing changes, others get carried along as well—the endless ceremonies that we'd previously respected as instances of an individual culture suddenly took on the appearance of repetitive mumbo-jumbo.

Father Hendricks continued for two whole days. He must have cured three or four hundred people, some of them several times. Everyone reported a slight but significant improvement and expected to be fully recovered in no time at all. But when we returned from Suva, at the end of April, all the old people were exactly as before. Nau—who had sat in that chair at least twice—still could scarcely stand up or walk. Well, the people of Waitabu had had two days of euphoric pleasure—at the expense of quite a number of tabuas and finely woven mats.

* * *

We sat in our house, trying to work, as the village became like Mecca or some Christian equivalent. On the second day Koleta escaped to 'Orovou to help her school teacher friend who was desperately trying to prepare six final-year students (none from Waitabu) for an English exam. The time came for Father's mass and I went along, together with a couple of hundred others. This I didn't record. Father Hendricks gave a sermon, just in English, with no translation. One sentence stuck in my mind. "Even Saint Augustine,"—he said Agustine but I think that's what he meant— "even Saint Augustine was once a little boy, then he grew up and became Saint Augustine." (Augustine wasn't mentioned before or after this in the sermon.)

I'd now finished a first draft of *The Price of Love* and was working intensively on a grammar of Boumaa Fijian. Originally my plan had been to do a bit of work on a few odd grammatical topics. But none of the existing grammars (all dealing with the standard dialect) were terribly satisfactory so I decided to do it properly and write a full grammar of the Boumaa dialect.

First off was a chapter on phonetics, and phonology, which describes how a particular language makes use of various sorts of phonetic contrasts to carry meaning. An account of which vowel sequences are diphthongs and which aren't. Then a chapter on "word." For most languages, a single unit "word" can be defined, with certain grammatical properties (it is generally words that take inflectional endings) and also certain phonological properties (a word will typically include just one stressed syllable). But

7. A Divine Visitor

Fijian, I discovered, had two different kinds of words—grammatical words and phonological words. There's a way of making a verb into a noun: you put *i-* in front of it. *Sele* means to "cut or slice"; *i-sele* refers to a "knife." As a noun is used in a sentence it must be preceded by the article *a* (a bit like English *the*). So *a i-sele*, "the knife." The fascinating thing was that the *a* and *i* form a diphthong on phonological criteria. *Ai* is one word and *sele* another. But on grammatical criteria *a* is one word and *i-sele* a second word.

I was sitting at the table tapping this out on my portable typewriter when Sepo entered. Tearing myself away from the train of thought I squatted on the floor. "Yes, Uncle?" He had a request. Not for himself, I must understand (Sepo had enough sensitivity to be aware that I was preoccupied). But could *polo ni wai* be healed in the house and also have the house blessed by Father?

At least, I *thought* he said *polo ni wai*, which means "ball of water" What on earth was happening? How could water be made into a ball? Why should Father Hendricks want to bless a ball of water? And why in our house? Well, after the events of the last few days I was ready for anything. "Yes, Uncle, of course Father Hendricks may attend to the ball of water here."

The mistake was elementary, and phonetic. Sepo had said *Paulo Ni Wai*, which was a man's name (I'd heard *o* rather than the diphthong *au*). The first name was based on the Biblical Paul. And the second one? Well if a Fijian can be called "gun" why not "of water"? Paulo Ni Wai used to live in Waitabu but he'd gone away before we arrived and only just returned. This is why I wasn't familiar with the name.

So Paulo Ni Wai came in, with his wife and assorted relatives. I sat solemnly on the floor, envying Koleta in 'Orovou. (She later told me they had scones with jam for tea. Get that—jam!) Each person sat in turn on my chair and was set on course for an imaginary cure. Then Father Hendricks blessed a cup of water and splashed bits into each corner of the house.

When Koleta returned I told her of the strange incident for which we could think of no explanation. Why our house? Anyway, it didn't seem very important. (There, as it turned out, we were entirely wrong.)

What we were looking forward to was returning to Suva for a half-time break. How were we traveling?, Tui Nasau asked. Well, plane... There was another way. The chief was excited as if discussing a fine meal. A boat, the *Princess Ashika*, had just begun a regular run. Waiyevo to Savu Savu on the island of Vanua Levu then on to Suva. We were doubtful. The plane was so quick. A boat might be cheaper, but... Oh, and better! The chief left no shadow of a doubt. There were three lounges, a bar, several restaurants, videos. We said we'd see.

After Father Hendricks left everything relapsed into routine. We could return to speculating over whether Qito was pregnant or not. I saw her one day sitting on the front step—I knew this is supposed to be taboo, but Qito always was a law unto herself—with her dress wet after washing and clinging to her stomach. I had no doubt that the opinion of 99 percent of the village was correct.

We also speculated about when the new store might be occupied. Construction work had been completed by February and then there was a wait to buy louvres and install them (the wait was getting the money together to buy the louvres). It was ready by March, but not occupied save for a recent yaqona party in the evening. Nor by June. Nor by the following June, when we made a return trip. Sepo had a straightforward answer as to why they'd gone to such effort and expense to build a new concrete-slab store and then left it unused. "We like the old wooden one," he stated.

Our housekeeping chores basically amounted to sweeping the floor each morning with a saasaa broom made from the spines of coconut leaves. I'd sometimes do this while Koleta was having a morning bath. It was all right so long as no one saw me doing women's work (for the shame this might bring on Koleta and on me).

We still did the washing jointly, at six a.m. when there was no one there to see. But I shouldn't help peg it out back in the village. One day I just plain insisted... If I could share the job at the washing pool, why not at the clothesline too? A lady came out of the next house to watch. "Oh, Roopate is *maopo*," she said. This was a new word (and we knew it must be special to the Boumaa dialect, since there is no *p* sound in Standard Fijian). "What does that mean?" asked Koleta, on the defensive, "does it mean 'like a woman?'" It turned out that *maopo* is "helpful." They didn't think any the worse of me for assisting Koleta. It was just that their own menfolk were lazy and useless, the lady said.

Up until mid–March we'd kept the camera hidden away, so as not to be identified as tourists. It was gotten out for the first time for a shot of Sepo's son Pete, Sepo, Bogi, Maarawa, and little Vilimaina. Qito refused to join this group but I took one of her a couple of days later, sitting on the step—and was rewarded with an uncharacteristic smile.

Then it was time to go. As we walked off toward the bus Koleta turned back and said, fondly, "Goodbye, our little house." I saw Bogi give Sepo a worried look, the import of which didn't become clear until much later.

7. A Divine Visitor

Almost the whole family accompanied us to the *Princess Ashika* (for we found we really had little choice in the matter of transport). Young Filo—denied school that year—desperately wanted to go to Suva and stood on the wharf with tears in her eyes.

The trip was just plain awful. There were two lounges, with quite comfortable seats but a video blared in each continuously from midday, when we left Waiyevo, until four a.m., when we arrived in Suva. Koleta can sleep through anything but I can't and I loathe videos. (I didn't then own a TV.) There were benches on the deck but with dividers between the seats which didn't make for a comfortable place to lie. The ship had no bar and the one meal—served at arbitrary hours—was fish curry and rice. Take it or leave it.

There was one distraction. We wandered up next to the bridge and were invited by the Indian captain-owner into his private cabin for a drink. He was extremely drunk. (Luckily the helmsman and the rest of the crew were Fijian, and they stayed quite sober. But what would have happened if the captain had given them some foolish drunken order?) Anyway, he told us he loved money more than his wife and children, and after a polite period we excused ourselves, to go back to the blaring video lounge.

Once in Suva, in the early hours, there was confusion about disembarking. A couple of lorries (the *Princess Ashika* carried everything) were revving their engines; we were requested to squeeze through a tiny space between them with—as I saw it—a real risk of being crushed like a pancake. Deprived of rest and quiet I lost reason and told the crew of the *Princess Ashika* exactly what I thought of them.

(The *Princess Ashika* was later sold to Tonga as a ferry between its islands. In August 2009, the vessel was inundated by a huge wave and sank, with 74 people reported drowned plus an unknown number of stowaways. Earlier, the boat had been judged as unseaworthy by an inspector in Fiji.)

It was great to fall asleep at the ANU flat in Suva. And to be able to go to the toilet without anyone calling out to me "Roopate, where to?"

8

A New House and a New Baby

We bought the *Fiji Times*, wandered along streets full of shops, went to the cinema, had a Chinese meal. I even visited foreign embassies to read newspapers from overseas. At the British and Australian High Commissions you just wandered in, but the American Embassy was guarded by locked doors and fierce Marines with those menacing low brims on their caps. Eventually they did let me into the library. At American Embassy reading rooms all over the world they'll let members of the public photocopy things free of charge. The Indian overlooking the Suva reading room agreed that was the case. I did one page of one magazine. One page of another. At the third one he exploded, and said that I could do no more, shouldn't have done any in the first place. And no, I could *not* pay for it.

What I yearned for was the real heart of Western civilization. Not Suva or Sydney or Canberra but New York and London. I sent off a subscription to *The New Yorker*; the first copy arrived in Canberra the week I returned there in July. And a friendly lady at the British High Commission let me have half-a-dozen back issues of the London *Times*. I kept a couple to take back to Waitabu. There is nothing quite like waking up on a Sunday morning in a remote Fijian village and sitting up in bed (on the floor) to read a weeks-old copy of the *Times*. It produces a very odd feeling.

We did carry on doing fieldwork, but in a rather undemanding way. There are three versions of each possessive pronoun in Fijian, depending on the nature of the thing possessed—whether it is to be eaten, or it is to be drunk, or neither of these. The "to be eaten" pronoun begins with *'e-* in Boumaa (*ke-* in Bau), the "to be drunk" pronoun begins with *me-* in both dialects, and the "other" pronoun begins with *o* in Boumaa and *no-*

8. A New House and a New Baby

in Bau. So you say *'ena dalo*, "his/her taro," *mena wai*, "his water," *ona isele*, "his knife."

But it isn't quite that simple. Tobacco takes *'e-*, for instance, and shellfish are *me-*. A pill, such as the doctor prescribes, is *me-*. Eventually I worked out that *'e* is used for anything that undergoes a change of state as it is being consumed—food is bitten and chewed before being swallowed, tobacco is burned and only the smoke inhaled. *Me-* is used for anything which does not undergo a change of shape or state as it is being consumed; water is just drunk down, a shell-fish will be sucked out of its shell, and a pill is swallowed whole.

But there remained the question of how jelly (or jello) was classified. What we did was go into quite a number of cafes, order jelly and see how the Fijian lady behind the counter referenced it—by an *'e-* or *me-* pronoun. Sometimes it was one and sometimes the other. We decided it all boiled down to whether or not you chew jelly a bit before swallowing it. Some people do but others don't.

There was a Russian cruise ship in harbor, out from Sydney with a couple of thousand Australians. They let us wander around inside for an hour. And we made sure not to do any shopping in town while it was there—all prices skyrocket in Suva when there is a foreign ship in. The Indian shopkeepers employ Fijians to hang about on the wharf, grab any tourists that appear, and escort them to the various emporia on Cumming Street.

We waited until the following week before making our purchases. In one shop I asked the cost of a set of pearl-shell coasters. "Six dollars." "But it says thirty dollars on the ticket," I pointed out. "Look on the other side," the shopkeeper showed me "in top corner, local price six dollars. The thirty dollars is for tourists, they love to bargain." That they don't. Most Australian tourists don't know how to bargain, don't even know one could bargain. I do, though, and I got him down to four dollars and fifty cents.

It was nice just to be able to sit and work in total quiet. Koleta devised tables and graphs and correlations, and made copies of questionnaires for when we got back. The first thing I had to do was choose the texts that would be included at the back of my grammar, since there'd be references to them in each chapter. I wanted texts that included instances of a wide range of grammatical constructions. That fine tale by Falaavia Matavesi about the Prince of Boumaa and the Princess of Waini'eli had to be included. One of Suliano's village announcements. And, for something completely different Siriloo Saabai's Christianity-tinged story of the war with Tonga and the cession of Fiji to Britain.

We called on Paul Geraghty, of course, and he was able to explain all sorts of things—linguistic, social and political—that had been puzzling us. I passed on to Paul a Monday edition of the London *Times* that I'd finished with, since I knew of his interest in soccer and it contained accounts of Saturday matches from three weeks before. "I don't admire the politics of your paper," he said, "but then I don't suppose they offered any choice."

I worked systematically through all the texts. There was one notebook for all those tiny modifiers to a verb, a page for each and all examples of it entered. I collated together the instances of each grammatical relator, things like "whether," "in order to," "or." There's one very frequent conjunction, *ia*, which means "well, then, but," of which I had about sixty examples. *Ia* had been given very short shrift in all previous grammars—generally just a couple of lines and one example. Because of that it was the first thing I looked at in detail, writing up an eight-page account of its meaning and functions. (This was précised down to two and a half printed pages in the final grammar.)

Grammarians sometimes assume that every other language has the same construction types as English. But each part of the grammar of a language must be justified on internal criteria within that language. Take relative clauses, for instance. Fijian has no relative pronouns parallel to English "who," "that," "which." Could it be said to have relative clauses? Perhaps constructions which have sometimes been translated by relative clauses (things like "You look at the cross which I am holding") are really just the coordination of two main clauses ("You look at the cross. I am holding it").

To investigate the topic I went through the texts and gathered every example of putative relative clauses. There are a number of subtle criteria which suggest that it *is* valid to say Fijian has relative clauses. A main one is meaning. One sentence from Elia Waqa's story of the olden days might be translated "There was little of our ancestors' food which was boiled." If this consisted just of two apposed main clauses they would have to be translated "There was little of our ancestors' food. It was boiled"; that is, they had only a little food and it was all boiled. But in fact he was saying that they had lots of food only a small portion of which was boiled (because of the scarcity of cooking pots at the time). To get the intended meaning, it must include a relative clause "which was boiled," qualifying "food."

Then there were things to buy for going back. The poshest type isulu Fijian men wear is a tailored garment with a pocket and a belt—rather like a tailored ladies' skirt in our culture. Sepo had lent me an old one for Sunday church, but it was rather small and needed pulling down all the time.

8. A New House and a New Baby

"You can have one made in Suva," he suggested. This struck me as quite a good idea. "Or get three or four," he went on with typical Fijian abandon. "Wear them for lecturing in Canberra. People will see you and exclaim: 'Ah! Here is a Fijian man.'" I didn't like to tell Sepo that if I lectured in a tailored skirt at Canberra people would certainly exclaim, but that wouldn't be what they'd say!

In the end I didn't buy any, simply because the shopping list Sepo and Bogi had supplied for the family's needs was so extensive and costly. Qito had handed Koleta five rolls of film to get developed at twenty dollars a go! We had three done. Then there was a dress and panties for Mariana, shorts and shirt for Elia and so on, for half-a-dozen more of Koleta's siblings. Sepo asked for a garden spade and a three-pronged fork. I got the spade all right but the only three-pronged forks were for haymaking. I wasn't sure if that's what he meant. Anyway, we'd already spent over four hundred dollars on solicited presents, so I decided a spade should suffice.

* * *

On Friday, April 26, we caught the plane back to Matei. (No more *Princess Ashika*, thank you.) The taxi stopped at the single Matei store and we bought the usual rice, flour, sugar, oil, salt, curry powder, tea, soap and so forth.

Sepo saw us arrive and waived the taxi around to the far side of his house. Our bags were taken into his house. Why couldn't we go directly to our own house? Well, it had been like this back in January. There was the timber frame of a new structure, just back of Sepo's place. "Oh," I remarked, "building a new kitchen, Uncle?" The old one was a real disgrace and he'd often spoken of the need for a new kitchen.

"No," Sepo replied, "that is to be your new house. I am building it tall, Roopate, so that you will not bang your head."

Then it came out. Our old house had originally belonged to Paulo Ni Wai. He'd left the village and sold it to Sepo. Since the only material that hadn't come from the forest was the roofing iron, that was what Sepo had paid for. Seventy dollars. (Which he'd borrowed from Jim Henning, the white man who owned a plantation nearby and was married to his sister.)

Then Paulo Ni Wai returned in mid–March and wanted his house back. Offered to refund the money. There had been fierce arguments and a series of meetings, of which we'd been kept completely in the dark. It had been incorporated into the on-going feud between Mataqalis (Paulo Ni Wai being a member of the other one, Waiso'i). Eventually Sepo had been forced to capitulate but as part of the compromise it had been agreed

After a month's break in Suva, it was good to return to Waitabu, seen here from the high hill to the east.

that they wouldn't move in until we'd left for Suva. That had been why Paulo wanted the house blessed by Father Hendricks and why Bogi had looked so worried when Koleta bid such an affectionate adieu to our erstwhile abode.

We'd live with them until the house was finished, Sepo said. The frame and roof were done. All that was needed was to build up the foundation and then add walls and doors. Just a few more days.

That was just great! I had nine weeks left, in which to finish off a grammar, living in a one-room house with eight other people. And as for Sepo's few days! I'd seen how Fijians went about things. One day this week, maybe a day next week and then a third day a week or two later. Time just doesn't matter to them. It did to me—I had to be back in Canberra for the semester that began in July.

Well there was nothing we could do about it. Our table was in Sepo's house piled with washing and lamps. First of all we sat on the floor and drank a cup of tea. Tui Nasau came in to say hello—it was nice to see the dear old chief again. We got out the presents and everyone seemed pleased. "No fork," said Sepo, "oh well, it's a nice spade." We had bought

8. A New House and a New Baby

a torch for Tui Nasau and he fiddled and fiddled around with it, eventually asking why the bottom didn't unscrew. How could one replace the batteries? We showed him how they went in at the top, in this model, and he happily slipped them in and out, getting the hang of it.

Qito was feeling sick. She was propped up on a bevy of pillows on the floor, looking flushed. But she did seem to appreciate the dress we'd bought her.

Then it was time for lunch. Back to that long grace and the elaborate thank you and ask-to-be-excused at the end. You two rest after the journey, Sepo advised, and then do a little work.

Rest? Work! Qito had the radio on loud. Vilimaina was crying. Bogi and a couple of daughters clattered pans as they washed up. Our table was piled with junk. Sepo wasn't available, he'd gone off somewhere with the village wheelbarrow. Work?

Koleta slipped off to talk to the women and fill out a few questionnaires. I put on my oldest shirt and shorts and went in search of Sepo. He was digging out earth from the hillside near Main Road Pipe. "No, no, Roopate," he said. "It is my responsibility to build a new home for you. Please return home and get on with your language study."

Disappointed as we were, it was impossible not to have the most enormous gratitude and admiration for Sepo. He'd tried to keep our old house and, when that battle was lost, Sepo had built the frame of a new one all by himself. A couple of dozen massive logs for the verticals and horizontals of the frame. The new house was nine feet tall, so I wouldn't bump my head. Sepo had gone into the forest with axe and knife, chopped, trimmed and carried them home. Dug deep holes for each upright. Tied all the joints together with a native twine he got from the forest. Put on corrugated iron for the roof, on a gentle slope from front to back. Placed two layers of stones six inches high, around the outside to inclose the foundation. And fetched umpteen barrows of earth to almost complete the foundation. He'd done all this while we were in Suva, sleeping in beds, eating jelly and visiting the cinema.

"Some people must have helped you, Uncle, others from the Ito'ato'a?" He shook his head. "Or Maarawa, your own son?" "No, Roopate, I do it all on my own. Now, we need about twenty more barrows of soil for the foundation, then sand to go on top. For the walls we shall require many reeds—some of the cauravou will go into the forest and cut them for us."

I insisted on helping. It would be impossible to do much work until we again had a house of our own so the only sensible plan was to build the house during all daylight hours. Sepo dug earth from the hillside, threw it into the barrow. I then trundled this across to the house-to-be and dumped it onto the foundation.

Pio the halfwit was ecstatic to see us back. He stood around as Sepo and I filled the barrow, grunting and jumping with excitement. I started to heave it off but Pio pushed in. "Let him help," Sepo advised, "he has little brain but plenty of strength." So I did. Pio loved being allowed to push that wheelbarrow. He set off at a great pace with me running after. The only thing was, he went in the wrong direction—heading for his own house instead of toward ours. I ran in front of his path, waving hands and legs and yelling "*Ele, ele!*"—which means "Stop! Stop!"—until he did. Then I started him off again more slowly, along the right path.

This was a source of great amusement to the whole village. Bogi had tears in her eyes as she recalled it weeks later. Anyway, Pio certainly did help. He was so eager he'd try and take off with the barrow, from where Sepo was loosening more earth, when it was only half full. (Actually he wasn't so totally stupid; it was a lot easier to push it like that.) I'd gently disengage his hands and say "Wait!"

We almost finished the foundation that afternoon. Sepo and I spread out the earth and built more stones around the perimeter of the house. "Six more wheelbarrow loads I think, Roopate. But I will do it by myself." "No, Uncle," I said, "I will help you. It will be good for me to learn how to build a Fijian house. When do you think it will be completed, so we can move in?" Sepo considered the question. "Perhaps on Wednesday or Thursday," he suggested.

People in the village seemed happier than before. Inoke explained why. Tui Nasau had called a grand meeting at which every person was encouraged to pour out their grievances, all those imagined slights that had been festering within. Some went back generations, to when a father or grandfather had been owed a favor and it was never repaid. Most were more recent. There were hot denials and some fiery exchanges, Inoke said. But just talking about imagined wrongs had somehow washed them away. The feud was over. Everyone went to church in everyone else's house.

Sepo asked Qito to come to the eating mat for supper but she was too sick. Not too sick to eat heartily though, from a sprawling position. Then there was nothing to do but sit around and chat until it was time for bed.

Sepo's house actually did have two beds, behind the curtain in the private part of the house. Both were gifts from Peteroo. There was one single bed with a mattress and on this sick Qito slept. We had a double bed that lacked any mattress. We just lay on a mat on boards, just as the

8. A New House and a New Baby

other members of the family did, but on the floor. It was rather less comfortable than the springy coconut fronds under the floor mats of our old house.

Koleta has the happy knack of just going out, like a light, as soon as her head hits pillow. I don't. For the next few hours I'd doze and wake, doze and wake. Everyone seemed to be asleep but then a child would start whispering to Bogi. Another joined in. There'd be silence for a while and then the same thing again. Sepo crept in after a brief couple of hours around the yaqona bowl. He tried to be quiet but the hinges squeaked and then there was an extensive whisper between him and Bogi. Qito seemed to moan. Silence. Another child woke and attracted its mother's attention. The night seemed already to have lasted for hundreds of hours. Then I did fall into a deep sleep.

"*Koleta, e bu'ete o Qito.*"

Who was that talking? Oh it was real. We were in Sepo's house. Bogi leaning over the bed, very agitated, trying to wake Koleta. She was saying something about Qito. What is *bu'ete*? Oh my goodness, *bu'ete* means "pregnant." What was Bogi saying? The baby was coming … now…

Qito had wakened her mother at 2 a.m. and confessed she was in fact pregnant. The whole village had known this months before. But Qito denied it and Sepo and Bogi believed her. They thought she simply had a stomach upset. But now the birth contractions had started.

Sepo didn't believe it. Everyone got dressed. Sepo wakened Suliano, asked if he could use the village phone, which was in his house, to call a taxi from Waibula. (There are no ambulances in Taveuni.) The Indian at the other end said there'd be a surcharge for it being the middle of the night.

Other households woke up. Bogi and Nana Maa and other women fussed around Qito, who had got from her bed to the floor. We waited. The taxi should not take more than half-an-hour. Still Sepo didn't believe it. Three o'clock came. Quarter past three. Another phone call. It wasn't clear what had happened; maybe the taxi driver had just gone back to sleep.

Eventually he did arrive, around four. Pillows were arranged in the back of the van. It took four of us to lift Qito into the taxi. "Oh, Roopate!" she gasped in flirtatious joy as I took hold of one thigh (it was just like the attention I'd had from Qito during our first two weeks).

Bogi, Sepo and Koleta also climbed into the back of the taxi. First they went to 'Orovou for Kalisita, the district nurse, in case the baby chose to be born along the bumpy road to Waiyevo. Kalisita, all by herself, looked after the health needs of about two thousand people in eight villages—the whole of Boumaa and Waini'eli (there was no doctor on our side of the island). She was a marvelous, well-organized person, with tons of common sense.

Sepo still didn't believe that Qito was pregnant; he just couldn't accept the fact. Kalisita had to speak quite harshly to him and to Bogi, saying they must have known Qito was pregnant—everyone else in Boumaa did—and that she should have been in the hospital a week ago.

The rest of us grabbed another snatch of sleep before the drums went for church. Poor Qito! And poor Sepo and Bogi! And pity our new house; this was certainly going to upset the completion schedule. No, not if I had anything to do with it. I was busy with spade and shovel before six o'clock. The six final barrow-loads of soil were on the foundation by the time young Filo—left in charge of her brothers and sisters—called that breakfast was ready.

Koleta telephoned from the hospital to say that they'd got there all right and Qito was now under professional care. I caught the ten o'clock bus around to Waiyevo, to find Sepo sitting in the waiting room, looking desperately unhappy. "Roopate," he said, "Qito is pregnant." It had finally percolated. "Yes, Uncle," I replied, "It is good news. The birth of a child is a wonderful thing." I was talking to a staunch member of the Catholic church. But neither that nor his traditional religion were of much concern to Sepo at that point. He thought only of the shame, how people would laugh at him. And of how Qito had broken a central rule of village life—it is forbidden to conceal a pregnancy, partly because there are definite rules about what a pregnant woman may do and who is allowed to associate with her.

Just then Koleta came in with the news: Qito had had a lovely baby girl. "Is it alive?" asked Sepo. "Yes," Koleta told him, "and she's crying and hungry." "Oh!" Sepo relapsed once more into unhappy silence, as if the whole world was against him.

We discovered that we were hungry too. Sepo, Bogi, Koleta and I walked down the hill to Lesuma's, bought bread and some cheese and oranges. It was only a couple of hundred yards back to the hospital but a steep climb and the new grandparents were exhausted, so we took a taxi.

We sat on the hospital lawn to eat. Bogi had scarcely ever had cheese before; it wasn't an accustomed taste. When she went back inside Sepo told us his worries. Now that Qito had a baby she would find it less easy to find a good husband. We knew that Qito was a special favorite of Sepo's and he wanted her to make a good and happy match. Well, it could be

8. A New House and a New Baby

adopted. What? Sepo had scarcely heard this word, and we had to explain. He said the idea had possibilities.

There were just two adoption agencies listed in the phone book, both from the Suva area. Lunchtime on Saturday isn't the best time to make a business call but I did talk to a couple of helpful people. Adoption is almost unknown in Fiji—someone from the extended family will generally take over any baby. But it was possible; I scribbled down the procedure and told Sepo.

Qito wasn't terribly well at all. During the last weeks, she'd gone off into the bush to try to end her condition. The result was a serious infection, which they were treating. It was possible that she might have to have a leg amputated but the doctor hoped not. The baby had been popped into a humidicrib, which wasn't a very good sign either. But it did look beautiful.

Koleta and I caught the four o'clock bus back to Waitabu. Sepo and Bogi would sleep at the house of a relative who lived nearby. They wanted to stay close to Qito.

* * *

The next day was Sunday when it is forbidden to do any work. We needed to get our breath back. Sepo arrived in mid-afternoon. He'd done a lot of thinking and come to terms with the situation. Thanks for finding out about adoption he said, but he and Bogi had decided they would bring up the baby themselves, as if it were their child.

There was little friendship or sympathy from other members of the village toward Sepo's family. Qito had behaved in an unforgivable way. Not so much getting pregnant as trying to conceal it. No prayers were said for her in church. No one even inquired how she and the baby were. Sepo had to go into the chief's house and present him with a tabua in a solemn ceremony of repentance for his daughter's sins. After that other members of the Ito'ato'a were cautiously communicative, but as far as the rest of the village was concerned we might not have existed.

On Monday Sepo went back to the hospital. Our new house stood there, neglected. What had he said? That there should be a layer of sand over the earthen foundation? I could certainly do that.

Pio—of course—came along as well, lolloping around in glee as I took wheelbarrow down to beach. He pushed a couple of loads back, getting up speed and taking an arbitrary direction so that again I had to run and shout to get him to stop. Sand weighs more than earth and I could only fill the barrow part way. The third load was at first too heavy and Pio couldn't manage it. I took a bit out but he wouldn't try again, wasn't interested. I fetched twenty or thirty barrows of sand that morning and covered the whole foundation.

Now to do just a little linguistic work (so that I didn't forget what we'd come for). There is a fascinating set of verbs in Fijian that include *ti'o*, "stay, reside," *tuu*, "stand," *to'a*, "squat," and a couple more. They can be used as a main verb or they can be auxiliaries, following another verb. They then have a special meaning—*ti'o* seemed to be something like "do it for a period of time," *tuu*, "done permanently," and *to'a*, "done unsatisfactorily." I was trying to investigate this topic systematically by checking to see whether *ti'o*, *to'a*, and *tuu* could be used with each of a representative sample of thirty verbs and adjectives, and what the meanings were.

This bit of research had been started before we went to Suva and now I'd like to continue it. But with whom? Inoke and some friends had gone to visit another village; no one knew how many days he'd be away. Goodness knows when Sepo would have time for linguistic work. The only course was to expand my range of consultants so I called on Pelasio.

A front door isn't closed during the day in a Fijian village so a visitor can't knock on it. What they must do is hover around outside until seen and invited in (no substantial conversation should be conducted across a doorway). "Come in, Roopate," Pelasio invited. I entered and sat cross-legged: "I was wondering whether I could ask a few questions about language, if you are—" I used the adjective *galala*, which means "free, unoccupied." Pelasio smiled: "*Au galala tuu.*" "I'm always free," he'd told me. Since his stroke Pelasio had been unable to garden and just sat in the house all day. The nice thing was that he'd already given me an example of what I'd called to inquire about, the auxiliary *tuu* (following adjective *galala*) meaning "permanently." Pelasio was very helpful that morning (but still didn't quite compare with either of my master consultants, Sepo and Inoke).

There'd been changes while we were away. This included a new village secretary. And guess who had been elected? None other than Show-off Person. It was not that the villagers respected that man—but they thought it was about time he pulled his weight and (who knows) the responsibility might bring out the best in him.

And it seemed to be working, at least as far as we were concerned. Tuesday was the day for "village work" and six youths were despatched to bring back gasau reeds for the walls of our house. An hour and a half later they returned each with a bundle containing sixty or seventy reeds, nine or ten feet long (and with cross section slightly bigger than a lead pencil). Then back for another bundle.

8. A New House and a New Baby

Sepo built the frame for our new house and I helped with earth and sand for the foundations. On Tuesday, youths of the Ito'ato'a fetched bundles of gasau reeds for the walls.

This made me very happy indeed. "We can start putting the walls up this afternoon, Uncle?" Sepo looked askance. "No, Roopate. We will start early tomorrow." The message I received was that one task was quite enough for a single day. "How long will it take?" "Oh just a few days. You and Koleta should be living in the new house by the weekend. Or sometime next week."

Koleta had gone off that day to visit Qito in the hospital. I decided to take the afternoon bus to Qeleni and do some linguistic work with a man I'd met briefly in February, Ranato Bulavakarua. He was the father of a lady in Waitabu called Teresia (who used to wear a T-shirt saying LOVE THY NEIGHBOR BUT DON'T GET CAUGHT, except that I'm sure she had no idea what it meant).

Waiting at the main road for the bus I saw Sepo scrabbling in a hedgerow. "What *are* you doing, Uncle?" "I am just getting this barbed wire, Roopate." He emerged holding a rusty tangle, trying to roll it up neatly. "It belongs to us and I am getting it back, it may be of use in house building tomorrow." Everything seemed to be getting curiouser and curiouser, as Alice remarked. Well, it was an unfamiliar culture.

Renato had been to a Catholic seminary in his youth. For seven whole years, but then he failed the course. "It was not the will of the Lord that I should be a priest," he concluded. He had been taught Greek grammar and mentioned tenses and cases, prepositions and particles—in both Greek and Fijian. I'd thought this might be helpful but in fact it wasn't. Renato spoke of grammatical categories that are appropriate for Greek but not for Fijian (things like present tense and locative case); he'd find something in Fijian that had a specious similarity. My questions about *ti'o*, *tuu* and *to'a* with various verbs were translated into Greek-style terminology, which just confused things. But a number of young men gathered around, interested in my line of questioning (perhaps partly the novelty of it), and their responses were rewarding.

The bus—on which Koleta should be—wasn't due for a while so I walked to Waibula. Guess what one of the shops there had? Ice cream! Little chocolate covered frozen rectangles. Well, they weren't rectangles any more. There had plainly been a certain amount of thawing and refreezing so that the block now had several crooked angles. Fijian-packaged ice cream tastes pretty poor, but that didn't matter. It was the triumph of actually being able to buy an ice cream at Waibula. (They never stocked it again. When I inquired, the Indian shop keeper just shrugged.)

The next morning, we were to start building the walls. At six-thirty immediately after church? "No, Roopate, we will start after breakfast," Sepo replied. "Mika and Eroni, Nana Mau's sons, have promised to assist and it will soon be finished."

Sepo did have a pre-breakfast task, though. He tied a rusty length of barbed wire—which had been retrieved from the hedgerow—between two trees. Sepo took one end and I was sent to the other. We were to remove the barbs, by knocking them to either end where they could be slid off.

"What are you doing?" Koleta asked, in amazement. "Getting the barbs off," I explained, "then we'll have clean, strong wire for reinforcing the walls." Sepo hadn't said this but I'd inferred it (there had to be some reason for the task). "But we bought six rolls of wire from the store," Koleta said. "Yes, I know, but this is stronger wire," I told her. Which it was.

The barbs were rusted on. Each one had to be hit with the back-edge of the blade of a cane knife, and it would take twenty hard hits before it budged. Then the barbs were gradually knocked along the wire to the end, tied to a tree. In an hour Sepo cleared perhaps three yards and I'd done a yard and a half. There was an awful lot left to do and my hands began to ache.

Perhaps there could be another approach. I walked down the wire.

8. A New House and a New Baby

On Wednesday, wall-erecting began, but for one day only.

"Uncle?" "Yes, Roopate?" He didn't stop banging as we spoke. "Uncle, you don't have a pair of pliers, do you?" "No, Roopate. This is the only way to do it."

The following year Koleta and I returned to Waitabu and of course took presents for all the family. A nice shiny new pair of pliers (from K-Mart) for Sepo. He examined them. And then opened a drawer and took out an old pair of pliers—that he'd had all the time—to compare!

After breakfast the house-building did commence. Only we never used that unbarbed wire. It wasn't even mentioned. In fact it just stayed, strung up between the trees, half the barbs rusted in place and half pushed to one end, for the next two weeks. Then, one morning when no one else was around I took it down, coiled it up, and put it under Sepo's house, next to another roll of fully barbed wire.

All we needed for wall-erection was the gasau reeds, a few impromptu bobbins and thin fencing wire. About six rolls, Sepo had estimated a couple of days before. The village store had exactly six rolls in stock, so that would be just right. What if one needed more than six? Perhaps Koleta should buy a couple of rolls from Morisi in Somosomo; we could use four from our store and there'd be two left in case Sepo had underestimated. No. He firmly rejected this suggestion. Koleta must *not* buy more from Morisi (it was given as an order). What was in the store would be enough.

The first step was to tie horizontals into place along a given section of wall. Three gasau were wired in from one side of the front door to a corner post of the house frame, and repeated about every foot-and-a-half up and down so that there were six horizontals up the height of the wall.

Then the wall itself was erected, a thin column of gasau. They were put in three or four at a time. A five-inch wooden bobbin on which some wire had been wound was threaded around to fasten each batch to the horizontal. We had two teams, Sepo and Mika, Eroni and Inoke (all men from the Vunivesi Ito'ato'a) one working eastward and the other westward from the front door. Tui Nasau sat on the foundation between, whittling out wooden bobbins and winding an appropriate quantity of wire onto each one. I was given a sharp cane knife and told to cut the raw gasau down to an appropriate size.

The work fairly whizzed along. Just before lunch the front wall was finished and each team turned around their corner, quite a tricky task. I was fearful that the work might not recommence after the midday meal (Fijians being highly adept at the siesta) but it did. There weren't four people working all the time mind you. They did tend to come and go. But I was ready to make up the second member of a team when necessary.

Koleta returned from 'Orovou with a big smile on her face, seeing that almost half of the walls had been finished in one day. We might well move in by the weekend.

Bogi had returned from Waiyevo with the news that Qito and her baby were both doing as well as could be expected. Maarawa and his wife Emelia now went to stay in Waiyevo; they'd visit Qito several times each day and fetch anything she might need. Filo and Elena were to visit her the next day, returning on the evening bus. Three-year-old Vilimaina wanted to go as well. Her parents said "no." So Vilimaina cried. She cried non-stop for three whole hours. If there were any kind of marathon crying competition—like people who dance or play the piano all night—that child would have won it. Anyway, roll on the completion of our house.

Life can't be all work, especially not in a Fijian village. The commencement of the walls of a new house must be celebrated with a christening party. After supper mats were placed on the sandy floor of our half-finished residence, a yaqona bowl brought in and a dozen men turned up to drink its health, including members of the Waiso'i Mataqali who had wandered past and made comments during the day but never offered to help. Show-off Person came, and Suliano and of course Sepo, Eroni, Mika

8. A New House and a New Baby

and Inoke. Koleta and I popped in for an hour and partook of three or four quarter-filled cups. I found that that much yaqona to be pleasant, similar to drinking a small bottle of beer in Australia. What I don't care for is twenty or thirty full-sized cups, which would be a regular evening's consumption. (You'd often hear men vomiting into the grass on their way home after midnight.)

There'd been about six hours of house-building that day and it was followed by seven hours of yaqona celebration. I took a photo of how the house looked at the start of the second day. And for how many more days? Everyone seemed quite hungover and it was clear that they had no intention of devoting another day to our house for quite a while yet. Vilimaina was just starting her daily wail…

I knew how to do it. And Koleta was perfectly capable of helping, although of course it was absolutely unheard of for a woman to join in such work. Bugger their taboos—we wanted our house that week, not next month. We made a good team and had completed another foot or so by breakfast.

Then Tui Nasau—perhaps feeling that his entire village was being shamed by our industry—came to join in. Sepo had been wandering around sheepishly, doing various jobs. Eventually he joined in too. We had two teams, Sepo and Koleta, Tui Nasau and me. So it progressed, much more slowly than on the previous day but still quite steadily.

There wouldn't be quite enough gasau. Sepo said he'd get Mika and Eroni to fetch two or three more bundles the next morning. At four o'clock Sepo announced that work must stop for the day. But there was still quite a pile of gasau. They weren't long enough, Sepo said. Some of them were. I could see that and so could he. But Sepo had made up his mind. There'd been enough work for that day. Couldn't we just finish a corner that was only a few inches away? Corners were tricky and I would appreciate Sepo's help (goodness knows where he might be next morning). "No, Roopate. We do not have the materials. It will be a simple matter to do that tomorrow."

Another four bundles of gasau did arrive, before breakfast (there would have been well over a thousand gasau used altogether). We did the corner. But would there be enough wire? The question was put at nine-thirty, before the morning bus went. I did an estimate and was convinced we'd be short. Sepo looked into the matter. "No we have enough, Roopate." "But Uncle, Koleta could catch the bus to Waibula…" "Roopate," he ordered me with restrained patience. "I have been building houses all my life. The wire we have left will be sufficient."

We worked on for an hour, just one team, Sepo and me. Then at about ten-thirty he announced, in a spirit of someone making a vital and unanticipated discovery. "Roopate!" I waited. "I do not believe that we will have enough wire. You must accept my apologies. We have been using it faster than expected."

The bus had gone and wouldn't be back for four hours. So Koleta set off to walk to Waibula—two and a half miles each way. Sepo disappeared to other tasks. I struggled along with the back wall all by myself—it's possible to work alone, but quite slow.

In the old days, they'd used twine from the forest to bind gasau into a house wall. Nowadays everyone employed fencing wire which was much stronger, and quite cheap (about a dollar a roll). You were supposed to twist and tie it just with the finger. On my return to Canberra I bought a house and there were a number of jobs to do which involved wire. Of course, I used pliers. Then one day I tried to do the same task just with fingers, Waitabu style—it was slower, less efficient and hard on the fingers. Sepo had a pair of pliers—as we discovered the next year—but chose not to use them.

Koleta was back in less than two hours. She'd got a lift most of the way to Waibula with an empty taxi (who she'd smiled at) and a lift some of the way back with the district agricultural officer. This was lucky—you could walk along the road on our side of Taveuni and not see any vehicle for a period of several hours.

We carried on building that back wall. Men and youths would stop by to watch but never offer to help. Then another Mika, Teresia's husband from the house at the back, did take pity on us. His father-in-law—old Renatu, the Greek scholar from Qeleni—was down on a visit and they showed us how to tie the last gasau into place.

So, there it was, all done, midway through Friday afternoon. The walls were finished—but we still needed doors. Packing case sides, as in our old house? Sorry! Phone calls to three possible sources on Taveuni provided the same reply—none of the stores had any old packing cases at present. Oh dear!

Then Koleta had an idea. She'd once spent a year in Japan. Why not collect the bits that had been chopped off the ends of the gasau and string them together to make a hanging door, the gasau parallel with the ground? The whole assembly could just be suspended from a couple of nails at the top of a doorway. Sepo wasn't too sure about it, but had no better suggestion to offer.

This would have been hopeless in a cyclone. If there was even a light

8. A New House and a New Baby   175

So I had to finish off the job myself, with only odd bits of help, and it was finished late on Friday.

breeze off the sea at night the door would blow in, so we put a chair against it. Neither would the roof have lasted long in a cyclone. The horizontals under each end of the corrugated iron were far too short—there was nothing sticking out to tie to the upper horizontals, holding down the iron roof. But it would do for the mild winter months. We'd be gone long before another "murdering wind" could invade this corner of paradise.

Now we'd need coconut fronds for the floor, to go under mats. "Tomorrow..." "No we will get them today, Uncle." Koleta and I took a knife, and a couple of her younger sisters and set off into the forest. There were heaps of fallen fronds: we cut off stalks and dragged vast armfuls home. The only difficulty was they were wet, and would have to be fully dry before being placed on our floor.

By this time the whole village was taking an interest in the manner in which we were cramming several month's normal activity into a few days. Paulo Ni Wai's wife had a suggestion: put them in the copra drier overnight. Great idea! This was a building on the edge of the village used to smoke coconut kernels before they were sold. Someone who had a measure of authority over the drier said it would be all right.

No one had ever done this before. (No one had ever been in our sort of hurry.) Nana Maa came over to say it was a terrible idea. We must on no account put our fronds in the drier. Just wait until tomorrow, the sun will soon do the job. Just wait! Don't use the drier! As Nana Maa was saying this, and Koleta was thanking her for such useful advice, I was gathering up handfuls and lugging them off to the drier. "No, we won't do it Nana Maa," said Koleta, as we did.

The drier didn't quite banish all moisture but—Nana Maa was right— the morning sun soon did. Bogi got together mats from our old house. Moving in was just a few hours away.

Then Sepo and Renato started walking around, inspecting the design. Was the roof quite correct? Probably not. Move that support—they pointed up—a few feet further back. Put another one in just before it. Yes, yes, that would make it different, perhaps even better. Of course, the roof would have to come off first. Shouldn't take more than a few days.

Finally on the Saturday we were able to move in and I could sit at my table, working on linguistics (rather than house-building).

We felt a sense of panic. "No Uncle, this is a good house. It is entirely sufficient for us." Sepo and Renato looked doubtfully at us, at each other, at the roof again. "Our house is finished, Uncle, it is entirely completed," my voice rose with nervous excitement. "And we are moving in this afternoon," Koleta concluded, in terms of the utmost finality.

Three minutes later we were arranging dried coconut fronds over the sandy floor. Sepo and Bogi brought in the mats. Our table. Two of Sepo's chairs. The large carton that we'd left behind, with sheets, pillows, buckets. Bogi put the curtain up in front of the sleeping area. Then the mosquito nets (holes and all).

8. A New House and a New Baby 177

Eight days after returning from Suva we were able to move in and start work properly. Eight weeks left, to complete a grammar.

* * *

The new house was in several ways a good thing. The efforts we'd put into building it vastly affected our standing in the community. For the first three months we'd devoted long hours to language learning and study. Except that sitting at a table writing in a book or going around the village asking questions isn't what a Fijian calls work. Then, for one week we devoted long hours to an activity they could appreciate—building up a foundation, erecting walls, devising a new sort of door, collecting coconut fronds for underlay. We didn't work for a day and then take two or three days off, we worked one day, then the next, then the next, only ceasing when the house was finished. Now we were back at our books—eight or ten or twelve hours a day on them. That must be another sort of work—for we certainly seemed to be workers. Luckily, they didn't take the train of thought too far. Work is forbidden on the Sabbath. But no one minded us doing language study, and helping with it, on a Sunday. It wasn't "work" to that extent!

The new house had a much better location; on the other side of Sepo's. No longer could Nau peer right in, or Tui Nasau's coughing echo through the night. Looking through the side door, where I habitually sat, there was just Nana Maa's kitchen and the forest behind. The kitchen had been built by her sons a couple of months before and had a traditional-style high thatched roof. Nana Maa would sit outside, peeling cassava or taro, chatting to other ladies as they came back from a stream that wound around in the forest behind.

The house itself was better. Taller, so that I never bumped my head. And the walls came down to the foundations so that toads could only enter over a door step. They were controllable. We had a healthy, toad-free dwelling. Sepo put a spare piece of corrugated iron at the bottom of the outside back wall, to deflect water coming off the roof and keep the foundation dry. That's where the toads lived. Pull it back and you'd see a dozen hunched forms, big round eyes staring up. One day I tried to take a picture of this menagerie. It took a while to get most of them looking at the camera. I'd tried to pick a time when there was no one around. But there was always someone lurking at Waitabu. They stood watching, at a respectful distance, thinking I was quite mad.

Attitudes to Qito were softening just a little. Nana Maa and a couple of other ladies from the Ito'ato'a brought in a gift of oil (made from a plant

Top: Looking through the side door there was a restful view of Nana Maa's kitchen and the forest behind. *Bottom:* Toads couldn't get inside the new house but if you pulled away the piece of corrugated iron against the back wall—there they were.

8. A New House and a New Baby

in the forest) and baby powder and soap, the traditional gift for a new born child. No matter that it was a week late. Bogi sat, very appreciative, during the solemn presentation.

Another tourist came to stay, someone Sepo had met at Waiyevo that week and invited over. Sepo never could resist a foreigner—I suppose we shouldn't have complained about this!—but it did seem an inappropriate time. A bronzed Australian with knapsack and surfboard, he arrived on the last day we spent in Sepo's house. The idea was that he'd leave on the six-thirty bus the next day, to go across to the island of Qamea. Sepo had said: come and stay with us again on your return—stay a few days or a week. And the tourist had promised to do just that.

I awoke the next morning at six. All of Sepo's family were sitting in silence, watching the soft bed with a mattress on which the stranger lay. "Have you woken him?" I asked. Heads were shaken. They hadn't liked to. I had no such qualms. "Hey, come on, didn't you want to get on the early bus." He shot upright and hurriedly dressed. I provided an escort to the edge of the village, making sure backpack wasn't hoisted too soon, and then I took him up to the main road. Qito was due back in a couple of days. I knew Sepo's family couldn't really cope with an awkward stranger in the house just then. So I delivered a parting message: do not, on any account, come back here.

As soon as we moved in, the drain of *'ere'ere* recommenced. Only small things, but they soon accumulated. On the first night in our new house Bogi begged a headache pill for Mariana, followed by Sepo who requested three dollars, the contribution levied on each household for a pig to be consumed at the funeral feast over a dead elder in some other village.

Sepo's two daughters just older than Qito—Rosalia and Seini—were married to soldiers, who had just gone off to Lebanon with Peteroo. They'd both come to stay and Rosalia had in her luggage a video player together with a benzene-powered generator (there was as yet no TV in Fiji, but lots and lots of videos). Sunday began with an *'ere'ere* from Rosalia and Seini for the bus fare to Qeleni, where Rosalia's mother-in-law lived. Then Sepo brought in his toothbrush to *'ere'ere* a smear of toothpaste for it (we'd brought him back a whole tube from the recent shopping expedition). Filo cut her foot and came to *'ere'ere* two sticking plasters.

On Monday Inoke came to do some work with us. We'd finally been able to unpack and presented a pair of long trousers, his present from Suva. "Oh," Inoke said, "how much did they cost?" That was a normal Fijian response (for a people who say they don't value money, there's an awful lot of interest in it). We told Inoke that the trousers were a present and in Australia it was considered very rude to ask what a present cost. Inoke listened politely, refrained from pointing out the obvious, that we weren't in Australia now. "How much did they cost?" he repeated the question. Twelve dollars.

That evening Sepo organized a film show with Rosalia's video, in front of the new store. Admission would be twenty cents, ten for children. And he came to *'ere'ere* our benzene light. We tried a mild protest—wasn't Sepo's benzene light working. Yes it was but he'd need two. Oh—and Sepo advised us not to come. We had valuable belongings and if our new house was left unattended something might get stolen.

What a wonderful evening! We'd been told not to attend the picture show (not that the movie had appealed to us anyway) and couldn't work, since we had no light. Just a minute—you don't need lights at a picture show. The main necessity is dark. After a while I went along (Koleta was already asleep) and found both benzene lights hanging on posts, extinguished. Sepo let me take ours back—and I was able to pour over the diverse usage of the grammatical relator *me* "should" for an hour before bed.

The next morning Bogi came in before breakfast to *'ere'ere* twelve dollars. It was to go and see Qito in hospital; she'd be returning on the late bus and promised faithfully to return the money that evening. Koleta and I pooled our resources—eleven dollars and twenty cents, that was all we had. There were a few more *'ere'ere* that day. Mariana requested a battery, Filo asked for our bar of washing soap and brought it back an hour later. Then she requested the same item again and this time it didn't return. Tui Nasau humbly begged twenty cents but we had to say with regret, that there was not a penny left in the house. Bogi had taken it all.

Sepo popped in after lunch to express his deep gratitude for the eleven dollars and twenty cents we'd let Bogi have. Unfortunately they wouldn't be able to return it that day, but he would repay us without fail on the following Monday.

Now here was a pretty kettle of fish. On the next day, Wednesday, May 8, we'd planned to go to Waiyevo. To collect more money from the bank, visit Qito—and especially to have a quiet gin and tonic and a cheese and tomato sandwich at the Castaway International Hotel, which we felt we deserved after the trauma of the past ten days. But how to get there? From what we'd told Sepo and Tui Nasau all of our money was exhausted. This wasn't in fact quite true—both Koleta and I had a $20 bill hidden away for emergencies. But to resort to this would blow the credibility of everything we'd just said about our finances.

8. A New House and a New Baby

There was one solution. Do as a Fijian would and *'ere'ere* the money from Sepo. Koleta was a little doubtful but I thought it might show we had really assimilated. So I went hesitantly in through Sepo's front door. He was discussing some village matter with Show-off Person. I sat in the humblest position, close to the door. They both looked up. "Uncle," I adopted a quiet and solemn tone, "Uncle, I have the most serious request to make of you. All of our money is currently exhausted. We wish to go to Waiyevo to see Qito. I *'ere'ere* our outward bus fare, which we will repay this evening." Sepo went to the back of the house, took down a jam jar full of money and counted out three dollars, the exact sum needed.

I felt quite proud of that episode, of behaving like a Fijian. But then we did do a slightly un–Fijian thing, and gave him the three dollars back after supper. Several weeks later Sepo offered to repay the eleven dollars and twenty cents but we declined, saying that it was a contribution toward the exceptional expense he'd incurred over the birth of Qito's baby.

The stream of *'ere'ere* continued at an alarming rate. We came back from Somosomo with a pack of twelve boxes of matches, which someone in the family saw. The next day a child came to *'ere'ere* a match, so we gave them a whole box. The following day another *'ere'ere* for another match so we handed over another box. And the same each day. They must have been building up a store of matches against the time when we should leave.

And the *'ere'ere* wasn't confined to close relatives. Litia, the wife of Show-off Person, asked for a torch—to keep, not to borrow. We said we needed it. Well, will you buy me one when next you go shopping, she asked. We said we wouldn't, that we didn't have sufficient money. (If we had acceded to that request, thirty more ladies in the village would have each wanted one.)

Sticking plasters and headache pills were the items in most demand, and those we kept a goodly stock of. One day I was sitting writing when Tui Nasau called. We had a somewhat awkward chat, from which I could tell that he was working up to an *'ere'ere*. Finally it came, a humble request for a *pedola*. This was a new word—and an interesting one. There is no *p* in Standard Fijian so any word with *p* has to belong to the Boumaa dialect. I knew that pill was *vua-ni-'acu*. So *pedola* must be a name for sticking plaster, and I gave him one. No, no, no. Eventually we got it clear and the chief went away with a headache pill.

On Koleta's return I told her of the new word. Oh, this was interesting! What could *pedola* have referred to originally? Its meaning must have been extended to cover "headache pill," a recent introduction into the culture. Koleta went off to consult Nau, her expert on traditional Boumaa words.

And she came back laughing. It was something Tui Nasau had invented, based on the name of the pills, *Panadol*. In Fijian the letter "d" is pronounced *nd*. He'd made out of the English word *panadol* a Fijian word *pedola* (adding a final *a* since every word in Fijian must end in a vowel and changing the first *a* to *e* for no reason at all.)

9

"Oh dear! Roopate is getting ready to go!"

After about two weeks Qito came home with her baby, who was called Paa. The doctor had said that Qito should make a full recovery but for the time being she moved very slowly, on a pair of crutches, and only left Sepo's house for the needs of nature.

Paa was a great little baby. Tui Nasau would bounce her up and down on his lap and sing a traditional Boumaa lullaby, a lilting melody punctuated with *oooh*, *ee-ee-ye*, and *koo-koo-wa*.

The chief seemed very fond of his new great-niece, and he was also a trifle deaf. One day at lunch Sepo said "Grace, Koleta." She began to recite it, just as Tui Nasau chose to amuse Paa with a series of dog imitations. "In the name of God the father, Him the son, ..." The chief let out a high-pitched whine. "Lord please bless this our—." *Yiiiiii* and a series of yodels from over on the left. Tui Nasau was absorbed with the child, completely oblivious to what was happening around the eating mat.

The standard of food had dropped off markedly in May, partly because Bogi and Filo were too busy to go fishing, what with looking after Qito and the baby, washing nappies and so forth. Often we had just plain rice for breakfast. We'd buy cans of fish (imported from Japan) at the store or from Teliva. The Waibula shops often had a big fish or two in their freezer (if it was working). One day we brought back a huge one. "Where is this from," Sepo gasped. "We caught it this afternoon," I replied nonchalantly, "Kilipati-style." All I knew about kilipati fishing was that it involved a number of young men with spears and quick reflexes. Anyway, it brought a laugh.

One day Bogi announced there was to be a special treat for supper, and wouldn't tell us in advance. Finally we saw. Chicken legs! Bits of sinews with minuscule pieces of unappetizing meat that could be chewed off with considerable effort. To Sepo's family, brought up on fish, any sort of meat was a treat. We tried to show a tiny bit of enthusiasm.

We'd been befriended by Mere, the wife of the catechist in Viidawa village. Often, seeing us return from a late afternoon stroll, Mere would come out with one or two ripe paw-paws. At first we handed them over to Bogi since she provided our meals. But after a bit we didn't. I'd smuggle them into our house, wrapped up in a rain jacket, put them in a plastic bag to keep the ants out, and we'd have a couple of slices of paw-paw in the late afternoon.

There was one hidden snag connected with walking barefoot on the beach. Every so often a grain or two of sand would work their way under the edge of a big toe. It would swell, turn red and really hurt. Sepo revealed that everyone got it from time to time. Luckily Koleta had a penicillin-based ointment that halted the infection; we had no wish to lose a toe or two.

The weather was now cooler but scarcely cold. You might need to pull up a blanket in the middle of the night. We had one cold snap, of about three days, when two blankets were needed (Bogi, bless her heart, lent us a second one). But it was a bit chilly doing the washing at six a.m., especially since we got considerably wet in the process. By now everyone knew that I helped, and didn't seem to mind, so we'd go along at any old time.

One morning, on the path to the washing pool, we met a ten-year-old boy with an improvised "machine." It had a long stick and then a small stick nailed on at the end, at right angles. At each end of the smaller stick was half of an empty fish can, as a wheel. There was a nail near the top of the longer pole, on which the handle of a bucket could be hung. It was a device for bringing a bucket of water back from the pipe, without actually having to carry it. "Hey that's good," we remarked, "who invented it?" "I did," the boy told us, with pride. No one had seen anything like this before and it was quickly christened *va'a-qiqi* literally "wheeled thing."

And of course there was still church. Always church. No question about church. We'd met Jim Henning, Sepo's white brother-in-law who had a small plantation just over the hill. I asked about Jim's religion. "He is Anglican," Sepo reported, "but goes to church only very seldom." Later I asked the same question of Jim directly. He replied that he was an atheist, there was no god in it whatsoever. Jim must have told Sepo this, but he just wouldn't accept such a statement. (It was a good job that I hadn't tried to tell the truth about my lack of belief.)

9. "Oh dear! Roopate is getting ready to go!"

There was a new young Fijian priest who now came across from Waiyevo to conduct mass on the last Sunday of each month. He was the son of Iowani, who ran the postal agency in 'Orovou. What amused us was that each called the other "Father," the younger man on filial grounds and the older on religious grounds. Iowani soon made one important change. Instead of following the 7 a.m. mass at Lavena with one at 11 in 'Orovou he changed the second service to two in the afternoon. This left a lot more time to hear confessions. Boumaa now had a priest visit for a full day each month, instead of just half a day.

And, as church moved around the village, it came to our bright new house. There'd be a full congregation just because people were curious to see what it was like inside. So many people, in fact, that Tui Nasau was sitting almost up at the back wall with Suliano. I was positioned just by a side door, next to Sepo and behind Elia Waqa who was wearing a T-shirt in tasteful dark blue with the legend SPEED-E-GAS.

A toad appeared on the doorstep (they seemed somehow to be attracted by church) and I knocked it away. Then, on the mat I saw something much worse. A centipede. How did that get in? It inched past Sepo

A large congregation attended when it was our turn to host church services, to see what the new house looked like. Here it is, empty.

who flicked the insect forward with the corner of his hymn book, toward Suliano. The centipede was about two inches away from a prominent member of the other Mataqali, who was singing away lustily, quite unaware. That was all we needed—for Suliano to be bitten by a centipede, during church at our house. I leaned over and flicked it a couple of feet off, toward the wall. Another toad appeared on the step, to be dispatched outward.

We were in the middle of a solemn religious occasion. All movement had to be covert. My eye never left that centipede; only when the last worshipper left could it be dispatched. Koleta had watched the entire episode from near the front door, with great amusement. We finally collapsed in laughter and relief. Church was never like this in Australia!

* * *

Now established in the new house, we were able to work. Inoke was only available occasionally, going off with some of the other youths to work on a coconut plantation for weeks at a time. But Sepo—enjoying it and at the same time feeling responsible about his critical role in our endeavors—popped in once or twice each day to ask "Have you any questions for me?" Koleta would generally go first, if she had anything outstanding, and then I used up whatever time Sepo had left. I always did have a grammatical point or two in need of elucidation.

Koleta also got assistance from some of the old women, particularly Nau. The funny thing was that if she played a tape at normal volume and asked Nau to help transcribe it, the results were not very good. But turn the volume down low and Nau could hear much better. It came from years of eavesdropping on far-away whispers, we decided; that was what her ears were most attuned to.

My grammatical study was based on examining the structure of the texts we'd recorded in January, February and March. On the basis of these I evolved tentative generalizations and then tried to check them out by a few well-chosen questions; these required a level of intellectual sophistication which only Sepo (and Inoke) could properly supply.

Most of the time Sepo was happy for me to decide on our agenda. But not always. One day he came in with a fifth grade school textbook and insisted on reading out one lesson about whale's teeth—with a few minor adjustments into the Boumaa dialect—for me to record. I had no wish to. But at least it only lasted a few hours, not a whole week like that history of the Ca'audrove Cooperative Association.

An ideal day would go something like this: I'd pick a grammatical

9. "Oh dear! Roopate is getting ready to go!"

Sepo had thought about language all his life and now explained to me, with clear insight, the intricacies of lexical meanings and grammatical patterns.

topic and sift through the examples of it from about six until seven-thirty. Sepo would call in before breakfast and I'd quiz him for half-an-hour, filling in a few obvious gaps in the data. Then during the morning and afternoon I'd study the topic very thoroughly, writing up a draft account. A number of queries would arise. Sepo might pop in again around six and for half-an-hour—until we were called for supper—I'd check out these outstanding queries. An hour after supper would suffice to make revisions in the light of the second session with Sepo. Days like this occurred infrequently—sometimes Sepo wouldn't turn up for several days, and then he might be available for a full two hours one afternoon—but were very satisfying when they did.

There'd be diversions like Nana Maa calling for someone. A Fijian would never just shout once. They'd carry on and on, even when it became apparent that the person had no intention of responding, perhaps couldn't hear. I counted the repetition one morning: Nana Maa called out "Eroni" (for her second son) no less than nine times, with an interval of about a minute between.

For a while, things would be peaceful in the village. And then all hell could break loose. Voices raised in angry vituperation with a series of screams and a single cry of pain. It was two teenage girls, bosom pals. One had been staying over at the other's house and her hostess remarked that the visitor's blanket smelled. That apparently is about the worst insult one Fijian can hurl at another. They fought with words and then fists and finally a piece of wood in which two rusty nails were embedded. We could see how in the olden days Fijians were so feared (and still are today, by the opposing side in a war or a rugby game). Anyway, nurse Kalisita in 'Orovou inserted several stitches and the victim didn't lose the sight of an eye or anything. Not this time.

Va'a-qiqi—that wheeled vehicle to carry a bucket back from the pipe—was catching on. There were now several dozen in the village. Every teenage boy and many girls had one. Little children demanded their own, just as a toy. It was fascinating to watch how the fad spread, way beyond Waitabu. It took a couple of weeks to reach Viidawa then another week or so to catch on there. Toward the end of June we went down to Lavena and the va'a-qiqi craze was just getting into its stride there, a couple of months after it had started in Waitabu (and when it was on the wane in its place of origin).

I'd often read, in books by prehistorians, how some technological innovation would start in a certain place and gradually spread over a wide area. The hafting of axes, for example, or use of iron tools. Here was a miniature example in quick motion, of invention, diffusion and loss.

I'd done quite a bit of work on the song-style of Aboriginal people in Australia and was looking forward to finding out something about Fijian music. That was before we got there. The youths of Waitabu would sing, sometimes all night, but to our ears it had a wishy-washy sound, a sort of dirge, vaguely based on Hawaiian music, accompanied by one or two acoustic guitars (not even Hawaiian-style instruments).

"Ah," Elia Waqa said, "what the cauravou sing nowadays is nothing. We'll have to put on a traditional Fijian Me'e for you." That would have been terrific. The few fragments we did hear sounded really interesting. But they never did get around to it.

At the end of May we took a four-day trip to Labasa, a town of about seven thousand people on the northern side of Vanua Levu. This was to see a bit more of Fiji and to get a break from the village routine (which could get claustrophobic after a while). We took the morning bus to Waiyevo, a great little motor boat (with no videos!) across to Buca Bay and then a minibus along the dirt road to Savusavu and over the mountain to Labasa.

9. "Oh dear! Roopate is getting ready to go!"

It was peaceful in the Great Eastern Hotel and I was able to sort out all my notes on possessives. There are five different ways of marking possession in Fijian depending on whether the "possessor" is a proper name, a pronoun, a human common noun or a non human, and whether the possessed is some inherent part—such as "head," "leaf," "name"—or something else. Sometimes there appear to be two alternative methods and I needed to frame a number of questions for Sepo to try to clarify this.

Court was in session at Labasa just then and the judge—a very solemn-looking white man—was also staying at the Great Eastern. I noticed him ordering just one egg for breakfast but they brought two (at many places eggs come in twos). If that had happened to me I'd probably have eaten both, but not this rather precise judge. He carefully put one egg on a side plate, and ate the other.

Labasa is a sugar-growing center with a large Indian population. We had a tour around the sugar mill, with a very helpful Fijian who was a trainee engineer. And we also lost an umbrella in Labasa.

It's not hard to lose things in Fiji. During the first week a penknife dropped out of a hole in my trouser pocket between our old house and the new store. I mentioned it to a few people thinking that someone was sure to find it, and hand it back. That was what would have happened in an Aboriginal community in Australia, where I never locked my room and nothing was ever taken.

But not in Fiji. Little things would disappear. I bought another folding knife and kept it on a ledge at the top of the house frame almost invisible from the outside. That went. While we were in Suva I'd left behind a rain jacket with a roll of scotch tape in the pocket; the jacket was there on our return but not the tape. Someone borrowed a torch and returned it with apologies that the bulb had gone, then we found that they'd taken the batteries.

It was raining one day when we went to an Indian restaurant in Labasa for a dollar-fifty lunch and I put the umbrella next to me on a bench. Then the weather fined up and I forgot it. Thirty minutes later we did remember and went back to the café. The proprietor said that a regular customer had sat there after us, a Fijian lady called Anna who worked at the Department of Agriculture office nearby. Yes, he had seen her leave with a black umbrella.

So we went across to the Agriculture office, and found Anna. "You were in the restaurant after us—," I began. "I wouldn't take your umbrella," she interrupted, "see I have my own," pointing to a green one put out on the balcony to dry. There wasn't much we could say. But the funny thing was we hadn't mentioned the umbrella—she had. Later we found the umbrella's little canvas bag, in our hotel room, and resisted a temptation to take that around to Anna too.

* * *

We flew back from Labasa to Matei, only to find that disaster had struck once more in Waitabu. A tiny whirlwind swooped down one evening, accompanied by torrential rain. It had been centered on our new house so everything had been removed to Sepo's place and the mats had been put out, to dry in the sun.

Things were back to normal. Except for a few of our belongings. There'd been three packs of cigarettes under the pegs in a plastic bag hanging up in the wall; now there was one. I had a thin carton half-full of typing paper. Someone in Sepo's house had pulled this out to see what it was, put half of it back (doubled over sideways) and kept the rest. These were all minor things but they did annoy me. "Fijians are habitual thieves," I said to Koleta in a mood of disillusionment.

Qito was now taking a bit more interest in the baby but she didn't really seem to be trying to get well. What was the incentive when she could loll on pillows all day while Bogi and Filo worked hard and long doing all the chores? Sepo eventually insisted that Qito should crawl across the floor and sit cross-legged at the eating mat during meals. But she didn't walk outside the house, even on those crutches.

From Labasa we'd brought small gifts. A different colored plastic bangle for each of Qito, Elena and Filo. Within a couple of hours Qito was wearing all three. It was the *'ere'ere* system at work, coupled with a pecking order principle which states that an elder sister can take anything from a younger one.

Sepo had now discovered, from Qito, that the father of the child was a soldier boyfriend she'd had in Suva. And now he too was away in Lebanon.

Sepo's family had a new craze: videos. No longer did they go away to the new store. Video shows were now held in Sepo's house—admission 20 cents for adults and 10 cents for children. Filo came in with an *'ere'ere* for sixty cents, being movie money for six kids. I gave her 58 cents, which was all the loose change I had. But, I ask you, having to pay to see a movie that is being shown in your own house!

Rosalia's husband had left behind a stack of about 23 videos, some—like *Alien*—quite unsuitable for children. Sepo didn't show just one or two movies in an evening. They sometimes went through five, one after another. The benzene-powered generator was outside his side door, right next to our house and it made a terrible row. I gingerly complained and it was moved around to the front door. Even then there was still the din of raucous soundtracks turned up as loud as possible. I finally got to sleep when the movies ended, at four o'clock. (Koleta slept right through every time.) The slight consolation was being able to check that one could include two negators in the sentence: "It was not possible for me not to hear the noise" (that is, "I couldn't help but hear it").

Not only I was tired and unable to work very well. Sepo was exhausted and had no time at all to help me; it was as much as he could do to organize the shop and fit in a little gardening. The day we got back from Labasa was a 4 a.m. finish. The next day, midnight, then the following day, Saturday, another 4 o'clock end. Sundays were blessedly video-free and I got one hour of Sepo's time. Tuesday we again hit midnight and on Wednesday there were four videos—Sepo predicted a one a.m. finish but I'm sure it was much later.

There honestly seemed to me no point in my staying on at Waitabu. I value my sleep and got cranky when it wasn't available from about ten o'clock until the lali drums went for church just before six. My queries were piling up. I'd done draft chapters on four or five topics and been unable to check any of the outstanding points with Sepo.

It was affecting his small children even more. Elia and Mariana only ever went to school on two or three days each week but now when they did they'd fall asleep at the desk. Silipa, Koleta's schoolteacher friend, came across on Wednesday to give Sepo a good telling off. He listened with respect. "We only have four more videos to see," he answered her, "they will be shown tonight and then it is finished!" (What an amazing logic—why not show one a week over the next month?)

A couple of days later I went across before breakfast and found Sepo and Qito on the floor, concentrating, each writing something very carefully in a small book. They were doing Elia's and Mariana's homework (while these two children weren't even nearby) so that they could go to school that day without fear of a return visit from Silipa!

After that things did improve. When Sepo came in one morning I executed a very earnest *'ere'ere* on him: "Uncle, you are invaluable to my work. I have only three weeks left. I *'ere'ere* one hour of your time each day." "Yes, Roopate, of course," he agreed, "one hour or two or three if you wish!"

Sepo was good, but it was never possible to rely on him. Or on anyone else. We wondered how to say "rely on" in Fijian. You'd never guess. The only possible word—Capell's dictionary gave it and Sepo confirmed—is *nui-ta'ina*, whose central meaning is "hope for." (This seemed a remarkably pithy summary of the Fijian worldview.)

Inoke was back from work occasionally, but he would only sometimes find the time to help us. I was making good progress with complement clauses, clauses that can be "object" to a main clause verb as in "I want *to go*," "I know *that we will come*," "I doubt *whether he will come*," "I appreciate *her having helped me*." In English a complement clause can be introduced by *that* or *whether* or *to*, or has *-ing* on the end of the verb. In Fijian these are introduced by *ni* or *se* or *dee* or *me* or have a verb which is like a participle. I was investigating which verbs can take which kinds of complement clauses. It depends on the meanings of the verbs and the meanings of the kinds of complement clauses.

We took a break from complement clauses and Koleta, working at the table, asked "Inoke, how old did you say you were?" He thought a moment. "Twenty-two. No, twenty-one." "When's your birthday?" I inquired. "It's in August," Inoke said, and then corrected himself, "no April."

This really broke us up. That Inoke, the cleverest youth in the village, didn't have any idea when he was born. Stung into action, Inoke went over to the chief's house, rummaged in his suitcase and returned in triumph, waving a birth certificate. "Inoke Soqu-O-Viti. Born 11th May 1961." Which made him 24.

The same level of vagueness seemed to pervade most aspects of life in Fiji. One day a post-office engineer came to remove the village phone. The bill hadn't been paid. There was a huddled meeting. People were supposed to leave payment for each call made in a box on Suliano's shelf. But it didn't add up. Sepo fetched twenty dollars from funds of the copra cooperative to make up the short fall. Sorry, the engineer wasn't authorized to accept money he just had to take the phone. The next day we were going into Waiyevo and we took the money to pay the bill. The following day the engineer had another round-trip drive of more than two hours to return our phone. No wonder, with such use of labor, that the lines weren't properly maintained. The line to Waitabu was above-ground at the main road but got lower and lower as it neared the village, being enmeshed in vines a good deal of the way. Within the village it just lay on the grass, and you had to be careful not to trip over it when hurrying to catch Teliva. No wonder if was difficult to hear anything over the Waitabu phone.

Show-off Person was like a different man since he'd taken over as village secretary. He came in one day for a chat, which would never have happened before. Koleta took the opportunity to ask whether he dabbled

9. "Oh dear! Roopate is getting ready to go!"

in traditional religion, conjuring up devils and that sort of thing. "Well, I used to at one time," he replied, with remarkable candor, "but not any more."

Show-off was still, however, regarded as a bit of a laughing stock around the village. He'd make his own village announcements and after one a woman thrust her head out of a window and called "What's that you say?" (Something that no one would have dreamed of doing to Suliano.) Show-off was forever strutting around blowing the conch shell, to announce the official beginning or ending of some activity. Mostly people ignored him. Litia, Show-off's wife, didn't give up the *'ere'ere*. "Could you buy me earrings when you next visit the shops?" she asked Koleta. We ignored her too.

Way back in January, when Tui Nasau used to come in, sit down and chatter away ten to the dozen, I couldn't wait to understand Fijian well enough to follow everything he said. Now I could, and it was so disappointing. All the chief did was blather. He'd rattle on about this and that, changing topics halfway through. We'd only be half-listening. But then there might be a serious question. "Do you have any problems?" Now in Fijian that is literally "Is there one problem to you?" "Just one," I replied, half-thinking. "What?" Tui Nasau sat up very straight. Luckily Koleta had been listening a little more carefully: "No problems at all, this is a perfect village." "Yes," I hastily added, "we are very happy, Big Uncle, in your heavenly village, this chiefly village of Waitabu." The chief responded with a big grin.

One thing we did want was a photo of him in that T-shirt from our first day, the PHANTOM CLUB CALIFORNIA one. Koleta asked him, as a special favor, to wear his green shirt the next day. But then he turned up in a different green shirt. We tried to be more specific. "Oh," Tui Nasau turned to his wife Nana Vero, "that is gone. It is now with a cauravou from 'Orovou." Oh well, things move around in Fiji. Whether by *'ere'ere* or whatever, our chief's shirt was now being worn by a youth in another village.

Koleta was trying to gather as much information as possible on the language of sevu ceremonies. She wanted to discover how much consisted of fixed formulas and how much might be original each time. She'd already recorded several sevu of a request for permission to enter a village. Sepo said he and Tui Nasau would perform for her a sevu presentation of the first crops from a harvest.

Sepo indicated that the ceremony was ready to begin. "*Ah, oi, oi, oi,*" Tui Nasau responded, together with a rhythmic clap. Then they went on. The thing that is to be presented must be downgraded. Suppose you gave someone a dress, you'd say "please accept this insignificant fragment of cloth." A parcel of groceries might be referred to as "a few crumbs of bread." Then quite a few references to the Christian God and the final ritual responses.

A few days later, at breakfast, Sepo mentioned another sevu ceremony, begging forgiveness for some wrongdoing. "Would it be possible to record such a ceremony?" I asked. "It is possible," Sepo affirmed, "but not a real sevu. Your Big Uncle and I will enact one for you."

The chief was having a happy time bouncing baby Paa on his lap, but he returned the baby to Qito and followed Sepo across to our house. We all four sat cross-legged and poker-faced. Sepo invented a transgression and apologized for it in the most humble and abject manner (he really was a terrific actor). Tui Nasau went along, playing his part, granting forgiveness. The final speech from him should have been *Oi, Oi, Oi*, each pronounced loudly and clearly. What the chief said was *Oioioi*, running it all together in a single perfunctory breath since it was only a pretend ceremony.

Then he did a perfunctory *'ere'ere* for a packet of cigarettes. There was only one left, but we reckoned he deserved it.

* * *

Considerable consternation throughout the village. People rushing around looking purposeful and stern. "What is it?" I asked Koleta. "Pio is lost. Disappeared." "Oh, he'll come back," I replied. " "He's been gone for hours, and they don't think he will."

The half-wit would wander around but never too far. He might walk up to the main road to watch the bus come and go. Or accompany his father, Keelepi, to Keelepi's garden. Or he'd go with us to a bathing pipe. (I'd taken a photo of Pio by the high pipe and Sepo's family had thought this decidedly odd. Who'd want a picture of the half-wit?) Pio had never gone by himself as far as the next village.

Pio's mother had set off on the bus that morning to visit relatives on the island of Vanua Levu. It's possible that someone had indicated to Pio her destination, pointing inland toward the forest. (Although in fact she had to travel around the rim of Taveuni since you can't go over the mountainous center.)

Anyway, Pio must have taken off into the forest. If not found within a few days he'd perish. Keelepi and some friends set off immediately to search. Other men called a meeting to decide what to do. (Surely no people loves meetings as much as Fijians.) We went along to do whatever we

9. "Oh dear! Roopate is getting ready to go!"

could. Well, I didn't know the forest so all we could really do was lend every single torch we had. A dozen men and youths searched well into the night but there was no sign of Pio.

Keelepi cried and moaned all through the night, we were told (our house was on the far side of the village), bewailing his son who might never be seen again, and blaming himself for not keeping a sharper eye on him.

When day dawned a proper systematic search was begun. It wasn't often that anyone really stirred themselves to do anything at Waitabu, but when they did the degree of activity could be astounding (compared, that is, to their everyday inertia). A coordinating station was set up on the main road by the bus stop, with each married man and each youth being assigned a patch of forest to comb.

Sepo set off after breakfast as if for a major expedition: hardhat, cane knife, packet of taro for his lunch and a flask of hot tea. If he found Pio, Bogi reasoned, the half-wit would certainly appreciate a hot drink of tea.

Pio, the half-wit, followed us around everywhere. One day he disappeared but not for long.

I can't imagine any couple more devoted to each other than Sepo and Bogi. Each worshipped the other. "Now that your father is going to join the search, Pio will soon be found," Bogi told Koleta, with total faith that Sepo's presence would auger success.

The only people left in the village were women and children and me.

I sat there, half-thinking of Pio, working on transitivity. In most languages about two-thirds of the sentences are transitive (with subject and object) and about one third intransitive (subject but no object). In Fijian almost every verb can be used intransitively (with no ending, like *la'o* "go") or transitively (with an ending, such as *la'o-va* "go for it"). Unlike most other languages, the great majority of sentences are intransitive. A chief will look at a youth and say, "Those logs should be stacked," rather than "Will you please stack these logs." People will remark "Our dinner has been cooked" in preference to "We have cooked our dinner." This habit makes discourse rather impersonal.

A sad feeling descended on Waitabu. Would they ever see Pio again? Someone who had been regarded as a nuisance became, overnight, a treasure. People didn't realize how much they loved him. "Well at least Roopate got a photo of Pio," Bogi said at lunch.

The afternoon wore on. No word of Pio. The search parties were fanning out further, going up the mountains. He'd be spending another night alone in the forest. "He'll die," Koleta suggested. "Oh no," I said, "it's not cold out there—plenty of water. He'll survive for a few more days."

I was still mulling over transitivity when there came the sound of a lorry. Suddenly a cry went up from a house near the end of the road. It was taken up in the next and then echoed, sweetly, around the village, "*O Pio, saa boo.*"

The lorry stopped before his house. Pio, standing on the back, grinning sheepishly. He jumped down. All the ladies of Waitabu converged on him. Each wanted to give dear Pio a special hug. Poor Pio! He'd never been the center of such attention before.

Some youths from Wai, combing the forest back of that village, had found him. (The lorry was from Wai.) A conch shell was blown loud and long from the coordinating center to tell all the searchers that Pio was found.

But that wasn't in fact what they'd said. There is a transitive verb *bo-'a* "find." It has an intransitive version *boo* "to be visible." The cry that had gone around the village was *o Pio saa boo* "Pio is now visible." They hadn't used the transitive verb *bo-'a* "find" or even its passive *bo 'i* "be found." Rather than "Someone has now found Pio" or "Pio has now been found" they preferred to say "Pio is now visible." A lovely example of the preference for intransitive sentences.

Waitabu reverted to its sleepy routine and we to our more active one. Each morning and evening we'd each fetch a couple of buckets of water from the pipe, as our contribution to household jobs; this would be used for cooking and drinking and washing-up. We may have done rather more than some of the male members of the family. I remember on the evening of one fine day Koleta asking Maarawa: "What have you done today, brother?" "Oh," he replied, as if speaking were itself an effort, "I've just been sitting in the house."

On our last shopping trip to Waiyevo and Somosomo we were given a long list of things to buy for the family. And not just verbally. Qito wrote everything down (on one of those pieces of typing paper they'd snaffled) so that no item could get overlooked. Quite a number of things for Qito's baby, and some clothes for the children and a few kitchen items. Together with ten large D-size batteries. We'd bought them yet another torch on the last trip and it took two batteries. Ten seemed a little excessive but we complied with the order.

That evening—just two hours after we'd handed over three large cartons of groceries, baby things and ten batteries—Sepo came in for an 'ere'ere. Can you guess what he wanted? Two D-size batteries. "But we bought you *ten* batteries, Uncle," I almost shouted the number ten. "Oh yes, Roopate, and we are most grateful for them. But those are for the radio Rosalia left here. It is a big radio and requires ten batteries." It made a big noise too; we were supplying the batteries to blast away our quiet. "Now I am asking for two batteries for the torch which you bought us," Sepo continued, as if we were the ones who were trying to be unreasonable. So he got them.

But then something went wrong with their torch. Perhaps it got dropped in the water. Two days later they came to 'ere'ere ours. "Sorry," Koleta said, " it's not working," which was true. What had happened was that one child had borrowed it, given it to another to bring back but they'd used it for an hour or two and passed it on to someone else. We did retrieve it in the end, after a Sherlock Holmes–like hunt, but minus batteries and bulb. And we had no spare bulb. That was the "public" torch. We did also keep a "private" one hidden away, then we had something to use ourselves, for reading in bed and such like. At breakfast the next day Qito was heard to remark very loud: "They said they didn't have a torch but I saw a light last night from Roopate and Koleta's house." (The gasau reeds had by now shrunk and readily let light in and out.) "Sshhh!" Bogi reprimanded her. We just ate our plate of rice, pretending not to hear.

* * *

All the stories that had been recorded were good and interesting, but the stand-out was undoubtedly that by Falaavia Matavesi, concerning the

Prince of Boumaa who had asked the Princess of Waini'eli: "Do you want to live or do you want to die?" Shortly before leaving, I went over to 'Orovou again and Falaavia agreed to tell another tale of olden days, about a Bird Princess. Like the earlier story, she spoke very fast and fluently. In fact, I didn't get to transcribe and analyze it—with the invaluable help of Sepo—until a return trip in December 1989. Here's how it goes.

> Quite a long time ago, there lived a King of Waini'eli and his wife got pregnant. There grew in front of their house a small coconut tree (called a varavara). The Queen gave birth to a bird, which flew to perch in the varavara tree. Once it had perched there, all the leaves stuck straight up, inclosing the bird. Then the tree grew and grew until it was higher than the roof of the house. The Bird Princess called out in a melodious voice which could be heard afar, even in Natewa Bay.
>
> The Prince of Natewa heard it, and traveled to Waini'eli to ask for the Princess's hand in marriage. Her parents replied that if he could climb right up the tree he could have her. He climbed higher than the roof of the house, still climbed but couldn't get to the top so came down and went home. The Bird Princess again cried melodiously and the Prince of Qamea came to Waini'eli to ask for her as his wife. He climbed and climbed and climbed but couldn't reach halfway up that coconut tree and he too went back home.
>
> Then the sweet sound of her voice reached the Prince of Ca'audrove who arrived and addressed the King of Waini'eli: "I've come for the Princess of Waini'eli, to make her my wife." The King told him: "All right. She is outside there. If you can climb up to her, you can take her to be your wife, and if you can't, well, there'll be nothing for you." The Prince went out and tightened his clothes. He told his companions to sing at the base of the tree to provide encouragement for him as he climbed. The Prince climbed and climbed, as night became day, still climbed, day and night, while his youths sang below.
>
> He climbed and climbed and then arrived at the top of that tree, stood there and called out: "Princess of Waini'eli, Princess of Waini'eli!" Then the leaves of the coconut tree opened up—one, two, three. The leaves folded down and remained there, just like a normal tree. "What's happening?" the Bird Princess asked. "Come here, I'm going to take you to be my wife." The bird flew down and perched on his shoulder. As soon as that happened the coconut tree shrank down to its normal size.
>
> The Prince of Ca'audrove and the Bird Princess of Waini'eli settled down in Ca'audrove. The Prince's sister, the Princess of Ca'audrove, became great friends with the Bird Princess and they spent each day together. One day, the Prince went off into the forest hunting, leaving the two girls together. The Princess of Ca'audrove fell asleep.
>
> Then a former girlfriend of the Prince came in and clubbed the Bird Princess, so that she fell down. The girl kept hitting and hitting until the bird was dead. Then it turned into a beautiful live girl. Well, she changed into a person, and hid under the bed. No one could see her. The sister-in-law woke up and when she saw the bird lying dead started to cry in sorrow. She cried and cried and cried and cried. Cried that she had slept when the bird was being killed.
>
> The Prince of Ca'audrove returned from the forest and didn't hear the voice of the bird. "Oh dear, where might the Princess of Waini'eli have gone, her voice cannot be heard." He came in, saw the dead bird and began to cry. The brother and sister cried. The dead bird was buried in Ca'audrove and still they cried. Then the Prince fell asleep on a bed, his sister on the floor.

9. *"Oh dear! Roopate is getting ready to go!"* 199

The Princess of Waini'eli was still hiding under the bed. Then her grandmother came from Waini'eli and asked her why she had no pity for these two, the brother and sister, who were still crying all the time. So the Princess came out and, with her grandmother, lifted the Prince of Ca'audrove off the bed onto the floor, while he still slept. They spread a new mat on the bed and a tapa cloth, then the two of them lifted the Prince back onto the bed. "Well, that's good. I'll go, I'll go now," the grandmother said.

The Princess of Waini'eli lay down and slept. Early in the morning she woke and went to light the fire to cook their food. When it was cooked, the eating mat was spread out, and the two of them still slept. Then the Princess of Waini'eli wakened them.

The Prince woke up and she asked him: "What have you been crying for? I am the Princess of Waini'eli." Then he woke up his sister and she didn't believe it. But the Princess of Waini'eli said: "It's me, I am a person now, I'm no longer a bird, I'm a person. I am standing upright here." Then the Prince hugged his wife, and cried and cried and cried for joy. They all went and ate there. After eating they were all very happy.

Then the Prince of Ca'audrove said that the person who had clubbed and killed the bird must be found and punished. The Princess of Waini'eli would recognize her assailant. So the King of Ca'audrove ordered that all the people of Ca'audrove were to assemble in one house and no one should be absent. All the mothers, all the fathers, and all the children came, so that the house was really full. The Princess of Waini'eli looked over them, looked over them again, and said that the young woman who clubbed her was not present.

The King had the absent girl, and her father and mother, fetched. The Princess said: "This is the girl who clubbed me, the one who stands here." The girl was asked if she had done it and began to cry. After that, the Prince of Ca'audrove said: "Well that's all right. You just rest, and let a lovo (earth oven) be heated up." So a lovo was prepared, with glowing red coals to heat the stones for the oven. The culprit's father was told: "Your daughter here clubbed to death the Prince's wife. Well, her punishment has arrived today. Now it is her time, to be taken and pushed into the lovo."

The young girl was crying. She was taken, taken to the edge of the lovo. Then they pushed her into the interior of the lovo, and covered her over with earth. When she was fully cooked, the lovo was opened up. They cut up her body into pieces, for them to eat her.

In true deprecatory fashion, Falaavia added: "Well, that's that. Roopate, It wasn't very long, and it didn't sound too good." I assured her that it was a magnificent legend and that I was honored to have been permitted to record it. (Falaavia passed away the following February.)

* * *

The time was drawing near for my departure. We planned to fly out on Sunday, June 30. I'd go back to Canberra and Koleta would have a couple of weeks in Suva before returning to Waitabu for another four weeks, or however long it took to finish off the fieldwork tasks she had planned.

"Isa, Roopate, e va'a-rau la'o." More and more people were starting

to say this. "Oh dear, Roopate is getting ready to go." One of the things implied was—how would I manage in Canberra? Who would cook and clean for me? The Waitabu ladies—and men—would have been shocked to hear about "division of labor" in Australian households. And the idea that a man could enjoy everyday cooking, could do the lion's share of it…! A woman's place was by her man, looking after him.

But men do cook the feast for a special occasion. (There is an analogy with Western culture. Until recently all the major chefs were men, although women are expected to look after day-to-day cooking). And we had a feast coming up. Elia Waqa's son Benedito was getting married.

Elia had purchased a cow and it—together with several score taro—would be cooked in a lovo earth oven in traditional style. The lovo was just beyond Nana Mau's kitchen. First a pit was dug, a fire lit and some stones heated right through. The meat, wrapped in leaves, was buried under the coals. Then the beast's head and all those taro were placed on top. They were covered over with coconut leaves, then piled high with earth.

For special occasions such as a wedding (or my departure) a "lovo" or earth oven is employed. A hole is dug, heated coals placed in it, meat wrapped in leaves put below the coals, then the cow's head and lots of taro on top.

9. *"Oh dear! Roopate is getting ready to go!"*

Here, the oven is covered with palm fronds and earth heaped over it.

Everything was left alone for a couple of hours. I went off to work alone. (No one could possibly bring themselves to work with me while a lovo was cooking. It was just like waiting for a cyclone.) When it is judged ready, the earth is raked off. Steam rises from the lovo. The leaves are taken off. Cooked taro is placed in ready-woven coconut leaf baskets. A couple of the choicest are taken off to be offered to an appropriate elder, just like a first fruits presentation.

The wedding took place in the Tunuloa shed that had been re-erected for Father Hendricks. A priest drove over especially from Waiyevo (for a suitable fee). Benedito and Luisa, his bride (who came from another village) wore long skirts of printed masi cloth, made from the bark of the paper mulberry tree. Benedito had on a white shirt and—of all things—a tie.

The wedding was at midday and I'd expected the feast to follow quite soon. After all, everything had already been cooked. But first we had a snack in Elia Waqa's house. Cake and scones and jam—all the things one didn't see except on a feast day. Koleta was working at the school in 'Orovou and she missed both service and snack. "You mean you had jam!" she exclaimed, "and I missed it." But she was there for the wedding feast,

Leave it all to cook for a couple of hours then rake off the covering—steam will rise up, mingled with a mouth-watering aroma.

at four o'clock, in the Tunuloa shed—beef cooked in every imaginable way and eel, turtle, octopus, chicken, taro and greens. A bevy of ladies sat off to one side with huge cauldrons from which they replenished the bowls on the eating mat.

The only flaw was that you couldn't take your time—neither for jam snack nor for wedding feast. There were so many guests that they couldn't all sit down at once. We needed three sittings so you had to eat rather fast and then retire and make way for the next shift.

I was just about going to finish my work in the time available. With Sepo and Inoke's help. Which was, as always, variable. "I have six days left and I must have six hours with you, Uncle, one each day." "And so you shall," Sepo promised, sitting down then and there to explicate with amazing clarity some of the problems that had been plaguing me about possessive constructions.

I scribbled. Then Sepo spoke, sharply: "*Namu, Roopate!*" Namu is "mosquito" and there were plenty around Waitabu, even in winter. One would alight on the clear expanse of my bald head—when we were doing linguistics, or during a meal—and there'd be a warning "*Namu, Roopate!*" The head being sacred they couldn't touch mine and kill it for me. I didn't

9. "Oh dear! Roopate is getting ready to go!"

know exactly where it was—mosquitoes don't worry me too much, and there is no malaria in Fiji—so I'd slap the flat of one hand hard on forehead, hard enough to squash any insect, and get on with what I was doing.

We went on to the relator *me*, the hardest and most interesting bit of Fijian grammar. "Uncle, is it possible to say—" "*Namu, Roopate!*" Slap. One dead mosquito. "Thank you, now Uncle, is it possible—."

The little children were going to miss us. My name Roopate had been abbreviated to Pate. Now, as we set off to do things that no adult Fijian would ever contemplate—bathe or jog or just saunter along the beach because it was a relaxing thing to do—a whole group of toddlers would call "*Bula, Pate.*" Pate became a general term they used for any white-skinned person (in place of the normal common noun *paapaalagi*); even Koleta was called "Pate."

"*Isa, Roopate, e va'a-rau la'o.*" People were now becoming really mournful. "Oh dear, Roopate is getting ready to go." Well, we had been there six months. We were related to every person in the village by adoption, and we had all got on reasonably well together.

But the cries were all about Roopate going, no mention of Koleta. When she returned to the village alone Koleta told me that the cry was then "Oh dear, Roopate has really gone." No mention at any stage of "Oh dear, Koleta is getting ready to go." It simply is a chauvinistic society, with overt attention focused on the men.

On one of our last nights there a full moon was due to rise up over the sea. "Hey," I said to Koleta, "let's go for a walk along the beach, see what the traditional priests are up to?" "I don't think that is at all a good idea," came the reply. Of course she was right. All those hours of sitting cross-legged in church, all that investment, might be squandered if anyone saw us on the beach with a full moon (even though I had no intention of taking my clothes off and dancing naked). Still, it was tempting.

My last Sunday. Felise the catechist devoted a part of his sermon to "the two chiefly foreigners, Roopate and Koleta, who have lived among us here, joined in with our activities, and have been regular attenders at our church."

Then the last day. We were to have a feast as well. Not with a cow, but there'd be a lovo with pork, taro and lots of other goodies. No—we weren't allowed to contribute a penny, it was our farewell feast.

Of course there must be a farewell speech. Now I considered that I knew enough of the language and the social conventions to write my own little speech. But Sepo insisted on writing it for me. I don't believe it was lack of confidence in me, just that Sepo liked to be in charge.

He wrote it out, two full pages on some of that typing paper they'd nicked. Obeisance to the chief, salutation to everyone in the Yavusa of Naisaqei. How we'd appreciated being part of the village, learning the Gato (glottal stop) dialect of Boumaa, our gratitude for the help we'd received… Those were all the things I wanted to say, and Sepo had done it for me. I copied out the speech into my own handwriting and then took off into the forest to rehearse, practicing all the stresses, and rises and falls in intonation.

Sepo and Inoke and all the other men from the Vunivesi Mataqali were cooking the lovo. They'd have no more time for linguistic work. That was okay, I'd just about finished with first drafts of twenty-five chapters for the grammar (some very short, a couple quite long). Now what order should they go in? As the lovo progressed outside I sat and pondered the question. There were grammatical criteria to support certain analytic decisions. Justifying the syntactic status of incorporated objects requires reference to predicate modifiers, so the predicate modifier chapter must precede that on object incorporation.

Bogi and Nana Maa came in, with several children and Qito, who was now walking around and getting accepted again in the village. They brought farewell gifts of mats, fans and brooms for use in Canberra. It was a solemn presentation. Sepo sat next to me but I did make the thank you speech all on my own. Koleta wanted to make one too but Sepo then stopped the proceedings. (He thought the world of Koleta, but there is a time for men and a time for women in Fiji.)

Then the feast. We were each bedecked with a garland of artificial flowers made from dyed voivoi vines, with real hibiscus blooms intertwined. I sat at one end of the eating mat, with Koleta next. Opposite me was Tui Nasau, then Felise as senior representative of the other Mataqali (Elia Waqa was away at a wedding in Lavena), then Sepo. I read out Sepo's speech and Tui Nasau replied. Then we had to move quickly away from the mat, to make way for a second sitting.

At breakfast the next day we said a special thank you to Bogi—using every one of the laudatory adjectives—for that meal and for every simply wonderful meal over the past months. She had tears in her eyes, dear Bogi.

A few minutes left for packing. Tui Nasau entered, sat down and gave his personal goodbye. He'd left the village on an errand—on purpose we were sure—by the time our taxi arrived. The whole village stood by, for farewell hugs. Even Show-off Person. "Goodbye, village secretary," I said, "thank you for your help." And Suliano and Atalemo, Nana Vero and Nana Maa. It was sad to go.

Epilogue

During the last half of 1985 I wrote a second draft of the grammar, in long hand, and then revised and typed out a third one. I sent a copy of this to Sepo. When we returned, in June 1986, he'd read the first half and offered detailed comments and corrections on the example words and sentences. Sepo continued to read the draft and in November sent me a notebook with comments and corrections on the remaining chapters.

The villagers had found that Show-off Person, during his time as village secretary, had been subverting village funds into his own use. He was stripped of office and left Waitabu.

Almost a year after Qito's baby was born, Sepo wrote a stern no-nonsense letter to its father saying that he should be ashamed of himself, getting Qito pregnant, and why didn't he do the decent thing and marry her? A reply came. This was the first he knew he had a child. It was wonderful news and of course he'd be more than happy to marry Qito.

The father, who was from the village of Urata, about ten miles north of the town of Savusavu on Vanua Levu, came to Waitabu with a group of relatives. They first presented a gift of whale's teeth to atone for getting Qito pregnant. Then another gift, asking for her hand in marriage.

The wedding, at Urata, was arranged to coincide with our return visit in 1986. (We bought the pig.) Qito was a different person, happy and lively, quite unlike the sullen face of old. She had a fine wedding with Koleta as a bridesmaid, decked out in brightly printed masi cloth. Urata seemed to be a much more modern village than Waitabu. Qito showed us over her new house—kitchen with a real stove, four rooms… "You'll be able to have lots of children," I teased, "and fill the house up." (She now has six, four girls and two boys.)

Koleta completed a good Ph.D. dissertation and had a couple of offers to publish it, but declined them. Koleta and I parted ways a couple of years later, and she moved into new fields of endeavor.

The novel which I had written at Short Sand between January and March 1985 (then revised and typed up in Suva during April) went the rounds of publishers. One commented that he liked the characters, the setting, and the plot but (and he didn't quite know why) he didn't want to publish it. Others were more matter-of-fact. *The Price of Love* molders at the bottom of a carton on a high shelf in my study.

A Grammar of Boumaa Fijian fared better. In late 1988 the University of Chicago Press published it in hardbound and paperback editions. The royalties (not that they amounted to much) were sent to Sepo.

By the time I made a return visit over Christmas 1989, Pio the half-wit had died. And my Big Uncle had also passed away, so that Sepo had succeeded to the office of Tui Nasau, village chief. Saddest of all was the death, in January 1994, of Sepo's wife Aquela Bogi (my Nei, "mother-in-law" or "aunt").

I visited Waitabu again in late 2006. "*O tautauvata Moomoo* (You are just the same, Uncle)" was my greeting. Sepo was always Sepo—welcoming, unfailingly helpful, and forever determined to call the tune. He recorded a long text summarizing what had happened in the village during the seventeen years since my last visit. We calculated that Sepo now had fifty grandchildren (an equal number of each sex). Of his twelve children only two daughters (Maritina and Elena) were living in the village, the remainder being spread afield—in Labasa, Suva, Canada, and Europe.

Inevitably, things had changed in Waitabu. There was now running water, but still no electricity. A proper church building had been constructed so that services no longer rotated around houses in the village. Rules for behavior were weakening—no one seemed to mind bags being worn over the shoulders.

Josefa Cookanacagi (Sepo) passed away in the hospital at Labasa on Wednesday, January 27, 2010, aged about seventy-five. He was one of the best friends I ever had.

References by Chapter

Chapter 1. Getting There

- Quotations from pages xv, xxv–xxvi of Lorimer Fison, *Tales from Old Fiji* (London: Alexander Moring, 1907). Drawing of "Widow-strangling in Fiji" is facing page xxii.
- Other books referred in this chapter are, in order of mention:
    - G. B. Milner. *Fijian grammar*. Suva: Fiji Government Press, 1956
    - A. Capell. *A new Fijian dictionary*. Sydney: Australasian Medical Publishing Company, 1941
    - Paul A. Geraghty. *The history of the Fijian languages*. Honolulu: University of Hawaii Press, 1983
    - C. Maxwell Churchward. *A new Fijian grammar*. Sydney: Australasian Medical Publishing Company, 1941
    - Albert J. Schütz. *The Fijian language*. Honolulu: University of Hawaii Press, 1985
    - C. Maxwell Churchward. *Tales of a lonely island: Rotuman legends*. Sydney: Australasian National Research Council, 1939
    - C. Maxwell Churchward. *Rotuma grammar and dictionary*. Sydney: Australasian Medical Publishing Company, 1940
    - C. Maxwell Churchward. *Tongan grammar*. London: Oxford University Press, 1953
    - C. Maxwell Churchward. *Tongan dictionary (Tongan–English and English–Tongan)*. Tonga: Government Printing Press, 1959

Chapter 2. "This is paradise"

- Information concerning young women being strangled at Somosomo from page 36 of James Calvert, *Fiji and the Fijians*, volume 2, *Mission history* (London: Alexander Heylin, 1858).

Chapter 5. "Do you want to live or do you want to die?"

- Full texts and translations of the story of the Prince of Boumaa and the Princess of Waini'eli, by Falaavia Matavesi, and of the story of the war between the Ca'audrove region of Fiji and Tonga, by Siriloo Saabai, are on

pages 305–351 of my monograph, *A grammar of Boumaa Fijian* (Chicago: University of Chicago Press, 1988). Note that the Vanua of Narova no longer exists; it was inland from Waini'eli.
- The comment on Africans laughing at a misfortune is on pages 229–31 of *Return to laughter* by Elenore Smith Bowen, nom-de-plume of Laura Bohannan (New York: Harper and Row, 1954).

Chapter 7. A Divine Visitor

Diphthongs are dealt with on page 3 of the grammar section of *A Fijian and English and an English and Fijian dictionary ... and a grammar of the language with examples of native idioms*, by David Hazlewood, published in 1872 by Sampson Low, Marston and Co. in London and George Robertson in Melbourne; reprinted in 1979 by the AMS Press. (The grammar had previously been published by the Wesleyan Mission Press in Vewa, Fiji, in 1850.)

Index

adoption 34
alphabet 6
Arms, Father David 14
Australian Aboriginal people 8, 58–9, 70, 72, 91, 111

bathing places 35–6, 39–40, 118–19
battles 73, 105–6
Bau, Bauan 11, 38, 54–5, 67, 74, 96, 105, 122–6, 140, 158–9
Bible translation 11, 67
bird princess story 198–9
Bohannan, Laura *see* Bowen, Elenore Smith
Bowen, Elenore Smith 97, 208
Burr, Raymond 13
buses 10, 26–7, 108, 123

Ca'audrove Cooperative Association History 140–1, 144, 186
Ca'audrove dialect 54–5
Calvert, James 207
cannibalism 4, 8, 132, 135
Ca'obau 106
Capell, A. 12, 68, 137, 192, 207
Castaway International Hotel 22, 24, 117, 180
ceremonies 67–9, 149–51, 193–4
cession to Britain 106, 158
Christianity, advent of 111–12
church services 9, 42–5, 66–70, 110–11, 116, 129–31, 184–6, 206
Churchward, the Rev. Dr. C. Maxwell 15–16, 139, 207
complement clauses 192
coups 14, 124
cyclones 3–5, 81–90, 96, 131, 141–4

dance hall 63–5, 113–15
demonstratives 54–5

diphthongs 138–9, 155, 208
drum *see* lali slit drum

earth oven *see* lovo
'ere'ere, kerekere 9, 102–3, 115, 126, 133, 147, 179–81, 190–4, 197
euthanasia 9

farewell speech 203–4
feasts 68, 107, 116, 122, 200–4
Fijian Monolingual Dictionary Centre 7, 13–14
Fison, Lorimer 8, 207

gardening 60–1, 134–5
Geraghty, Dr. Paul 7, 13–15, 64, 96, 137, 160, 207
glottal stop 31, 37–8, 55, 67, 105, 124, 204
gods, traditional 20, 49, 62, 93, 111, 126, 145–7, 153
Gordon, Sir Arthur 8–10
greetings on the road 121–2

Hazlewood, David 139, 208
Hendricks, Father 144–56
house building 163–77

independence from Britain 123
Indian indentured laborers 10
intransitive verb *see* verb transitivity
Ito'ato'a 62, 64, 112–5, 141, 146, 163, 167, 169, 172

jelly (jello) 76–7, 118, 160

Kaba's guest house 22–6, 46
kerekere see *'ere'ere*

Labasa 188–90
Lakemba 11
lali slit-drum 42–4, 47, 118, 149
Lau group 11
Levuka 14–17
lovo earth oven 199–201, 203–4

mail 57, 59, 120–1
Mataqali 31–4, 62, 138, 141, 161
Matei 22, 24
meals 20, 40, 50–2, 77, 112–13, 124, 183–4
Milner, G.B. 6–8, 81, 139, 207
missionaries 11, 22, 39, 67, 69–70, 77, 96, 105, 126–7, 135, 137, 145
money-drink 128–30
Nadi 6, 9–11, 76

novel writing 6, 63, 98–101, 108, 118, 154, 206

Ovalau 14–15

Peace Corps 11–12, 20, 104
possession 158–9, 189
postal agency 57, 59, 120, 185
presentations 17–18, 21, 30–2, 72, 144, 149–51, 179
priests, traditional 145–7, 152, 192–3, 203
Princess Ashika 155–7, 161

Qamea 62, 107, 122, 198
Queen Elizabeth II 5, 12, 14, 143
Queen Salote of Tonga 5

Ralph 144–8
relative clauses 49–50, 160
religion, traditional 111, 126, 145–6, 192–3
Return to Laughter 97, 104, 153–5, 208

Schütz, Albert J. 15, 88, 207
sevu ceremony 193–4
sevu(sevu) presentation of first fruits 135, 193–4
shopping 75–7, 81–3, 97, 117–8, 132–3, 135, 160–1, 183, 197
snake 47

Solomon Islanders 139
Somosomo 22–3, 54, 73, 207
Soqulo 25–6
Suva 7–22, 157–61

tabua (whale's tooth) 18, 21, 30, 32, 67–8, 92, 147, 150–2, 154, 167, 205
tagimaucia flower 73
teevoro ("devil") 126
Teliva 122–4, 139, 183
Ti'ina 62
toads 66, 70, 177–8, 185–6
Tonga, Tongan 5, 11, 16, 18, 49, 74, 79, 105–6, 126, 159, 207
traditional gods *see* gods, traditional
traditional priests *see* priests, traditional
traditional religion *see* religion, traditional
transitive verb *see* verb transitivity
Tui Ca'au 74, 105–6
Tunuloa shed 63–4, 114–5, 148, 201–2

Va'a-Tunuloa shed *see* Tunuloa shed
Vanua 27, 34, 61–2, 71, 91–4, 107, 120
verb transitivity 108, 119, 140, 196
village announcements 114–5, 129, 159
village chief 3, 4, 84, 141, 206
village secretary 78, 114, 169, 205
village work 78–9, 114–5, 129, 124, 168, 193
visas 7–8, 14
vowels 138, 154
Vuna 19, 23–4, 38, 148

Waibula shops and taxis 75–7, 118, 133, 165, 170, 173–4, 183
Wairi'i 24–5, 54, 106, 110–11
Waiyevo 23, 82, 117, 155, 165–6, 188
waqona 125; *see also* yaqona
washing clothes 95–6, 156, 184
washing, words for 53
whale's tooth *see* tabua
widow-strangling 8
word, types of 154–5

yaqona (kava) 18, 30–4, 56, 61, 64–8, 71, 99, 114, 125, 129–30, 150, 172–3; origin 74–5, 106–7, 116
Yasana 62

www.ingramcontent.com/pod-product-compliance
Ingram Content Group UK Ltd.
Pitfield, Milton Keynes, MK11 3LW, UK
UKHW041959140426
5217IPUK00015B/876